Women

with

Altitude

Challenging the Adirondack High Peaks in Winter

Carol Stone White

North Country Books, Inc.
Utica, New York

Women with Altitude
Challenging the Adirondack High Peaks in Winter

Copyright © 2005
by Carol Stone White

ISBN 1-59531-002-9

Library of Congress Cataloging-in-Publication Data

White, Carol, 1940-
  Women with altitude : challenging the Adirondack high peaks in winter
/ by
Carol Stone White.
      p. cm.
  ISBN 1-59531-002-9 (alk. paper)
  1. Women mountaineers--Biography. 2. Mountaineering--New York
(State)--Adirondack Mountains. 3. Adirondack Forty-sixers
(Organization) 4.
Adirondack Mountains (N.Y.)--Description and travel. I. Title.
  GV199.9.W44 2005
  796.52'209747--dc22

                              2005025475

North Country Books, Inc.
311 Turner Street
Utica, New York 13501
315-735-4877
ncbooks@adelphia.net

To Dave,
whose ready wit and true grit
made all the ups and downs
peak experiences

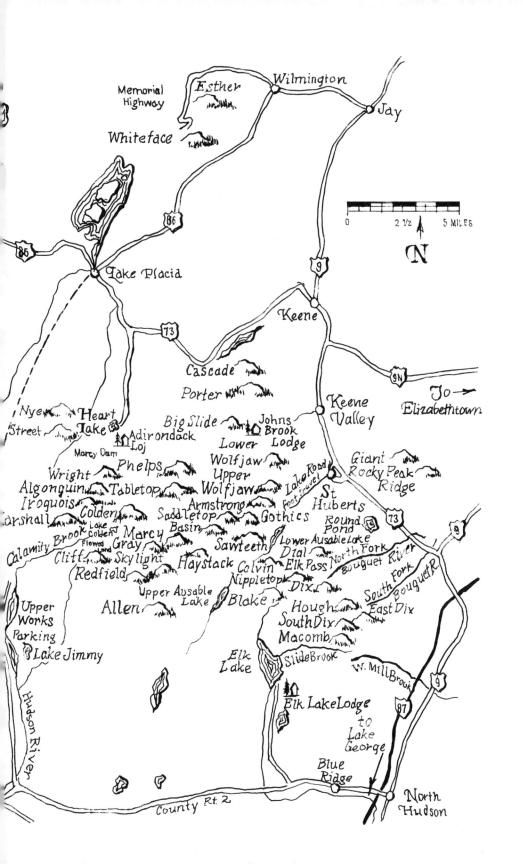

"I think we are to see in the title that "Altitude" and "Attitude" are to be interchangeable to varying degrees in each account. However close altitude and attitude may have brought these women to the brink of disaster, there always seems to be some conservative common sense, a survival instinct if you will, that keeps them from going stupidly over the edge as men will. In my years as a Ranger, I recall a number of non-life-threatening sprains and breaks and one death among women. In the meantime men got spinal fractures in avalanches, died at the rate of about one each year from stupid acts and left frozen body parts at our local hospitals, and more.

Recognizing women's survival instincts, I often addressed them rather than the cavalierly suicidal men in a party headed for serious trouble. I knew that the women could bring the whole thing to a screeching halt when the scale started to tip in the wrong direction. Thank God for women. This is an interesting read of women with attitude in a location of some altitude who are governed with a sense of reality."

> — *C. Peter M. Fish*
> NYSDEC Forest Ranger (Retired)
> Adirondack High Peaks Wilderness Area

"'That's pretty good for a girl' is not the kind of thing you'd want to say to the women you'll meet in this book. Having successfully conquered all 46 Adirondack High Peaks at least once—in the winter, no less—they don't take any nonsense, from people or nature. They're physically and mentally tough, feisty and determined, and their stories of ultimately victorious encounters with storms, spruce holes, below-zero nights, swollen rivers and skeptics (usually of the male persuasion) are inspiring to all of us."

> — *Neal Burdick*
> Editor, *Adirondac Magazine* and Forest Preserve Series of Guides to Adirondack and Catskill Trails (ADK)

TABLE OF CONTENTS

ACKNOWLEDGEMENTS

The sometimes hair-raising and always interesting stories in this book are written by a diverse group of women in New York, New Jersey, Vermont, New Hampshire, Maine, and Connecticut who share their fascinating lives with us and offer detailed mountain adventures in the Adirondack High Peaks in solar winter. I'm very grateful for the ready responses given by these women, who are not exactly spectators in any area of life! I now understand why Grace Hudowalski corresponded with so many hikers for so long.

The staff of the New York State Archives efficiently and helpfully supplied everything I asked for; they are meticulous about the handling and order of files and research. My husband, Dave, accompanied me once when we expected to be at the Archives for two or three hours. We spent the whole day, Dave immersed in riveting accounts of mountain climbing in the frozen High Peaks of New York. His spotting of crucial information, and throughout the project remembering our adventures and adding good detail to initial drafts, contributed greatly to the final product.

Ditt Dittmar, long-time Adirondack Forty-Sixer Club Treasurer, quickly responded when I needed information about contacting people. Tony Solomon and Mindy Jatulis at the Office of the Historian in Schenectady gave immediate help as the work progressed. Tony Goodwin, editor of "Adirondack Trails: High Peaks Region," reviewed *The 46 Adirondack High Peaks* section. Phil Corell, now Forty-Sixer Treasurer, supplied interesting information about the removal of the canisters.

"DEAR GRACE..."

"These are very precious experiences, and if you don't write them down you won't remember." So wrote Forty-Sixer Club historian Grace Hudowalski, who for half a century received and answered tens of thousands of letters from aspiring Forty-Sixers. To become an Adirondack Forty-Sixer, you climb the 46 highest Adirondack peaks and write to the Office of the Historian, P.O. Box 9046, Schenectady, NY 12309-0046 about your adventures.

Bob Marshall, renowned naturalist, was the first to climb all 46 peaks, those measured as over 4,000 feet on United States Geological Survey maps, with his brother George and their friend Herbert Clark in 1924. Grace Hudowalski was the first woman to summit the 46 in 1937. Since then over 5,500 hikers have succeeded in this quest, but only thirty-six women and 207 men climbed them all in winter as of March 2001, before the canisters on the trailless peaks were removed—the period covered in this book.

These few intrepid women have written in chilling detail to Grace about the ferocious winds, icy cliffs and deep snows of northern New York State's 46 highest mountains between December 21 and March 21 of the year, solar winter. Elsie Chrenko, in 1973, became the first woman to summit all 46 High Peaks in winter and she completed her third round at age 65!

The first recorded winter ascent of Mt. Marcy was in March 1893, by Benjamin Pond and John Otis. Gifford Pinchot, a pioneer conservationist who headed the Agriculture Department's Forestry Division in the 1920s, ascended to Marcy's summit in February 1899, when everyone else in his party had retreated from the extreme cold and wind; he suffered frostbitten ears in spite of wearing a sealskin cap. In 1904, the Sno Birds, a group of six, started snowshoeing and skiing up Whiteface. By 1920, the club had expanded to hundreds of adventurers who began climbing and skiing Marcy in winter. In February 1923, Bob and George Marshall and Herbert Clark reached the summit of Algonquin. Small groups began ascending Haystack and Giant; Jim Goodwin pioneered winter climbs of Gothics in 1927, Lower Wolf Jaw in 1931, and Colden's Trap Dike in 1933.

By 1948, the Adirondack Mountain Club (ADK) began awarding trophies for college outing club teams who succeeded to a summit first by skiing or snowshoeing. ADK's Winter Activities Committee established the "V-Badge" for climbing five High Peaks in winter. In 1954, the club began conducting Winter Mountaineering Schools at the Adirondack Loj. The first person to ascend successfully all 46 High Peaks in winter was Edgar Bean on March 10, 1962. Six men did so in the sixties and only sixteen more men and two women completed the Winter 46 in the seventies. The eighties saw a greater interest in the challenge, with thirty-seven men and eight women summitting the 46 High Peaks in winter, and in the nineties 117 men and twenty-three women did so. Three more women and thirty-one more men completed the Winter 46 by March 2001 before the canisters were removed.

Clearly, this is a sport that is rapidly growing in popularity and their stories tell why. Winter climbing is increasingly more accessible with the proliferation of how-to courses and books, clubs, hiking groups, and improved equipment and clothing. Earlier hikers in this book describe the impediments of snowshoes without crampons.

The first Forty-Sixer Club was formed in Troy, New York, in 1936, after Ed Hudowalski and Reverend Ernest Ryder of Troy's

Grace Methodist Church became the sixth and seventh people to climb the 46 Adirondack High Peaks. Only three people from this club climbed the 46 peaks during World War II, bringing the total to thirty-one by 1945. Interest resurged after the war and by May 1948, with recorded Forty-Sixers numbering fifty-four, the original club established the Adirondack Forty-Sixers. They created a questionnaire for new Forty-Sixers, appointed a committee to determine and mark the true summits of controversial peaks, and decided the criteria for a "peak": there must be at least a 300-foot drop between peaks, or a peak must be at least three-quarters of a mile away from another, to be considered a separate summit.

On September 15, 1950, the first canister was placed on Mt. Emmons. At the summits of nineteen High Peaks without maintained trails, the Forty-Sixers placed metal canisters that contained a notebook and pencil (on East Dix I had to sign my name with a chocolate bar!). You added your name and listed in your journal the names of the last three hikers to sign in. This information was sent to Grace; her now-expanded committee keeps records of all successful ascents and preserves the stories of hikers.

Forty-Sixer Club members "give back" to the mountains in numerous ways: in 1972, an Outdoor Leadership Workshop was begun to train leaders who take groups into the High Peaks; in 1978, the Conservation Service Award was established for those contributing forty-six or more hours of trail maintenance. The club awards grants for lean-to construction and trail maintenance. Members participated in Dr. Ed Ketchledge's summit restoration program to protect fragile and rare alpine plants.

Forty-Sixers meet twice a year and publish *Adirondack Peeks* magazine, begun with the Fall/Winter issue of 1963-64.

Most of all, aspiring Forty-Sixers corresponded with Grace about their progress as they climbed the 46. One woman wrote, "Thank you Grace, for all your letters and encouragement. Do you realize the thrill we get when we find a letter from Grace in our mailbox? Words can't describe how exciting it is." This correspondence is in the New York State Archives in Albany, a source of many adventures in this book. Grace told me she was happy that some of those thousands of letters she received are now being used for this book.

Who was Grace, truly a legend in her own time? She grew up in Ticonderoga and then Minerva, a hamlet not far from the old Adirondack Iron Works at Tahawus. When she was fifteen, she was invited to join a group of college students who were going on a three-day trip to attempt Mt. Marcy. In those days no one climbed Marcy in less than three days.

That was the beginning! She had none of the equipment we take for granted today. She walked around for a few days getting used to carrying a blanket roll which was pinned together with large horse blanket pins. Inside were her knife, fork, spoon, food, and clothing. Even though it was rainy and therefore muddy, the group pressed on to Four Corners Lean-to at the base of Mt. Marcy. Her dad had given Grace woods advice she was to remember all her life: "It doesn't matter if you reach the summit—but it does matter how you make the climb." She said she learned what that meant on the trek to Marcy—turn back or go on? Gripe or maintain cheerfulness? Do your share of what had to be done? Although mist and clouds surrounded the summit, for a brief moment the clouds parted and Grace saw Lake Tear of the Clouds, the Hudson River's source far below, and was elated! She talked about mountains, wrote about them in school papers, even spoke of them in public speaking classes. She wrote a class song on mountains.

After she married Ed Hudowalski, who had never climbed, she inspired him and he took boys in his church school class up to the Great Range. That started it. He and Grace climbed all the high peaks. "Forty-Sixer" was not yet a word. In a letter to Marta Bolton, Grace wrote: "When asked, 'Why do you climb?' I haven't any one answer—most of them are tied up with the spiritual values they have released in me. When we first went as a small group from Troy, NY, to climb it had to be on a Sunday. Back in the thirties one worked six days a week; it was Depression years. But we had our service on the mountains—that was important to us. The Vespers we have at today's meetings date back to that custom; today, realizing there are various religions as well as denominations, we do not use the name of Christ. But it is well to sing praises and recognize that there is a Supreme Being."

Grace was the first president of the new Adirondack Forty-Sixers.

She told me that she used a lot of her mountain experience while working at the New York State Commerce Department and on her WGY radio show, "Two's Company," recounting her many fascinating stories. She started keeping records for those who climb the 46, and as time went on she urged climbers to write about their experiences and adventures on the trail. Grace wrote individual letters on a typewriter, never a form letter, to each climber and felt this a very rewarding experience—getting to know so many climbers; many wrote intimately of their climbs and their feelings even though the correspondents never physically met. She learned more about the mountains and about nature from their many letters. "The climbers are my friends and I like to think I am theirs," Grace said. She especially loved responding to the children, who would write about animals and other things they saw in different-colored pens with decorations on the stationery. A proposal is under consideration to rename East Dix "Grace Peak" in honor of Grace Hudowalski, and South Dix "Carson Peak" for Russell Carson, author of "Peaks and People of the Adirondacks."

"Have you written Grace?" Barb Harris asked my husband Dave and me as we described adventures climbing eleven High Peaks. "Who's Grace?" we asked. We learned about this fascinating procedure, climbing these magnificent peaks and then adding to the growing literature that captures the wonders of climbing New York's highest mountains. Grace Hudowalski's insight that we need to describe our hikes has preserved the beauty and struggle and exaltation of these experiences. Grace died peacefully at age 98 in March 2004.

Page xiii, Line 13 should read "At the summits of twenty High Peaks without maintained trails, the Forty-Sixers placed metal canisters that contained a notebook and pencil..."

FOREWORD

I'll never forget learning that there are 46 High Peaks in the Adirondacks over 4,000 feet and that intrepid adventurers, Forty-Sixers, have climbed them all. Former weekend activities are replaced by poring over maps and guidebooks, learning strange mountain names like Couchsachraga, deciding what trails to take, acquiring map and compass skills. Peak bagging lures us to areas we'd never think of going and rewards us lavishly with wilderness experiences and panoramic beauty from many vantage points. One wonderful day you summit your forty-sixth High Peak, a magical moment forever etched in memory, a significant life event.

"Now what are we going to do?" people inquire, after completing their first forty-six. With the many dimensions of mountains—season, weather, time, humidity—"you don't climb the same mountain twice," to paraphrase a Zen saying. We love mountain climbing because it meets many elemental human needs. The mountaineer rightly claims a sense of accomplishment and pride. We learn about our body and its wondrous potential, about staying oriented in mountain terrain, about nature in her many moods, about equipment and survival, about pushing through self-imposed limits as we triumph over fatigue, fear, and challenge. As in yoga the competition is rightly with the self, gradually stretching beyond what one thinks one can do, building on greater capacities. An enlarged self emerges, more in touch with the essential human that evolved through millions of years in nature, more joyous and free of non-essentials. Thoreau put it well, "Most of the luxuries and so-called comforts of life not only are not indispensable, but hindrances to the elevation of mankind."

Climbing 3,300 feet to elusive Hough Mt. through six miles of untrailed forest on the shortest day of the year, we asked ourselves,

"Why do we do this?" Descending miles in fading light will be arduous and possibly dangerous. We won't know what adventures the new terrain has in store for us. We'll do what is required—sometimes profanely, but often cheerfully—for the mountain teaches patience, acceptance of what is at any given moment on the mountain or in our psyche, pleasant or not. In return the mountain transports us to states beyond the usual in its lavish beauty.

Squandering the daylight remaining, delighting in the summit views of this remote Adirondack five-peak range, time—at the back of our survival minds—is not important. What is important is the heightened consciousness granted by the mountaintop, that transcendent state accessible to those who climb mountains, for they are places where you experience happiness, and that is indeed mysterious. "To see heaven in a wild flower, eternity in an hour," as poet William Blake put it. There is timelessness to these wild days, like the endless summers of childhood. After a period in the mountains we feel we've experienced a great deal, been given sustenance until we can return. We do so at every opportunity.

However, climbing mountains in winter is a very serious endeavor that teaches us humility in the face of inexorable forces of nature. The stories in this book describe breaking through icy brooks, frostbite, falls, forced bivouacs, uncontrolled descents, whiteouts, scaling icy cliffs, being trapped in seemingly bottomless spruce holes or in slushy trail up to your thighs in a remote pass.

Dave and I climbed twenty-nine of the 46 peaks by ourselves; we were lucky. Duo and even solo hiking is not uncommon. Ambition to achieve what few others have done is a powerful motivator and can lead to getting in over your head—in this case, over your head in snow!

Winter is a favorite season for many reasons and first is, no bugs! Hiking is more pleasant in cold weather. Footing is easier because rocks, roots, scrub, and blow-down are buried under snow; sliding downhill is fun and reduces muscle pain caused by descent. Crossing lakes and walking up brooks on ice is magical and saves time on these short days, but great care is needed testing ice. In winter you can have an entire mountain summit all to yourself! Pick a sunny, windless day and you can tarry a long time; little else on earth rivals this experience.

The ability to hike all seasons has wonderful benefits: one stays in shape instead of having to get back in shape. Those of us who are older not only "keep up with our grandchildren," we challenge them. Aerobic exercise results in strengthened muscles, improved balance and agility, lowered heart rate, increased metabolism and bone density, and great sleep—except when one must arise in the wee hours to begin hiking before dawn! Natural highs replace stress and depression.

The "down" side of winter hiking is the inability to "bliss out" for a long time if summits are frigid and blustery; three to five degrees is lost for each thousand feet ascended and wind-chill above treeline drives you down fast. Keeping extremities warm can be a challenge. Treks require correct gear and know-how. For most people winter climbing requires a team effort for safety, for trail-breaking in deep, unconsolidated snow, and for climbing cliffs. The wild world provides many experiences to which we respond much as we do to the rest of life's ups and downs—an opportunity for self-knowledge, sometimes a dubious pleasure! Occasionally in the pursuit of peak bagging we abandon prudence and must live the consequences, as some of these stories show. Just as in life, be careful what you commit yourself to, for sometimes you can't bail out.

We climb mountains because it makes our bodies and minds feel great. Even the average out-of-shape body becomes capable of hiking for many miles. To stay in top shape, adventurers in this book run, bike, canoe, down-hill and cross-country ski, walk, kayak, weight train, water-ski, rock and ice climb, paraglide, wind surf, scuba-dive, roller-blade, backpack, fish, spin, sail, practice yoga and Pilates, competitive body-build, and play competitive sports. They range from those who never felt good in sports at school to accomplished athletes. Their ages span the decades from fifteen to sixty-five. They've experienced cancer, miscarriage, eating disorders, foot problems, addiction to smoking, poor circulation, asthma, but all are undeterred in pursuing "re-creation."

Among the satisfying aspects of mountain climbing is making friendships as easily as children do, based on shared experience. Differences that can divide people like economic status, political beliefs, age, or gender don't exist on the trail because human commonality—helping, cheering, marveling, struggling together—is more real. Families enjoy and learn about each other as individuals. Relationships are renewed while sharing new adventures; delightful, surprising and inspiring aspects of one's partner emerge. Meeting kindred spirits occurs frequently.

Why do we climb mountains? The analytical mind yields no final answer because mountain climbing is an experience of the body, the senses, the heart, the will—cumulatively, of the spirit. The reasons we keep coming back are as varied as the adventurers themselves, as inscrutable as the unplumbed depths of the human being. There is an "agony-and-ecstasy" quality to mountain climbing that gives it its peculiar delight; sometimes we say we hike because it feels so good when we stop!

These wild experiences give perspective to our life; everyday existence is newly valued and enjoyed—a hot shower and comfy bed. One begins to simplify wants. Thoreau wrote, "That person is richest whose pleasures are the cheapest." Nothing in life is cost-free; every choice exacts a price; playing it safe, however, exacts a higher price. It is more fun to risk and discover new trails on this journey of life. The challenge of a human being is to continually grow, move, flow, as does nature, and so discover the limitless human capacity for striking out in new directions and experiencing life more deeply.

Immersion in the natural world gives insight into the finer perceptions of those who have actually lived there, such as Native Americans, Aborigines, rain forest dwellers, who experience creation as hallowed ground. The Taos Indians say, "The Mother of us all is Earth...we are children of Earth, and do it no harm in any way."

The natural world touches a deeper part of the self that reveres our world's vast complexity, balance, and beauty. Black Elk writes, "At the center of the universe dwells the Great Spirit, and this center is really everywhere, it is within each of us." Perhaps environmental degradation and squandering of natural resources are a result of alienation from nature in the modern world. Once we have fallen in love outwards, we're in that sacred consciousness that will "do no harm." Explorer and lover of nature John Muir wrote, "In wilderness is the preservation of the world."

ELSIE CHRENKO

46er #766W

The sun had not yet appeared above the mountains that loomed over my village in the Swiss Alps when a softly spoken "Time to wake up" interrupted my sleep on Sunday mornings. My mother would have breakfast ready for Atti (Daddy) and me before our trip to the mountains. My father took me hiking when I was three years old; first easy walks to alpine meadows, then more demanding hikes to minor peaks where one would spend the night in the hayloft of a cow herder's hut before attempting a summit. So began my love for the mountains in the 1930s in Switzerland.

When I was ten, my father took me on roped glacier peaks with his friends. We also skied the mountains, climbing to the huts with skins on skis. The wake-up call came around 4 A.M., depending on the severity of the climb we had chosen. I couldn't sleep much. Would I be able to keep up? Would they laugh if I were afraid to jump across a crevasse? What about the weather?

It was a great success when I reached the summit of the Balmhorn. I was filled with contentment, jubilation, joy and pride. I could see my valley in the distance and mountains like Matterhorn and Mt. Blanc far away. I felt like I was floating on a cloud of happiness. I knew then that climbing mountains would always be part of my life.

My first ice ax was a birthday present from my parents, handcrafted by famous Swiss skier Edy Schild. The shaft was made of ash wood with a large adze of steel; it had my name imprinted on it. I was proud of my ax and I still use it today! Crampons made of solid steel and weighing a ton were another birthday present at age sixteen. I was proud to place them under the flap of my rucksack so people could see I climbed high mountains.

I met my future husband "on the rocks" near New Paltz. Richard worked at the G.E. Research Center in Schenectady and I had a job in New York City. We spent nearly every weekend at the Shawangunks, where Richard was a climbing leader for the Appalachian Mt. Club. After the birth of our first child, we'd pack climbing gear plus baby in the car and head to those cliffs. We would leave her in the pram on Carriage Road at the foot of a climb.

Richard also introduced me to the Adirondacks where we climbed many High Peaks together. We would drive to a trailhead where one of us would stay with the children while the other went hiking. Then he introduced me to winter climbing; he'd nearly finished his second round of the 46 and I was tired of staying home alone, so I braved harsh weather and cold feet and was intrigued and captivated by the beauty and exhilaration of winter climbing. I'd never snowshoed before; Richard found and fixed big, heavy Army bearpaws with gut lacing for me. I climbed my first Winter 46er round on those antiquated, weighty, expansive bearpaws.

Often the experience of driving to and from the Adirondacks for my winter climbs was as memorable as the climb itself. Once I climbed a minor peak with a new ADK member who had politely offered to drive. He said his winter climbing ability was very good, but he probably underestimated the Adirondacks. We had to break trail in deep, unconsolidated snow, and he tired right away. Driving back on the Northway, he suddenly aimed straight for the cable railings! I screamed and tried to reverse the steering wheel. My shriek awakened him, for he stopped abruptly before hitting the fence. He walked around to the passenger side and brusquely said, "You drive." Soon he was sound asleep—again. We hiked the 46 High Peaks in winter three times, every ascent a day trip from Scotia, NY.

I finally acquired a pair of modified bear-paw snowshoes. I'd thought of buying much lighter plastic ones, but a friend had trouble in deep snow with his (early made) plastic snowshoes folding in two under his weight. My loyalty to wooden ones was renewed; they served me well for many years. Last season I finally replaced them with the same kind. Winter skills grow with every gained summit; one feels more at home in all kinds of different conditions. Winter climbing is an ongoing process of maturing and enjoying. I wouldn't want to have missed the great memories of climbing the Winter 46.

Much of my climbing has been in the Northeast: Catskill 3,500ers, Northeastern 4,000ers (called 111ers) that include peaks in New York and New England, and the New England 100 Highest. In winter I finished my third round of the Adirondack 4,000ers at age 65, and in 1994, I completed the forty-eight White Mountain winter 4,000ers. I've climbed a number of Colorado 14,000-foot peaks and have done non-technical climbs in Canada and Alaska. I hiked in Patagonia and did the Milford and Abel Tasman Treks in New Zealand, climbed Kilimanjaro in Africa and Illiniza in Ecuador. I broke an ankle climbing in Ecuador. What an experience, getting home from the hospital with an improvised wood-wire-nails-crutch on one side and the ice ax on the other! The other ankle was broken when learning to paraglide in Switzerland in 1988.

In the Alps some peaks climbed were the Eiger, Matterhorn, Weisshorn, Dom, Wetterhorn, and Monte Rosa, with my husband as a climbing partner. Richard was surprised by the integrated bunkrooms in the Swiss mountain huts. The hut master assigned you a bunk if quarters were nearly full. I slept next to old fogies, handsome young guys, extroverts, and others you couldn't even get a "good morning" out of—but very seldom women. I'm glad that has changed!

In 1992, we retired to New Hampshire, and are surrounded by

sparkling rocky streams and waterfalls, trailheads to magnificent peaks, miles of forest to hike and ski on. What more can an all-season climber ask for? I still look forward to climbing Mt. Washington via Lion Head at least once every winter.

Algonquin, February 8, 1970:

Five men and I went on an ADK outing to Algonquin. Until the steep section above the Wright Peak junction, I had walked in the middle or near the front of the group. Suddenly I was being overtaken—I was slipping and sliding, finding no traction. The snowshoes didn't obey me any longer. What was happening? I wasn't tired, I'd had experience from Couchi, had pointers from Richard how to place the bear paws on a steep slope. The men seemed to watch me with glee; here and there I detected a hardly-concealed smile. I felt so inadequate, inferior, out-of-place! One remarked, "Your crampons don't seem to work very well." Crampons! Of course! They were in my pack. Richard had homemade ones that we could mount and dismount. I put my crampons on and my place was again in the middle or near the front. I could have overtaken them all—but in the '70s a woman knew where her place was!

Haystack, February 23, 1970:

An agonizingly slow and difficult ascent of the last part of Haystack taught me the lesson of listening to my gut feeling and being careful about leaving snowshoes behind. I was hiking with Guy and Larry when, at Little Haystack, Guy suggested we leave the snowshoes there. I wasn't happy with his decision, yet I made only a feeble attempt to voice my opinion. I wanted to take them at least down to the col between the two peaks where snow could have accumulated. The two fellows were adamant to go without.

We soon encountered a stretch of bottomless snow. I feared I would never reach the summit of Haystack. I was so-o-o tired and so unhappy for not having the snowshoes with me; it would have rendered the ascent much easier and more enjoyable. We reached the top; during the last stretch I wasn't even tempted to help break trail, as Richard had advised me.

Colvin and Blake, March 5, 1978:

Richard and I were coming back from climbing Colvin and Blake. I was in a happy mood because everything had gone very well that day. Richard had even paid me a compliment for my mastering steep sections of trails so adeptly. Then it happened. Without warning I stumbled near the Nippletop junction, slid off the trail and ended up head-down, snowshoes up in deep, powdery snow. I flung my arms around wildly, hoping to find support; my head and body were embedded in a sea of white splendor! The more I tried to free myself the deeper I sank into the all-engulfing white mass. I tried to swing my legs and shoes to the downhill but couldn't lift them out of the heavy snow.

"Are you alright?" Richard's voice came from above. "How could you ask—don't you see I'm in trouble?" I heard Richard's hearty laugh, probably supposed to cheer me up, but it got my blood boiling. I finally played dead. Then I heard, "Give me your hand." Richard managed to turn me right-side-up and pull me back to the trail. I gave him the silent treatment on our way back to the car. After all, my tumble was nothing to laugh about—or was it?

Seward Range, First Round, March 10, 1973:

One unforgettable trip was to the Sewards. Our friends had graciously offered to look after our two children, then two and four. We dropped them off the night before our climb. We got up at midnight, ate, and then could not start the car! It was a VW Squareback, the first year with a computerized fuel injection system. After an unsuccessful hour, we were desperate at the thought of having to waste a good day and cancel the trip. We called our friends to explain the situation, hoping they might offer us the use of their car. They did.

As we drove up the Northway we began to wonder if it was such a good idea. The car was a Ford Bronco. It was bitter cold, far below zero, when we left home. The heater couldn't keep the windshield clear. Fortunately, no other vehicles were on the road. The flapping, fabric-covered doors had big gaps and the cold wind was slowly turning us to ice. The thermometer read -20° when we drove through Saranac Lake. For once we were looking forward to getting out of the car at cold-cold Corey's.

We warmed up as we hiked. Crossing a brook that was partially open, we saw that large frost-fingers had formed on the tree branches; they were back-lighted from a setting moon. It was a most unusual and extraordinary sight, as each finger seemed to be illuminated by a supernatural glow in the bitter cold.

Seward Range, Third round, March 1990:

The range seemed so much more difficult this time. There was deep snow; I sank in up to my knees even on snowshoes. When there are only two people to break trail in such conditions, we should have stayed home! I was so-o-o tired on top of Seward; but after a good rest and helpful old tracks, the hike to Donaldson and Emmons was great. We were surprised to find we were the first ones up these mountains this winter. We decided to return via Calkins Brook and found a great steep slope right to the brook. The walk out by an almost full moon and a sky of sparkling stars, seeing all the shadows of the trees plus our happy faces, was delightful. No flashlights were needed.

Allen, March,1990:

Richard and I climbed Allen for my third round after a friend and I got lost while Richard babysat (Richard and I never had to abort a climb due to getting lost.). The weather was beautiful, but a huge ice-jam had demolished the bridge across the Opalescent River. There was open water, but ice-blocks were strewn in a big jumble across the stream. Were they solidly wedged together, or would they fall apart at the slightest touch? After the four-mile hike we were reluctant to turn around. Richard gingerly climbed from one chunk to another positioned much deeper down. Sometimes he would disappear out of my sight altogether! I felt very ill at ease.

After Richard arrived safely on the opposite side, he motioned me to cross. I was glad when this ordeal was over! Then it struck me: it will take time to hike the twelve miles to Allen and back from here; how will conditions be when we want to return tonight? Will the sun melt our back-to-civilization ice and snow bridges? Will we still be able to cross on those precariously positioned chunks? I can't remember if the fear of this return overshadowed my whole day—but we did cross safely after a long and strenuous hike. We walked out by flashlight under a sky of stars and a quarter moon with the sound of Richard's melodious yodeling (he can't carry a tune) filling the otherwise serene stillness.

Santanoni Range, Second round, March 1982:

The Santanoni's were always a challenge. Their remoteness meant more miles to drive and more miles to hike for our one-day climbs. Fewer people were in the mountains years ago; one was surprised to find a packed trail to a bushwhack peak. From Bradley Pond the trail is a steep ascent; the degree of challenge depends on the type of snow one encounters. The snow-pack was relatively hard and it was a pleasure to snowshoe easily up Panther Brook to the Panther-Santanoni ridge and to the summit of Panther. A marvelous view rewarded us; Santanoni Peak greeted us from above. "We shall be there a little later," our hearts sang. Couchie, our next objective, beckoned—oh, so far away. But we arrived at its summit sooner than we thought. Retracing our steps back up the ridge, we headed south toward Santanoni.

The sun's reflections off the icy patches on the summit cone blinded our eyes. The higher we climbed, the stronger the wind. Fighting to keep our balance, we reached the top. What an exhilarating feeling! Far away from any human being, almost touching the sky, in a cold and windy, yet so majestic environment, we were happy. Not so happy when, after one half-hour's digging, we still could not find the canister. We were getting chilled and a long way still lay ahead of us. So we had to give up. We so much had wanted to write in the register: "#46 third round in winter for Richard; #46 second round in winter for Elsie."

Santanoni Range, Third round, March 19, 1990:

I was always surprised and almost jealous reading the extraordinary and grueling tales about peoples' Adirondack adventures. All our exploits went according to plan—except on my last third round finish on Santanoni. The forecast was sunny, with snow showers the next day; time to climb the range. We started early; no more babies or children to take care of! The temperature was on the warm side. On the way in we heard the melt-water gurgle under the snow-covered trail and sometimes a snowshoe would sink deeply into the wet snow.

The climb up Panther was enjoyable. Bare ground down the ridge to Couchi showed in places; we even took the snowshoes off for stretches, unusual for winter climbing. The sunny sky, however, became cloudy and the first snowflakes began to dance as we approached Couchi. While eating on top we wondered: Would we be able to climb Santanoni before the weather worsened? Rushing up under heavily falling snow wasn't exactly this mature climber's dream! Halfway up the Santanoni-Panther ridge we found our tracks already covered with snow. We soon realized we had to abandon the fervent desire to climb Santanoni. The wise thing to do with the snow increasing and the visibility decreasing was to descend and go home. That was a drastic decision! It meant giving up the chance of finishing another 46er round this winter. We tried to keep our spirits up by telling ourselves we would return the next day.

Our descent was wet, wet. Snow on the trees was melting and changed to rain lower down. We took our umbrellas out (steady companions when weather is uncertain) and changed to dry clothing. For us, the four-and-a-quarter-mile hike down did not sound intimidating, but the miserable conditions made it feel much longer! The water-soaked snow was rotten and often a large slab would break off with us on it. That would dump us into water that was flowing freely like a stream under the snow. Dripping and gurgling and roaring sounds were all around us and made the woods unpleasantly alive. We knew that we'd be unable to come back tomorrow; we wouldn't be home till midnight, then return to this mess? It wasn't until March 18, 1992, that I finally climbed Santanoni, the last peak for my third round of Winter 46.

Big Slide, January 26, 1974:

I had been sitting at home one beautiful day doing nothing (if doing nothing means taking care of house and children, preparing lunches, cooking dinners, keeping books, volunteering for school library, and Info-line) and Richard must have felt sorry for me, because he suggested I do a solo climb during the week. We decided on Big Slide; I had climbed it before so was familiar with the route.

I bounced happily along the trail when, shortly before the Big Slide junction, I met two girls. They stopped me, asking where I was headed. They seemed impressed when I mentioned Big Slide. "Alone?" When I nodded, their friendly attitude changed to one of disapproval. Did I realize it was dangerous to climb by myself? Maybe too much snow would hinder me. Maybe I couldn't get up if I fell. The binding could break. I pointed out the fact that they were by themselves also, which was unusual at that time. They explained they hiked to Johns Brook Lodge only and there were two of them. And who was I? After they heard my name they smiled and said, "Oh, we know you; we've heard about your and your husband; you are a legend in your own time!"

Wow, that put wind in my sail! The snow did get deep and the going tough. When I arrived at the very steep section shortly after the junction to the Brothers, I didn't seem to be able to make any headway in the deep, fluffy snow. What should I do? I tried to take my snowshoes off, hoping to get more purchase. That, of course, was a mistake. In deep snow and a sheer drop-off, one should leave the snowshoes where they belong—on one's feet! I had an excruciating time getting my deeply buried legs back onto my snowshoes, which kept getting covered by surrounding, unsettled snow. The thought of being stranded there or having to forego the summit, however, never occurred to me.

I eventually reached the summit of Big Slide with immense pride and satisfaction. I enjoyed a grandiose view of many familiar mountains. The sun was shining brightly, I felt wonderful and believed winter climbing could not throw anything at me that I couldn't master! I was so happy, singing loudly all the way home. I looked forward to hearing Richard's complimentary welcome, "What, you are home already?"

Algonquin and Wright:

Richard always predicts when I should be back. On the route up Algonquin, I passed the Wright junction and braced myself for the steep section; my snowshoes performed splendidly and soon I found myself above timberline. The higher I climbed, the more spectacular was the view of one mountain range after another, all clad in their exquisite winter garb. At the summit I sat on the rocks, ate, and talked to people who were about to leave—so I didn't linger; I'd noticed climbers over on Wright and decided to climb that short extra half-mile one-way. By now, the sun had rendered the snow wet and mushy; I was sinking in deeply and snow balled up on my snowshoe crampons. I felt so hot and tired. It was an arduous job reaching the top; I didn't tarry. Richard's greeting this time was not complimentary. He only asked, "What took you so long?"

Elsie began Winter 46ing at age 37 and finished her third round at age 65.

DOT MYER

46er #914W

I was on top of Mt. Marcy just above a blanket of white fluffy clouds, and saw the highest High Peaks rising above. I was so impressed by this fantastic view that eventually I was to climb them all, once in summer and once in winter. On Mt. Marcy I was with the University of Vermont Outing Club; it was 1953. I was wearing street clothes, even shoes, on this highest peak in New York State. I was carrying an old army rucksack borrowed from the Outing Club. Real hiking boots and a knapsack of my own were to come later.

I grew up in the country and always "walked in the woods." I started serious hiking in the winter with the University of Vermont Outing Club. I stayed in Vermont and worked for the University for thirty-five years, mainly as a research assistant in community health research. I joined the Green Mountain Club and this began a lifelong avocation of hiking and other outdoor activities. I've remained active in the Green Mountain Club through my seventies; I've hiked the Long Trail in Vermont, the Northville-Placid Trail in New York State, and many High Peaks in New York, Vermont, and New Hampshire.

In 1970, when I was forty-five years old, I really concentrated on climbing all the High Peaks, first in the Adirondacks and later in New England. I'd climbed about half of the 46 Adirondack High Peaks, a point at which it becomes natural to want to finish them. I met Carlene, Jack, and Ralph who were to become my regular hiking companions throughout the rest of the 111 High Peaks of the Northeast. Ralph and I climbed all 111 in winter; I was the first woman and sixth person to do that. I bought crampons near the end of 46ing to climb the winter peaks in New Hampshire and Maine; I should have had them on Basin.

We camped in many places. The biggest difficulty for me, when camping, was cold fingers in the morning. While hiking, I often have to take my mittens off. Nights out weren't too bad; we had supper and went to bed. But in the morning my hands "froze" making breakfast. The most difficult camping was in the Seward Range at about thirty degrees below zero. One person got frostbite. Another time we cooked in the tent for two nights; everything got so wet that we were cold, even though it wasn't very cold at night. We learned from that. I have winter camped a lot after finishing the Winter 46, but would not do it so many weekends in a row again.

Sometimes we "camped" at Winter Camp in the Johns Brook Lodge area, an annual event that Ralph started and led for the Green Mountain Club. From that base camp we'd go on various hikes and have a party at night. One hike involved twenty-three people! We bushwhacked to Phelps and had to count off periodically to keep track of each other. We climbed Redfield with the ADK/AMC winter school, also a large group, and another time turned back just before reaching the summit of Algonquin.

I continued climbing a few High Peaks each year and learned about many great smaller peaks in the Adirondacks that I climbed with my friend Pat. In 2001, also with Pat, I climbed Mt. Redington in Maine that has been added to the High Peaks list; there are now 115 peaks over 4,000 feet in the Northeast. Redington is the only one I haven't climbed in winter. I completed the Appalachian Trail in 2003. I've hiked in Montana, the Canadian Rockies, Alaska, Norway, Scotland, Switzerland, and Bolivia.

I use my bicycle for regular transportation. I have ridden my bicycle to all 251 towns in Vermont, alone or with my old college friend, Lindy. (There's a 251 Club in Vermont whose members travel to all 251 towns). We've also bicycled around Lake Champlain. I'm currently Membership Chair of the Green Mountain Club and have always enjoyed working on trails and shelters. I coordinated the rebuilding of Taylor Lodge on the Long Trail.

The outdoors has been an important part of my life and I think it's important to pass on this interest to young people. I've worked at an Audubon summer camp and with the Girl Scouts, which I led for many years. In spite of breast cancer I remain healthy and plan to continue outdoor activities. I always say, "I can do anything I ever could, only it takes three times as long." The Winter 46 is the most adventurous thing I ever did. Sometimes the problems are even more memorable than the good times. For others contemplating it, persistence is important. Neither my partner nor I were exceptional hikers but we never gave up; we just kept trying even when things went wrong.

Haystack, Basin, and Saddleback, March 9, 1974:

One of my most dangerous adventures occurred on a hike on part of the Great Range. Ralph and I and someone named Bob hiked in to spend the night in the lean-to at Johns Brook Lodge. It was very icy and we had to be careful hiking in the dark. Our friends Jack and Carlene had not arrived by 8 o'clock and we decided to start without them. It was icy and some spots were very difficult, especially going up and descending Little Haystack. We climbed Haystack carrying our snowshoes and chopped steps in the ice in places on the descent. We met up with Jack and Carlene who were ascending, and waited for them to come back down.

The four of us went on to climb Basin; we met a woman descending alone—wearing crampons. We didn't have crampons that day or for the Adirondack Winter 46; we got them later for the White Mountains. After some difficulty finding the trail down the other side of Basin, we were descending well when suddenly I had one of the worst falls of my life! I tried to slide toward a little tree but missed it and went sliding down a long, steep snowfield at full speed, headfirst on my stomach. It happened too fast to think. I only remember seeing a large tree and thinking, "Should I slide into the tree, or continue all the way down the slope?" Either way could have been fatal. Fortunately the others were down ahead of me. Carlene, who is not particularly religious, said she prayed. Ralph caught and saved me. I only got a bruise on my leg. We went on to climb Saddleback and, although there were many very difficult icy places, we made it without further problems.

Tabletop, January 5, 1975:

I experienced an unusual fall coming back from an attempt to climb Tabletop. We had set up camp in the Johns Brook Lodge area and tried to bushwhack up Tabletop from Bushnell Falls. Unsuccessful, we were on our way back down and I was pushing through bushes so thick that I had no idea of what was a foot ahead of me. I pushed with all my might, finally forcing my way through and flew off a small cliff! I hit my head on a log and hurt my neck and leg. I was afraid that it might be serious, but I was all right after a little while. A little farther on Ralph fell off a cliff and hurt his leg. We both limped back to camp.

Algonquin, March 9, 1975:

Ralph, Joan, and I had a chance to use survival techniques when we got disoriented descending from Algonquin's open summit. We had backpacked up to the Wright junction where we set up camp. The next day we climbed Algonquin carrying just our daypacks and lost the trail in a whiteout on the descent. We tried to follow a compass course that we hoped would intercept the trail, but by 5:30 P.M. realized we would have to spend the night in the woods without our sleeping bags or other equipment.

My first thought was to walk as far as possible, but we realized that would have been foolish. We followed a small brook until we found open water and decided to camp. By sheer coincidence we found the remains of a slight shelter with a roof built of boughs. We dug the snow out, put boughs in the bottom, and added our snowshoes to the roof. Our fire never got going very well, even though Joan worked at it until nearly 11 P.M. We ate bread and fruit and shivered through the night, sleeping only occasionally. We had a small space blanket that kept the snow from melting under us, but otherwise it didn't do much good. Fortunately it was not a very cold night.

At daylight we started walking, which was much warmer than sleeping! We followed a compass course for two hours until we came upon snowshoe tracks. In a short while we came to the trail just a few yards from the junction of the Van Hoevenberg-Algonquin Peak Trails. We had paralleled the trail all the way down! We climbed back up the trail for our tent and equipment near the Wright junction. Except that we were tired and hungry, we felt fine.

Seward, Donaldson, and Emmons, March 12-16, 1976:

One of my most memorable hikes was when Ralph and I spent five days in the mountains without seeing a single other person. We got to Blueberry Lean-to at one o'clock and after that we were bushwhacking with map and compass. We went on to a brook, boulder, and lower ridge we remembered from a previous hike to Seward, but this time took a different route to avoid some steep pitches. We came to red flags, saw the ridge of Seward in the distance, and set up the tent. The next day it was drizzling and snowing and Ralph was tired, so we didn't start until noon when it cleared. We ascended a very steep ridge and saw Seward across a valley. We found a way down several smaller cliffs on our side and crossed to the bottom of some larger ones, where we made camp in a nice little hollow.

The next day we found a good route up Seward. The trees were covered with new snow—beautiful! It was a bright sunny day, but I got so wet and cold I had to hike with my heavy jacket on. It was a fairly easy hike to the top of Donaldson. We signed the canister register and started for Emmons. We scouted for another campsite and found a very pretty spot in the trees. We were a little wet and uncomfortable but slept well. The inside of the tent was getting wet with condensation from cooking inside. We learned from that trip to cook outside, no matter how cold it was.

The next morning was bright and beautiful and we started out for Emmons. The trees were thick and the ridge was confusing, but we finally reached the summit of Emmons. We decided to return via Calkins Brook and noted this in the can. We bushwhacked around Donaldson instead of going over it again. Descending to a flat area we headed northwest until we saw a very deep valley and started down, which took a long time. Calkins Brook is wide here and most of the ice was not safe enough to walk on, so we had to walk beside it through dense trees. We found a nice camping spot right beside the brook but couldn't break the ice for cooking! So again we melted snow. We hadn't planned on taking this long for the hike but fortunately had brought spare food.

The next morning we soon came to old logging roads and the going was easy; in the afternoon we found a place to cross the brook and found the road to the trail. About 4:30 P.M. a ranger came on a snowmobile looking for us. Friends had become worried, and after calling our work places, other hikers were summoned for rescue and the ranger was notified. For his report, he questioned us about our clothing (all wool, proper at that time) and what we did when we were "lost." We had a hard time convincing him that we were never lost—we just took longer than planned! The previous week we really did get lost in a whiteout on Algonquin, and nobody missed us!

Nye and Street, February 26, 1978:

We made seven attempts on Nye, each with a different problem. We usually tried to climb it by the Old Nye Ski Trail. One time we got a late start, the snow was very deep, and we ran out of time and had to turn around. Another time we reached a high point that was not the summit and didn't know where to go next. It was a cloudy day and we couldn't see much, but finally we saw a peak off to our right and headed for it. It was so steep and cliffy that Ralph had to pull me up in many spots. Finally we reached the top. There was no canister and no place any higher. By this time it was snowing hard. We couldn't see at all, but were pretty sure we were on the wrong mountain. I was afraid to go down the steep way we'd come, so we found a different descent route.

That was a Saturday; we stayed overnight and planned another try on Sunday. We met two people who seemed to know exactly how to do it. We went with them. We made very good progress and soon were on top of a mountain—the wrong one! There were snowshoe tracks partly buried in the new snow; we think they were ours from the day before. This time the weather was clear and we saw Street and Nye in the distance, but it was too late to try and climb them.

Another time we couldn't get across Indian Pass Brook near the beginning. We retraced and climbed Cascade and Porter, so the day wasn't lost. At the top it was so cold that my glasses froze and I had to take them off. When I tried to put them back on they snapped in half. We were shocked to see a couple with a tiny baby near the top of Cascade. We hoped they didn't take him all the way.

Still another time, we climbed Street from Rocky Falls Lean-to and hoped to get over to Nye also. We had a very good climb and finally reached the top of Street. Ralph was so happy, he kissed the canister! But the weather was so bad and it was late, so we didn't go on to Nye. We started back down and I soon fell in a deep spruce hole. I just could not get out with my snowshoes on, but somehow I was able to get them off. Ralph held my ankles while I went down headfirst to retrieve them. It was raining that day and when we got back down, Carlene, who had not hiked that day, said to me "You look awful!" I'm sure I did. Later it cleared up and we saw beautiful northern lights—amazing!

We tried so many times to climb Nye, one of the smallest of the High Peaks, that whenever we walked into the Hikers Building someone would say to us, "Oh, you're climbing Nye again?" We eventually did climb Nye. After six attempts we decided to camp part way up instead of doing it all in one day. We hiked until 4:00 P.M. and set up our tent in the snow. We had a comfortable night. The next day it was a surprisingly easy hike to the elusive Nye, which was named for a legendary Adirondack guide.

Dot began the Winter 46 at age 45 and finished at age 49.

NOLA ROYCE

46er #1399W

Growing up in the environs of a sedate and intellectually oriented family in Queens, NY, is not what comes to mind as the most likely beginning for a mountaineering enthusiast. It was a fine breeding ground, however, for developing my curiosity and my eagerness to explore.

Although my parents, especially my mom, had in mind that I'd do that exploration through a love of music, literature, and theater, I found that my desire to know about the world required my direct, physical participation; I am most joyous when being physical. In the mountains I feel whole, alive, and at peace. Discovering the Adirondack Mountains in the 1970s, when I first moved up to the Albany area, was delightful. I met other outdoor enthusiasts and developed long-lasting friendships based on that common interest. Hiking the 46 High Peaks of the Adirondacks was an excuse to get out and play, to unwind from the week's stresses and to enjoy good company. Hiking led to climbing, with the routes varying from mild to moderate to extreme.

I had the good fortune to have hiked with "old timers" from ADK and learned a great deal from them. As an "old timer" now myself,

I enjoy offering that gift to others. The ADK winter school is a great experience also; I highly recommend it. When I started, my gear was wool clothing, wooden snowshoes, and leather or rubber insulated boots, and a frame pack; today's gear makes things easier.

In the 1980s I also got interested in weightlifting as a means of getting my upper body strong for rock and ice climbing, and eventually engaged in several bodybuilding competitions. It was hard work and helped improve my climbing ability; the only part I didn't like was the dieting down for an event. You take a lot of pictures of how you look in that posing suit, because you can only fit into it on the day you show! It was fun, though, eating your way back to normalcy.

After I climbed Mt. Rainier in 1986 and Denali in 1988, I realized I was on my way to another level of travel and adventure. The quest for the Winter 46 was great training for my ascent of Denali and other mountains around the world. I was the fourth woman, in 1990, to ascend all peaks over 4,000 feet in New York and New England in winter. It was on Mount Elbrus, the highest peak in Europe in the Caucasus, that I met Skip Horner, with whom I went to Antarctica in 1993. After summiting Mt. Vinson, that continent's highest peak, I thought to myself, "I love this place—I'd go back in a heartbeat." Right though the mid-1990s I just kept on climbing and traveling and having a grand time in the mountains.

In January 1996, I had a big surprise. I was diagnosed with breast cancer. I was in shock and frightened, partly in response to the disease and partly because of what I imagined it might mean to a way of life I had come to love so deeply. I questioned whether or not I would ever be able to climb again, but I fully recovered. I got involved with Expedition Inspiration, an organization that promotes the physical and mental well-being of breast cancer survivors. Their motto is: "There's a climb until there's a cure." Founder Laura Evans formed teams of survivors and others to climb significant mountains to raise awareness and funds in the fight against breast cancer. In 1996, Expedition Inspiration was looking for sponsors and climbers for an ascent of Mt. Vinson in Antarctica; I had climbed Vinson in 1993, so I applied and was accepted as a member of that climbing team. I also climbed with them on Mt. Rainier and Mt. Aspiring in New Zealand.

Upon my return from the trip to Mt. Aspiring in 1998, I had a local recurrence of cancer and underwent surgery. I worked my way back into good health and good form. I've included Iyengar Yoga as part of my weekly routines for physical and mental well-being and continue to rock and ice climb, ski and snowshoe, bike, and play tennis.

Today I am still seeking adventure and companionship in the mountains and, with a climb of Kilimanjaro in August of 2000, have had the good fortune to have climbed on all seven continents; I recently trekked to Everest Base Camp to summit Mt. Meru, a 21,000-foot peak. The past three winters I've climbed ice in Ouray, Colorado, and spent a week ice climbing on the big waterfalls in Valdez, Alaska.

The Winter 46 was wonderful training ground for everything I've done. Winter 46ing reinforced my sense of self-reliance and interdependence. It stretched my physical, mental, and emotional limits. It put me in touch with myself and my environment in a deeply moving way. When I began the Winter 46 I had a lot to learn about snow conditions, keeping well hydrated and fed to accommodate the body's needs in extreme weather.

A few winter Adirondack peaks required more than one try. As I became more proficient in snowshoeing and selecting the time of year to attempt certain routes, the whole business got easier. Patience is necessary in this sport. I intend to keep on climbing and exploring, both in the mountains and within myself. The experience of climbing offers endless opportunity for both. It is a wonderful journey and I have been blessed with the ability to do it. For that, and much more, I am eternally grateful.

I decided that I wanted to work locally in the field of support for breast cancer and decided to join my friend and fellow survivor, Mara Ginsberg, at a non-profit she had founded in 1998, called To Life! We've created a safe haven here in my hometown for women and their families to receive all the support and information they need to deal with a diagnosis, treatment, and recovery. Having left my position as a school administrator the year before, I signed on with Mara and became the Program Coordinator at To Life! I've been with the organization ever since. I enjoy sharing my experiences with other women and encouraging them to take charge of their lives and their well-being. I am living what I believe and loving it. It is very life-affirming!

Rocky Peak Ridge and Giant, February 23, 1975:

I found myself hiking later and later into the fall season and eventually into winter. My first solar winter ascent of a High Peak was Giant Mountain, still one of my favorites. The route we chose was long and required an overnight. We came in from NY 9N in New Russia, camped, and traversed over the peak on the second day. Among my companions were Norm and Marilyn Fancher, Walt Herrod, and Craig Geiselhart, the chap who had introduced me to the Adirondacks a couple of years before. We took turns breaking trail in very deep snow. My snowshoes were long for my height and weight; my short legs (I have a 25" inseam) struggled to pack down the fluffy stuff. When it was my turn up front, although my effort was great, there was little to show for it. I usually stayed about third in line and thus reaped the benefit of packed terrain. There was little respite even in that position and I was most grateful when we reached the lean-to. We set up camp and hunkered in for the long night.

Plied with lots of hot drinks, soup, freeze-dried mush for dinner and more hot drinks, I snuggled into my sleeping bag and tried to sleep. Sleep, of course is interrupted by the need to relieve oneself from the copious amount of fluid one drinks to keep warm and stay hydrated. It was a toss-up between wetting the bed and freezing my buns off and I made several trips to the outhouse (back of the lean-to as the night wore on) before falling into a very deep sleep. With morning came the task of fitting all that fluffed up down and gear back into my pack, eating more mush and other frozen inedibles, and stomping more trail. The uphill section to the summit of Giant seemed interminably long; finally we were rewarded with a windy but relatively flat surface across its top. With this achievement, I began counting my Winter 46.

Seward, Donaldson, and Emmons, March 16, 1979:

We had one exciting bivouac after climbing Emmons. The climbs began by a challenging ascent of Seward in deep snow by bushwhacking and trail breaking, not on any direct herd path. Because

I'm short (almost five feet), deep snow always challenges me. En route to Emmons, we got turned around and wasted time. Rather than slog back over Donaldson and Seward, much of it in the dark, we agreed to head down from Emmons to find shelter at the Cold River.

I barreled down through deep snow off the top and we reached the valley by dark, finding ourselves on a log bridge—which meant we were near the Cold River Lean-to. Inside we changed into anything dry we had; all our stuff was wet from snow falling on us or from sweat. This was done long before I had access to the new fabrics and I was grateful for my wool gear—it kept me warm even when wet.

We huddled together under the one sleeping bag we had. I also wrapped myself up in my ultra-light emergency blanket. We had candy bars left and rationed them throughout the night. No one wanted to get extra water from the river, so we let that go until daylight—which took a long time coming! We were not in danger, but not terribly comfortable.

In the morning we waited until the sun was well up, gathered our frozen belongings and began trudging back to our base camp at Ward Brook Lean-to. It was a long, hungry, mostly silent trek. Once we were thawed out, we took photos at the Hermit's camp and nibbled the last scraps of candy bars. It was near St. Patrick's Day and back at camp, Kathy Gill shared some Bailey's Irish Cream with us—one cup of that in my hot chocolate and I was down for the count.

We slept late the next day. The 5.4-mile walk back to the car was mostly uphill, or so it seemed. The pack was unusually heavy and I was really tired. I had gotten to use a lot of the skills I'd learned, pushed myself really hard, and felt quite satisfied. It was all good training for things to come on bigger, badder mountains all over the world. I just didn't know that yet.

Macomb, February 3, 1979:

Another trip where there was so much snow that the canisters—in summer well above our heads—were buried, was my ascent of Macomb with Kathy Gill, Steve Sopko, Alan Via, and Bill Sewell. We took an unusual approach that brought us part way up Sunrise Mountain and then traversed over to Macomb's summit. The only way I knew I was there was that the metal crampon attached to my wood and rawhide snowshoe scratched across and caught on some-thing underfoot and threatened to dislodge itself from the rawhide to which it had been tied. I didn't lose the homemade crampon and we located the canister. What a good feeling that was!

The early part of that day was very brisk and clear. The view down toward Elk Lake was inspiring, which was a good thing, because the trail breaking over to the summit of Macomb was ardu-ous. This is not the typical way to go up Macomb, so it offered us another opportunity to stay warm by working up a sweat and slog-ging through untouched terrain. If I sound like I was complaining, I may very well have been; many ascents were tough going but well worth it.

All that training made future climbs seem reasonable when walk-ing on well-packed, crusty snow, especially with crampons. Snow-shoes will get you through stuff that no other footwear will plod though and during the period in which I did most of the High Peaks in the Adirondacks, we seemed to have had deeper, fluffier snow and fewer people on the trails…or maybe they were smart and waited until they heard about someone having packed them!

Gothics, February 18, 1979:

Companions Steve Sopko, Bob Grimm, Art Haberl, and I shared the task of breaking trail up the steep Orebed Brook Trail. The cables on the ascent to the summit were almost totally buried. The day was crisp and clear and we were all grinning at the sight of the summit and the vistas surrounding us. After traversing over to Armstrong we came back to the col between Gothics and Armstrong and bush-whacked down to Orebed Brook in deep snow that seemed bottom-less…and I didn't want to find out! While sliding on steep powder I found myself in a face-plant, after a couple of not-so-graceful pirou-ettes…a difficult maneuver, at best, on snowshoes. I had the feeling that if I went in over my head, I'd be found only after the spring thaw. This was a good, quick route off the mountain but one to be done only in appropriate winter conditions.

Allen, March 3, 1979:

After having tried the usual way up Allen, which is a miserable bushwhack in summer and even more miserable in winter, we decided that usual is not always the best approach. After waiting for late-season freezing and thawing to consolidate the snow, we selected a route paralleling the stream and well above its banks to avoid blowdown and the possibility of stepping into open, deep pools. We did avoid the traps and pools; however, the snow was deep and at the headwall, steep.

I and my companions, Kathy Gill and Steve Sopko, did reach the summit after one of our longer days on the winter trail. We were followed by another party one week later. Kathy ran into the group on another hike and had heard them comment on the uniqueness of the route they found up Allen Mt. and how easy it was. I'm not sure what Kathy said to this group; I am sure of what I might have said, but it's not printable.

Dix and Hough, December 22, 1979:

If a hike doesn't go past twenty-four hours, it's a day hike. The shortest day of the year is probably not the best time to plan a fifteen-mile winter climb of two remote Adirondack High Peaks involving bushwhacking! However, that's exactly what a group of my usual suspects, Steve Sopko, Rich Casler, George Tilroe, Bill Sewell, Kathy Gill, and I did.

We drove as far as we could on the road into Elk Lake, stopped by the snowbank left by plows. With another two miles to trudge on the road, we hefted packs and walked to the trailhead for Dix Mountain. Our plan was to go up Dix, traverse to the summit of Hough and return via Lillian Brook to the Dix trail, leaving us several miles of trail and roadway to get to the car. The distances and logistics of this trip, planned in the warmth and light of my kitchen, seemed very reasonable at the time. We also wanted to get a good jump on the season and bag a "so-far elusive mountain," Hough. The year before I had turned around on an attempt to reach Hough's summit in miserable conditions. Now Hough was on my hit list!

An early start put us on the Dix Trail at daylight and we made good progress until we reached Slide Brook, where we had to slither across downed, icy logs. This proved to be only the beginning of our adventures with interesting stream crossings and dicey conditions.

On the steep, uphill trail to Dix Mountain, we found continuously variable snow. This presented a challenge as to what accessories would work. Sometimes snowshoes would be best, other times full crampons would. No matter what we tried, we frequently discovered that we had on the wrong item shortly after donning it. In spite of the conditions and arduousness of the climb to Dix's summit, it was not too unreasonable, we thought. It looked as if the summit of Hough were just over the ridge from the Beckhorn.

Looks can be deceptive! As we bushwhacked toward Hough, we thrashed through thick brush and, surprise, surprise, no one else had been anywhere near this area since the first frost! The illusion that Hough was close dissolved quickly. We wallowed over, reaching the summit of Hough at 3:30 P.M. Now, of course, we had to get down the trailless, steep western slope. We were all well prepared with headlamps, extra food and drink, and appropriate clothing. The weather was cooperating, relatively warm and calm. We dropped down over the summit and took a bearing toward where the Dix trail would intersect Lillian Brook near the lean-to.

With Steve Sopko out in front and me close behind, with one eye on the compass and one on the terrain below my feet, I directed our progress as we slogged down from Hough. Sometimes it was evident that we were on a herd path and sometimes not. We stayed on our bearing and as darkness approached, stuck close together, plodding on. It was well after dark when we reached the Lillian Brook-Dix Trail junction and then, our nemesis of the morning, Slide Brook.

I was ready to find a comfy spot in the woods or at the Slide Brook Lean-to and bivy till morning, having no desire to deal with that miserable stream-crossing one more time. That idea did not resound well with my companions and they searched for a better way across. Finally finding one, we dragged our weary bones four more miles out to the trailhead and car. The ride home was slow and silent.

On one of my camping trips to bag winter summits I slept in on our retreat day. Kathy Gill and I tented together and she was first to get out. Bob Grimm was saying something about coffee brewing and Kathy asked if I wanted any; my response was, "Sure, do they deliver it with the *New York Times*? It's Sunday, you know." I won't repeat what either Kathy or Bob Grimm said. I can tell you though, that on my 46th winter peak, Bob did bring me the *New York Times* for that day and instead of coffee, poured champagne. And he didn't make me carry out the whole paper…what a guy!

Nola began the Winter 46 at age 30 and finished at age 38.

DIANE DUGGENTO SAWYER

46er #1843W

I have been teaching mathematics to junior high students since 1970 in Portsmouth, New Hampshire, and was Department Chairperson for twenty of those years. I began to hike during the early years of my teaching career, for two reasons: I wasn't interested in the usual things that young people find fun, and hiking was a way to be with friends and to enjoy nature.

I met my future husband Tom Sawyer, also a teacher, and the two of us began to hike every weekend and during school vacations. On my first hike with him and students in his hiking club to Mt. Clinton in New Hampshire, it rained; only a few opted to climb to the summit from the hut—including myself. Tom said he knew then that I had potential. That summer he invited me to go to Colorado to climb

14,000-footers. It was often more technical climbing and prompted us to take up rock climbing, which we have continued to this day. I plan to complete the dozen 14,000-footers I haven't finished after I retire (there are 54.) We climbed the other 14,000ers in the United States and the high points in every state except Alaska.

I've climbed all the 4,000-footers in England, Wales, and Scotland; Kilimanjaro; Elbrus, Europe's highest peak; and Orizaba, Mexico's high point. The peaks in Maine are hard to forget. We decided to hike the Adirondack Winter 46 as soon as Tom finished the New Hampshire Hundred Highest in winter. Because of low snow levels in 1982 and 1983, we completed the Adirondack 46 in just two winters.

We backpacked the Long Trail in Vermont in winter; camping out at twenty and thirty below zero, getting mired in spruce traps, snow-shoeing twenty or more miles in the dead of winter. We camped while climbing several Adirondack peaks in winter. We use bags good to -40° and a V24 North Face tent. We like to cook in the vestibule and always have hot drinks. We put two canteens of hot water in bed with us. We're always toasty—even once at fifty below. We often pack in using Mountain Smith sleds and use cross-country skis whenever possible. We bury water near the tent so that it won't freeze. We have favorite things to eat that help keep the spirits and energy up. Each experience adds to your skills.

I've grown in many ways because of my experiences in the mountains. I've learned to rely on myself and no one else for help—cell phones and other locating devices, even companions, can give one a false sense of security. The mountain will be there but you may not if you're too anxious to get to the summit. Tom Sawyer, the fel-low with restless feet, isn't happy unless he has a list to work on. I'm happy hiking for the exercise, the camaraderie, and to experience nature up close—at times too close! In Maine we just missed hitting a moose on a dark road!

I don't want Tom to hike these remote places alone. Mostly it's just us two, at least on the multiple-day backpacks to climb the win-ter 3,000-footers in New England. We leave each Friday soon after school; house and schoolwork are done by Thursday evening. Packing is an hour or less since some things remain permanently packed. Our house has one room devoted to outdoor clothing and equipment. During Christmas vacation we leave in the already-loaded van right after changing out of work clothes.

We put on chains when arriving at an icy logging road; spend an hour chopping a space off the road in which to park the van; prepare our sleds for a weeklong camping trip. Then we sled to the base of a group of remote mountains, navigating by headlamps, and set up base camp. Perhaps move our tent to shorten trips.

These treks are a transition from the hectic work world to the tranquil, frozen, timeless world we are entering. Our minds and souls are healed by returning to the lives led by our ancestors—the simple struggle for survival. Moose, deer, snowshoe hare, otters, grouse, even a fisher, lynx, or larger cat may roam the deserted, remote areas.

Temperatures vary from single digits to fifteen below during late December. Stopping to eat is difficult in the frigid atmosphere; taking off gloves is done only for seconds and it takes many minutes to re-warm hands; we struggle to do simple things without taking gloves off. We check each other frequently for frostbite on cheeks and noses or use facemasks; if the wind is ferocious we set up our tent. Dealing with tent poles is the most challenging job—gloves slide on the metal poles; frost-nip is always possible. Tom stakes the tent by burying sticks tied to the ends of tent poles. We must get water before total darkness by breaking ice in a brook, not an easy task! The banks are steep and slippery and we're wearing snow-shoes. Once I heard a horrible moaning. Tom was looking for water upstream and I thought Tom had fallen in! I shouted and he answered! Then we heard the mournful sound of a moose in the set-tling dusk. We found its tracks the next morning near our camp.

At night, water is heated for supper and water bottles; we bury water in a pot to use in the morning for hot drinks and oatmeal. We remove wind jackets, hats, mittens, boots, sock liners, vapor barri-ers, wool sweaters, long johns, and wash in heated water in the tent vestibule (it's imperative to bathe daily in order to keep warm). Tom makes us hot drinks like Jell-O or bouillon. Bagels with cheese and slices of ham are heated in the pot lid until the cheese melts; the main meal is usually a freeze-dried dinner followed by brownies and hot chocolate with a shot of coffee brandy. Then we rinse dishes, store food, and heat water to fill bottles for our sleeping bags; I use one at my feet and one near my stomach. Shuddering, I place my boots in the bottom of the bag—keeping legs curled up to avoid contact! Inevitably they would be frozen solid by morning. Our friends John and Pat Bickford join us for fun and challenging winter hikes. Tom and John do the lion's share of the breaking trail, but we all take turns at the head of the line.

I also enjoy reading, gardening, cooking, dancing, birding, and attending plays on Broadway and visiting Boston. I'm fortunate that Tom is willing to join me for both cooking and dancing lessons; sometimes he's be the only male in the classes. We're into white water canoeing. Because of back problems I thought I couldn't carry a pack, but I've discovered that a large fanny pack can hold an amazing amount. Recently I completed the Northeast Winter 111 peaks over 4,000 feet and am working on the winter New England Hundred Highest. I've done eighty percent of the New England 3,000-footers in winter; Tom is the first and perhaps will be the only person to complete all the 3,000-footers in New England in winter. We are planning to complete the Adirondack 3,000-footers in winter as well.

I've developed ocular Roseacea, which limits the amount of exposure to wind, cold, and sun I can be subjected to without risking permanent damage to my vision. This prevents a Denali climb; the doctor thinks I may have frozen my eyes. I can't imagine how! Try forty to fifty below in Maine or howling wind and blowing snow, ice collecting on your face as you hike for ten hours. Although I wouldn't have done many of these quests without Tom, together we've found enjoyment, completion, and much happiness in the mountains. I helped Tom to enjoy birds, flowers, and animal tracks, and he has helped me to find peace in the mountains. When I retire in 2005, we plan to bike from Maine to California on our touring bikes. In 2006, we hope to hike the Appalachian Trail end-to-end.

Panther, Couchsachraga, and Santanoni, February 14, 1982:

With friends John and Pat Bickford, we began the bushwhack up Panther Brook on an overcast day with flurries, about 12°F. We reached an established base camp at 3,200' and pitched tents, melted snow to drink, cook, and wash. After supper at 4:30, I snuggled down in my bag with my two canteens filled with hot water and read for a couple of hours before dropping off to sleep. We rose at 4:30 A.M. the next morning and Tom prepared hot cereal, warm Tang and Pop Tarts. The batteries in his headlamp died. At 5:45 we climbed Panther Brook on broken trail and at 7 A.M. we were standing on the summit of Panther; the 360° view was obscured by clouds. We used a compass and altimeter to follow the ridge west to Couchsachraga.

Later, on the bushwhack to Santanoni, we encountered a dense spot north of the col. Pat and I were behind the men; she disappeared into a horrendous spruce trap. She is five feet tall and was now well below the level of the snow, suspended on numerous spruce branches below. She is a real scrapper—a tough and resilient hiker and rock climber. This was the first time I'd seen her exasperated and frustrated. She was cursing at the guys, whose tracks she had been following. After all, they had stepped here before her and they were heavier—yet they had managed to float over this spot. I watched her struggle as I called unsuccessfully to John and Tom. I circled to find some way to help her and not fall in myself; when I reached across, the snow caved in around me and in seconds, I was eyeball to eyeball with Pat. She was none too happy that I had reburied her snowshoes and was now standing on them—making it even more difficult to move. We both worked for a long time trying to free ourselves. Each time we tried to kick a step into the side of the hole, hoping to work our way up, we would only discover another spruce trap. Finally the guys arrived, having retraced; why were we so long in coming? They roared with laughter when they spotted us.

There wasn't much they could do, as the entire area was a minefield of spruce traps. So they watched. Pat was finally able to make her way out. By then I was exasperated, discouraged, exhausted, and fearing I would never be able to get out. It was nearly an hour after first seeing Pat disappear into that God-awful spruce trap, that I managed to get out with a hand from Tom. By the time we were both out, the giant crater that had been created by our struggle was thirty feet across and seven-plus feet deep. We wondered what the next party would think when they found this spot!

Donaldson, Emmons, and Seymour, March 6, 1982:

It was a mild morning as Tom and I began our trek at 5 A.M. The stars were bright and twinkling in the unpolluted skies when we left on cross-country skis, snowshoes strapped to our daypacks. At the junction of Calkins Brook and Ward Brook Trail we switched to snowshoes and hid our skis. Bushwhacking up from Calkins Brook was easy going; we could generally ride on the crust and by 9 A.M. we had reached 2,950' with views of impressive cliffs. Continuing to 3,650' west of Donaldson, we encountered thick, steep bushwhacking for a few hundred feet—slow going but short-lived. We reached Donaldson at noon and came across fresh tracks. On opening the register we discovered we knew the last entries: Kip and Norm Smith, Bruce Brown, Pete Delig. The views were delightful on this beautiful blue-sky day. I was relieved that the biggest part of the uphill was done; it had taken seven hours to get here and we were hoping to get three peaks today. The rest would be a breeze in comparison. Also the path out was well packed. What a break!

We followed our friends' tracks to Emmons and met them on their descent. We shared plans for the day and how many 46er peaks each of us had left. We topped Emmons at one o'clock where we were treated to good views, though hazy; the temperature was mild. We didn't spend long here as we had only four hours to get to Seymour; it would be a shame to miss this one now! Retracing, we caught up to them on the north side of Donaldson and Tom took the lead. Mild temperatures had softened the snow and made it heavy; lifting snowshoes loaded with moisture-laden snow is brutal. Tom, though, always seemed tireless when he had a peak in front of him. I would spell him, but I was slow at this uphill breaking—though I had the endurance to continue indefinitely at my pace. I was usually in the lead on the downhill and this would give him a break.

Tom decided to head across to Seymour by slabbing the south side of Seward to Ouluska Col between Seward and Seymour. Pete, who had just completed his 46 and Northeast 111 on Emmons, was tired and decided to descend on his own. I looked back and saw that Pete's tracks didn't drop off the ridge in the direction I'd expected; I asked, "Should Pete be heading down that way?" Tom exclaimed, "Oh God, no!" He was descending off the wrong side of the mountain into a great wilderness many miles from a road—as fast as a snow-ball rolling down the side of a mountain! He couldn't hear us yelling; one of his group went after him.

We summitted Seymour at 5 P.M. and turned right around after signing the canister register; we needed to be sure the two made it out safely. We bushwhacked northwest, descending many cliffs, and found their tracks coming back up to the ridge and down toward the lean-to. We reached the lean-to at 6:15 P.M. and had Cold Duck to celebrate with Pete.

Tom and I trekked out; the moon shone through thin clouds to illuminate our way. It began to snow, making the night even more beautiful. We reached our skis at nine o'clock. Tom was exhausted. His efforts from the hard breaking and the long day had taken their toll; he fell several times and seemed totally depleted of energy. We stopped to eat and drink but it was too late; only a good night's rest would replenish him. I felt fine. I always seem to have enough energy, but I don't break trail for long periods like Tom. Also my metabolism is slower than his; I can get by on much less food, but even I was weary today.

Tom and I agreed to use headlamps tonight because I was worried about one of us falling and getting hurt. Now it was snowing harder and this limited how far we could see, in spite of headlights. Time seemed to slow down now. I worried about Tom; we had been on our feet for eighteen hours. Finally at 11 P.M. we saw the van; it was all we could do to crawl into it and into our King Tut bags. We made it! We fell asleep immediately; no energy left to stay awake to cook.

Sawteeth, Gothics, Armstrong, Upper and Lower Wolf Jaw, January 1, 1983:

These five peaks of the Great Range were the most difficult of the 46 because everything was coated in ice, covered by a light dusting of snow. This beautiful but steep and rugged range was challenging, my favorite because of that challenge and the spectacular views. The temperature was 24° and dawn was breaking on the horizon when we arrived at the well-patrolled boathouse at the end of Lake Road. We ascended up to Rainbow Falls, enjoying the relative warmth and the beauty unfolding as dawn progressed. Flurries added enchantment to the scene. The steep terrain approaching the col between Sawteeth and Pyramid was treacherous with its icy covering, as was the steep trail to Pyramid. The half-inch of snow over the ice made the going precarious; we shuffled along gingerly, carefully placing our feet, but in places slipping and sliding awkwardly off balance. The views of the many breathtaking cliffs from this trail were spectacular! Reaching Gothics at 10:45, the views made the climb well worth the effort—a panorama of dramatic cliffs and ledges. There is no other place quite like this in all of the United States!

We encountered a challenge descending Armstrong. Covered with ice and a dusting of snow, one false step at the cliff with the cable and ladder could lead to serious injury and possibly a fatality. We proceeded down the cable and then the ladder with much caution—after discussing the merit of aborting this route in favor of a much longer bushwhack around the cliffs. Reaching Upper Wolf Jaw at 12:45, we were greeted with another vista; at Lower Wolf Jaw by 2:15, then back at the trailhead at 5 P.M., it was a twelve-hour day. The Great Range in ice fully tested our limits, judgment, and skills.

Allen, February 19, 1983:

John and Pat joined us for the nineteen-mile round trip to Allen Mt. Six inches of old snow lay in the trail and we were able to boot it even though it hadn't been broken out; we took turns breaking trail. We spent the first hours catching up on the news in each other's lives. We grabbed munchies and warmed ourselves in the sun at 10 A.M. at a lean-to; the day had warmed from 5° to 25°. We began the four-mile bushwhack; conversation lessened as the going was more strenuous. We scared up a grouse that was under the snow; as we approached its hiding place it burst out with a hard fluttering of wings and a quick spray of snow. Deer tracks led to the brook where holes in the ice yielded water.

The muffled gurgle of partly frozen, snow-covered Allen Brook mingled with the crunch of snow under our snowshoes. I always found this time peaceful yet lonely, a time for quiet reflection and enjoying solitude.

How amazing to be out in these temperatures—and much colder ones—attired only in long johns, shorts, a wool sweater, hat, and gloves; how could the body provide the heat needed? How do animals survive in the harshest cold and winds of our Northeast winters? My favorite pastime in the woods is to watch the birds; I love to call them in. Chickadees are willing participants. I like to determine if they're boreal or black ones—boreal chickadees have a brown rather than black cap and a more nasal call, usually found at higher elevations in the northeastern mountains. They're adorable; we carry seeds for them. Suddenly a spruce trap would shake me from this reverie back to reality. The most exciting bird I've encountered in the Adirondacks is the pileated woodpecker; what a treat to hear and see one of these guys tap, tap tapping away looking for those elusive bugs.

Within 100' of the summit ridge we were forced to don our snowshoes. At 3:15 at the summit we stopped for a half hour to eat, sign the register, and enjoy the views. Our descent was slow despite the fact that we retraced. As dark approached, we didn't need our headlamps with the half moon's glow providing more than enough light. Tom and I made it a rule to try to travel by moonlight after dark. If the sky was very overcast, or if we were tripping or slowing down too much, we'd use artificial light, but we resorted to this reluctantly and rarely.

We talked quietly again on the descent about things that seem to come up after dark—things that frighten us or leave us confused. Why things work out the way they do or the sadness we feel about things in our lives we can't control. At first on these dark descents, I'd be nervous and couldn't relax and enjoy what the dark had to offer. It took many trips before I would learn that the darkness is not a scary time, but one filled with wonders not known or explored by many.

Dix and Hough, February 26, 1983—46th Peak:

Dix Mountain was our last of the 46 and what a great peak on which to finish. Although not the perfect blue-sky day, nothing could put a damper on our spirits. At Clear Pond, the gate across the road was locked with a cable due to the current logging. After two miles of walking the unplowed road, we took the trail to Slide Brook Lean-to, stopped to talk to three backpackers, and then followed a herd path that left the trail half a mile north of the shelter. It was good going until we reached a treacherously steep slide near the Hough-Hogback Col. We picked our way with care and planted the homemade crampons that were attached to the bottom of our snow-shoes very firmly with each step. It required the extra effort of stomping each foot against the ice slope. This slowed us down and required lots of extra energy, but the alternative was to risk life and limb in a fall down to the bottom of the cliffy area! We finally reached Hough summit at 1:30 P.M. with fine vistas to the west.

Following the herd path north again we found ourselves on a very unique, interesting, and narrow ridge approaching Dix. We had chosen Dix for last, with its 360-degree views. Putting down a piece of foam for a seat, we stopped to celebrate our last New York 4,000-footer with a bottle of champagne. We first sprinkled some on the mountain to thank the mountain gods for providing us with such unique and delightful peaks. We took a few swallows and quietly sat enjoying the view of the distant snow-covered mountains, even though it was 4 P.M. and we had nine miles to go. The sun was low in the sky.

On the return trip, we trudged wearily, lost in our own thoughts and happy that the long drives to New York would be over, but re-gretting that we would not be back here for a while; this area has a unique rugged beauty. We planned to be back in the summer but knew we'd be moving on to other challenges, and it would be a long time before we'd return to these peaks in winter. Also, I knew that in the quiet of this evening as the moon was throwing shadows onto the pristine snow, Tom was reflecting on the possibilities for our next goal.

Diane began the Winter 46 at age 32 and finished at age 34.

KIP SMITH

46er # 1647W

I grew up in Lake Placid in the Adirondacks, where my parents and their friends enjoyed snowshoe outings and had climbed Whiteface Mountain in the 1920s. While attending the University of Vermont, I joined the Outing Club, and on a freshman class trip climbed Camel's Hump. I did no more hiking until 1970, when my first husband planned to take our teenage sons on a Labor Day climb of Mt. Marcy. I objected to the exclusion of our daughters and myself, so this became a family trip. The six of us made our climb, leaving our backpacks at Indian Falls, but did not reach the summit until 6 P.M. After sending the boys ahead to set up camp, we finally got back to Indian Falls at 8:30 P.M. and hiked out the following morning.

We became charter members of the Ramapo Chapter of the Adirondack Mountain Club. This introduced us to the Forty-Sixer Club and climbing all 46 Adirondack peaks over 4,000 feet. Our family camped at Howard Lean-to near Johns Brook Lodge; we climbed Lower and Upper Wolf Jaws, Armstrong, and Gothics Mountains and camped at the Orebed Lean-to. We ran out of water on Armstrong; #1 son purified some from a puddle and then a June snowbank on Gothics saved us. We ate lunch under our dunk bags because of the black-fly scourge. The views, though, were inspiring and this trip whetted my appetite for the mountains. I had mountain fever and loved the solitude of the woods. My husband, however, swore off mountain treks.

I was active in the Scout movement in Nyack, NY, first as a Cub Scout den mother and then as an organizer and cadette troop leader in Girl Scouts. In 1972, an assistant and I trained the girls in hiking and backpacking, culminating in a Labor Day weekend climb of Mt. Marcy. Our only problem was that our Jamaican member suffered from altitude sickness. Yearly trips to the Adirondack peaks with one or more of my children, or solo, followed as I worked on my list of the 46. One time with #2 son we found newborn fawns on the Slide Mountain Trail as the mother snorted nearby. Another time on top of Mt. Colden, we watched thirty-five hawks soaring in the air currents. I joined the Ramapo ADK chapter on many of their hikes, first in Harriman Park and then in the Catskills. All of these outings added to my knowledge of skills, equipment, and clothing—much of which I made myself.

Through the ensuing disintegration of my marriage, I seriously turned to hiking and experienced the thrill of completing my 46th Adirondack peak on East Dix in 1980, as well as finishing the Catskill 3,500 peaks in both summer and winter. Winter Mountaineering School in the High Peaks added instruction in cold weather backpacking and camping; I was fortunate to have Guy Waterman as one of my instructors. Winter camping created a need for inventiveness on my part. After purchasing a pee bottle and corresponding funnel from Campmor, I created an appropriate opening in my long johns and thereby avoided the dreaded frigid exodus into the night. The method worked so well, in fact, that I then proceeded to make hiking pants with a zippered crotch for using the funnel alone. This arrangement was especially appreciated on later roped climbs.

After working as a district sewing teacher at Singer Company, I commuted to work in New York City as an instruction writer at a pattern company. A core group of friends inspired me to climb the Winter 46. Every Friday after work, I joined a group of other hikers and carpooled to whatever peaks we had targeted; we spent Saturday and Sunday in the mountains before driving home—sometimes not arriving until 1 A.M.—and then back to work on Monday morning.

A member of ADK's Ramapo Chapter invited me to join his trip to climb Mt. Katahdin in Maine. Doing the Knife Edge was a wonderful experience and I was introduced to a new area of mountains—and another list of peaks to climb! Our hiking group became close-knit with much friendly competition and esprit de corps, fostering long-lasting attachments. We also did a group trip to Mt. Rainier.

During the 1980s, winters were spent climbing the New England 4,000-footers as well as the New England Hundred Highest, which I was the first woman to finish in winter. I was also the third woman to summit the 111 peaks in the Northeast over 4,000 feet in winter. One scary memory was running out of energy after climbing Hamlin Peak near Mt. Katahdin and struggling to reach the trail down to camp; too much clothing had sapped my strength. We've climbed twenty-two of Colorado's fifty-four 14,000-footers and fifty-three of the 14,000ers in the lower forty-eight. I took rock climbing lessons, but in hiking boots, to be able to handle those peaks that demanded this skill.

I read about the Highpointers Club on our way out West the summer of 1989, so we planned our route to include a few state High Points. At the annual Highpointers Club dinner, a member announced that he had climbed all fifty high points after the age of fifty. That night I thought about us doing them all after the age of sixty! Because I was only fifty-nine when we began our High Points, we'd have to repeat many. Before heading home by way of Arizona, New Mexico, and Oklahoma we climbed Nevada's Boundary Peak and Mt. Whitney. We swung north to revisit Mt. Sunflower in Kansas, Mt. Elbert in Colorado, Kings Peak in Utah, and the High Points of Nebraska, Iowa, Indiana, and Ohio.

The next June we did a second climb on Denali, this time sixteen days, reaching summit on a spectacular sunny and windless day. As we climbed, we looked down on the volcanic ash deposited by the eruption of Mt. Spurr, just fifty miles away. The Denali Park Rangers had considered closing the mountain because of the ash, and were worried about getting climbers out. Ash could cause melting on the Kahiltna Glacier, opening of crevasses and a landing problem for our plane pickup; we did a nineteen-and-a-half hour descent to return—a bit much after a thirteen-and-a-half hour summit the previous day. In Talkeetna the next morning, Norm forgot he was not in a tent and took his only fall—out of bed! This climb made us the oldest married couple, at ages sixty-two and sixty-four, to summit Denali and I'm the oldest woman to have done so.

Among my most memorable trips was hiking the Annapurna Circuit in Nepal. We experienced a vastly different culture. The people are hospitable and friendly, and in desperate need of basic medical care and sanitation. Environmentally, I especially remember the garbage dumped in the river running through Kathmandu and privies that emptied into underlying streams. Pollution and recycling have became important concerns of mine.

The longest trek we made was a six-month adventure on the Appalachian Trail, for which I spent five-and-a-half months dehydrating and packing our food to be shipped weekly to us. More long-distance trails followed: the Colorado Trail; New York's Northville-Lake Placid Trail and Finger Lakes Trail; Vermont's Long Trail; the Grand Rondonnee Cinq from Lake Geneva to Nice; the Tour de Mt. Blanc; Peru's Inca Trail; and exploring the Canadian Maritimes. We've successfully ascended Africa's Kilimanjaro, Mt. Meru, and Australia's Mt. Kosciusko, the highest peak on that continent.

At home, life is a constant balancing act to maintain a cook-from-scratch vegetarian lifestyle, deal with housework (it doesn't go away), working out at the gym, keeping in contact with children and grandchildren, researching my family genealogy, designing and constructing items for various trips, and doing the repairs and cleanup after each adventure. For what it's worth, people seem to regard us as role models. We are constantly being queried about age, but being able to continue what we love to do is the important factor. The alternative is not appealing, so we keep striving.

Climbing mountains has become a way of life to us—a most satisfying recreation that is not only emotionally fulfilling, but also physically rewarding. Each peak has added not only another "notch on the stick" but usually some new bit of knowledge and a fresh experience. Other than the usual challenges of accurate compass work, breaking trail in deep snow, ice travel, a few falls in icy brooks, whiteouts, and staying warm in sub-zero weather, I've experienced no injuries while hiking except frostbite on my first Catskill winter climb. Winter is especially appealing to me for many reasons: The beauty of the snowy landscapes, no rocks or insects, and fewer people. Some of the greatest experiences involve meeting other hikers and developing new friendships. The Adirondacks will always be my favorites because it is home country and, having been born and raised in the heart of the area, I think I'll always find an excuse to return and continue visiting these mountains.

Skylight and Gray, March 21, 1981:

Although we camped on most trips, we climbed these two peaks as a daytrip from Kingston where we picked up a fellow hiker—a very long day! We began driving at 2 A.M. to reach the Adirondack Loj trailhead by 7:30. We started in by headlamp, breaking trail past Lake Arnold, and climbed Skylight first using full crampons. The views were obscured. On the return route we struggled our way up trailless Gray, floundering in up to five feet of white fluff near the top. We could not find the canister! Norm glanced behind himself and caught a glimpse of familiar gray barely visible through a hole blown in the snow heaped around one of the treetops at our feet. A little digging uncovered our target—so nearly missed!

We glissaded off Gray at top speed all the way down to Lake Colden, proceeded across that and Avalanche Lake, and reached the trailhead at 6:30 P.M. After dinner in Keene, we drove home in time for a couple of hours of sleep before commuting to work in New York City.

The Seward Range, March 6, 1982:

The combination of a 6:10 A.M. start, a glorious sunny day, and unerring compass work netted us all four Sewards in one twenty-four-hour trip, including travel time. Other hikers, Tom and Diane Sawyer, joined our group after returning from Emmons. We reached the summit of Seward at 9:15, Donaldson at 11:30, Emmons by 12:40, and then a route was laid to Ouluska Pass—cutting across precisely between the cliffed sections.

We had some excitement on this trip when Bruce O. Brown of the

New England 4,000-Footer Committee fell into a spruce trap and spent some time "swimming" his way out, never losing hold of his pipe that was tightly clenched in his teeth. We arrived at the base of Seymour in the Pass at 4:30 P.M., peaked at 5 o'clock and literally chute-slid down the north side to regain the trail below by moonlight and back to our camp at Blueberry Lean-to.

We camped out to climb the Seward Range, the Santanoni Range, Allen, Nippletop-Dial-Colvin-Blake, and the Dix Range. Sometimes we used a sled for gear. It is always important to carry emergency survival gear, as well as all the appropriate equipment for the occasion; I constantly upgraded my gear and equipment and, with experience, I became more confident and knowledgeable. These winter climbs and winter school were good training for my future climbing. I always enjoyed winter camping with the long nights in a warm sleeping bag and the crisp, fresh air, but getting out of that warm bag could be challenging, so I learned to dress while still in my cocoon. The next challenge was eating, but that could also be done while still "bagged."

Allen, February 28, 1983:

Our group included Phil Heald on our Allen climb; his Golden Lab, Charlie, provided quite a show when he "flushed" a large buck. The two had a standoff about twelve feet above us, with Charlie challenging the buck that was flailing at him with his front hooves. Our shouts to Charlie were to no avail. The tense situation was resolved when the deer leaped over a log and lunged down the slope, with his opponent in hot pursuit. Finally Charlie gave up and returned to us.

Porter and Cascade, 46th Peak, March 13, 1983:

However memorable all of our adventures and experiences were, they were all topped, if you'll pardon the pun, on our last climb. I'll give you some background: Because we had such heavy packs on our trip in to Flowed Lands, no champagne was carried to properly toast Norm Smith's finale on Redfield—his 46th! Such a furor arose that Norm and I decided to make it a double party on my upcoming 46th peak, Cascade.

Norm and I were joined by Forest Ranger Pete Fish, who opportunely scheduled a patrol. We climbed Porter first and then went up Cascade. The sky was socked in and the wind was a "Marcy blast." Because I was having trouble standing against the elements, my aim was a short stay and speedy retreat. Then Pete spotted something pink partly covered by snow, and not remembering any pink rocks there, we went over to look. What emerged was a bottle of pink champagne with a message on hot pink paper, all carefully wrapped in plastic. Phil Heald and Betty Maury had made a 6 A.M. climb on the day before to plant this surprise from "Charlie and Friends." Marvelous!

Kip began the Winter 46 at age 50 and finished at age 52.

JEANNE GOEHLE STERNBERGH

46er # 1960W

One of nine children, I grew up on a farm in Tyler, Minnesota, a Lake Woebegon-like town in a flat region of the state. Farm chores did not permit long vacations so I never climbed a mountain, but I played outdoors in all seasons and weather. I enjoyed reading and dreamed about seeing the world. I went to the University of Minnesota where I got a degree in English Education, met and married Tom Nylund. Our marriage lasted eighteen years and was a key factor in my winter backpacking. We joined the Peace Corps where I taught English as a foreign language in Morocco. While there, a colleague introduced us to the Atlas Mountains.

After we returned from the Peace Corps, Tom began grad school at Purdue University. I taught secondary school for two years, and although I enjoyed teaching I did not want to have it as a lifetime career. I went back to school and got a B.S. in Chemical Engineering, which led me to Eastman Kodak in Rochester, NY, and, ultimately, to the Adirondacks. Many of Tom's co-workers at Kodak backpacked; with their advice, Tom and I bought gear and planned our first backpack to the Black Forest in Pennsylvania. We hiked seventeen miles the first day! I was a runner and in good shape, so I was unprepared for what happened when I woke up; my legs were so cramped that I could barely walk. With a hastily fashioned walking stick, I limped the six miles back to our car. In spite of the muscle strain, I got the hiking bug. We took our first backpacking trip to the Adirondacks and the following January went on our first winter backpacking trip.

Our hiking buddies suggested we join the Rochester Winter Mountaineering Society (RWMS), a group that sponsors winter hiking primarily in the Adirondacks. New members must go on a beginners' trip before they can participate in any other. RWMS has a spring party with slide shows, sharing stories, planning the next season, and negotiating for trips that help us work towards our Winter 46.

I hiked with the RWMS until I earned my Winter 46, from 1979 through 1984. During that time I was the only woman active in our society. For these five years I was in the best shape I've ever been. I'm 5'6" tall and, at that time, weighed 125 pounds—all muscle; I even had a flat stomach! To keep in shape I ran nine long flights of stairs during my lunchtime at Kodak; during the season I ran them more frequently. I biked or walked two miles to work every day, and cross-country skied or jogged evenings and when I was not winter backpacking. I wanted to be a strong and capable hiker. Although I wasn't the strongest hiker in RWMS, I was nowhere near the weakest. I had stamina and was determined. Some of my fellow hikers called me "tough"—they may have thought, "for a woman." I carried my own weight—both on my back and in my participation; I never permitted the men to compensate for me. With time, I was just one of the group.

We were encouraged to participate in beginner hikes and in my third season I joined one to Big Slide. Conditions were great and I felt like I was flying over the Three Brothers; the beginners had fallen behind so I went back to check on them. They looked at me with new respect; the biggest and the tallest one said, "We thought when we saw you were on the trip, that this would be a piece of cake."

We did not necessarily follow trails. Using compasses and maps we took the most direct route to the summit, often following stream-beds or rock slides. We had to figure out the best way around obstacles and got into interesting dilemmas when we got lost or found a bit of topography we had not anticipated. I found this hiking exciting and had the most energy when we were bushwhacking. I think it kept my mind off aches and pains.

The part I found most strenuous was kicking steps in deep snow, especially up a steep slope. In these situations we used rotating leads. The leader took approximately fifty steps and then dropped to the end of the line. As we moved forward in the line, we worked harder and harder. When we dropped to the back we could rest; sometimes it felt that we were standing still. When the stronger hikers were in the lead, they did extra steps. I never did; I endured my quota and then moved back.

People ask me if it was hard to spend many weekends hiking and camping only with men—I didn't find it so. My work as a manufacturing engineer at Kodak was primarily with men. When I attended Purdue there were only a few women in my engineering classes. I was comfortable expressing my opinion and sharing ideas in these settings. I don't remember consciously dwelling on being the only woman. I'm sure being married made it easier for me; I only went on trips when my husband was there.

Things I found onerous about winter backpacking, such as personal hygiene and lack of privacy, were undoubtedly complicated by being the only woman. I like to wash my hands regularly, but because it took so much fuel to melt snow, we only used water for cooking or drinking—so I carried alcohol wipes to wash my hands and face. After two strenuous days in the mountains, when the car heated up we started to notice body odors; we joked about getting thrown out of restaurants for our smelly and scrubby appearance. For bathroom stops we had not-so-subtle clues, "Don't wait, I'll catch up." One must get out of sweaty garments quickly after setting up camp; I got adept at changing clothes in my sleeping bag.

Emotional privacy was more tenuous. Occasionally I wanted to hike alone and learned to say that I wanted some "alone" time. I began to transcend pain and tiredness, learned to zone out—I frequently felt that my mind was outside my body watching it climb the mountain. This created a sense of serenity, being alone with oneself even in a group—and it afforded me emotional privacy.

Cold was the worst; when we stopped I was one of the first to get cold. I found it more difficult to regulate my heat during the hike. I did that by layering; removing hats and gloves is the easiest way to cool off. When we stopped for a break, I put on everything or I quickly got cold. Setting up and breaking camp was trying; it seemed to take so much time. Nightwear was a one-piece navy fleece with a drop seat, very convenient for the early morning constitution. It was very warm but my knees got so cold if pressed against the chilly sleeping bag, that I would wake up several times nightly and lose valuable sleep. A thoughtful friend, Doug Wall, heard my complaints and he sewed fleece tubes to pull over my knees and they ended my sleepless nights!

I have not winter backpacked since completing my Winter 46. People ask me why. First, I had achieved a goal; second, I love trying new things. At Kodak I was invited to join an indoor soccer league that played on Saturdays during the winter months. I also learned scuba diving—a passion and a primary factor in choosing vacations. Finally, when I turned forty, two major factors had an influence on my spare time: I got divorced and I got promoted to supervisor, then management positions at Kodak. My time was devoured by work, caring for home and yard, and building a new single life.

Five years later I married a wonderful man, Jim Sternbergh. We had initially met on an ADK trip when I was married to Tom. Jim claims he instantly fell in love with me. He thought, "If I ever meet a woman like Jeanne, I'll get married." I saw Jim maybe once a year; I always thought he was a great guy—kind, with a good sense of humor. And he was an excellent cross-country skier, to boot. He was amazed that I could climb mountains. The year of my divorce, a friend invited me to a Christmas party; coincidentally Jim was there! He still had not found that special woman and asked me out; after a couple of years we got together for good.

After we were married, I earned my Masters in Management Technology at the Sloan School at MIT. Jim and I commuted between Rochester and Boston on weekends. When I returned to Kodak, I had challenging management jobs working both in the business and manufacturing units. Jim's division was sold to a firm that shut down all operations in Rochester; we moved West and bought a fixer-upper in the vineyards of Sonoma Country. I plan vacation trips from the Canadian Rockies to Utah. This seems so far away from winter backpacking in the Adirondacks. It all goes back to why I winter hiked in the first place—to share an activity with my former husband. We didn't have children and spent most of our week at work. Another motivation was escaping the city and recapturing that solitude in the outdoors I'd enjoyed growing up. I feel like I have come full circle.

Big Slide, January 6-7, 1979:

Big Slide was my first winter backpack with the RWMS, a month before my thirtieth birthday. Our trip leader was Ted Robinson, quite a character. Seasoned RWMSers teased him about being so thin. For his New Year's resolution he'd made a monetary bet with a friend—whoever lost the most weight by Christmas would have to pay off the other. The following summer the friend had lost a significant amount of weight. So Ted went on a cabbage diet; he claimed he only ate cabbage. He won the bet and celebrated by eating a couple pounds of fudge.

As we climbed the mountain, Ted was encouraging and supportive. My husband was also on this trip as a beginner. When we got to the campsite, Ted said that it wasn't acceptable for spouses to stay together on a RWMS beginners' trip (his rule, of course). So he put me in his tent and Tom in another. The next day as we bushwhacked down, Ted decided to put us through our paces. He mocked our pristine Gore-Tex and gleaming snowshoes (aluminum Sherpas). I felt that he was especially hard on me, wagering that I could not keep up. Well, that brought out my determined (or stubborn) streak and I decided I would show him! I bushwhacked through some of the toughest sections of the decline. However, I don't think I really proved anything to Ted. He knew all along that he was showing me that I had the capability to be a full partner in winter climbing in the Adirondacks. When we got to the bottom I was satisfied. And so was Ted.

Street and Nye, February 3-4, 1979:

My second winter backpack was a combination cross-country ski and snowshoe trip. I was just learning how to cross-country ski so I had some trepidation before the trip. I had not skied with a backpack before, and it seemed to have a mind of its own. When I tried to turn, my backpack went straight. No matter how I tightened it around my body, I continued falling every time I tried to make a turn. I had decided to abort the trip when a caring fellow hiker, Jack Freeman, suggested we switch to snowshoes. He claimed he did not enjoy skiing with a backpack either. Tom, who was skiing successfully, also chose to join us. I still felt badly that I had signed up for the trip, thinking I had ruined it for everyone else.

The trip leader had planned that we drop our skis at Wanika Falls. When we three snowshoers arrived there three-and-a-half hours later, we discovered that the fastest skiers had beaten us by only fifteen minutes! I felt a lot better because we had not significantly delayed the trip. We snowshoed up Wanika Creek on an unusually well broken trail. Near the top we met five hikers who were looking for a downed plane that had crashed around Christmas; this search party asked us to look for signs of the crash. We kept our eyes peeled but did not see signs of the plane.

We reached the summit of Nye in late afternoon. The sky was clear and we had absolutely magnificent views. We camped just below the summit on the way to Street. The temperature dropped below zero that night. The next morning we bushwhacked to Street; the view was awesome. The old-timers identified all the mountains we could see, including Mount Mansfield in Vermont. On the way out I threw my skis over my shoulder and snowshoed out; I realized how fast I had snowshoed in our attempt to keep up with the skiers. That gave me confidence. I would be the first woman in the group to complete the Winter 46.

Colden, January 24- 25, 1981:

At a spring celebration while I was trying to convince other wives to join RWMS, we hatched the idea of having a special family trip, called the "slower-paced" trip. We would choose a mountain with a great view that could be climbed fairly easily; we would waive normal expectations for a winter trip. The purpose of the trip was to provide an enjoyable experience where family members could appreciate the work required to winter backpack, but mostly see the awesome scenery and enjoy the solitude of winter mountain wilderness.

The RWMSers would be the tent leads, carry the communal gear, and do most of the lead hiking. We planned a slower pace, more breaks, brought extra fuel, and set up camp early so participants had more time to settle in and clean up. We chose to do the trip early in the season when the regular RWMSers were still getting in shape. I volunteered to be the leader of the first trip and chose Mount Colden, an incredibly beautiful summit.

Giant and Rocky Peak Ridge, March 20- 21, 1982:

Billed as our annual family trip, I officially cancelled it because of the forecasted cold and stormy weather. Three of us decided to take the hike anyway. Our challenge was to bag Giant and Rocky before spring officially began. Banking on being able to hitch a ride on Sunday, we parked the car on Route 73 and began a one-way hike. There had been a lot of snow that season and the trail signs stuck barely two feet above the snow. The climb was quite easy and we reached the summit of Giant before noon. Unlike the predictions, Saturday was sunny and warm so we had a leisurely lunch at the summit.

We then lunged down Giant, taking a great ride down a long chute. The climb along Rocky Peak Ridge was exceptional with excellent views of the High Peaks; we reached the summit by early afternoon. We decided to camp at Dickerson Notch. After a satisfying dinner we had amaretto and hot cider to help ease our aches and soften the night, already beautiful with the star-filled skies and surrounding white birch.

We expected the hike out on Sunday to be easy. But when we

descended Bald Peak, we took a bad compass reading and had to take a long traverse to get back on track. The cold temperature had arrived, turning Saturday's melted snow to ice and forming a hard crust on top of deep powder. When our snowshoes broke through the crust, they got caught. We tried hiking without snowshoes but inevitably broke through and sank deep in the snow. We put our snowshoes back on! The last two miles of descent were treacherous. Two of us waited with the gear while the other hitched a ride to get the car; it arrived just as the snowstorm did.

Marcy, February 19-23, 1983:

It was a couple of years before I reached the summit of Marcy. It was partially because of my ego. I was not going to be lured by Mt. Marcy just because it was the highest, but when I did, it was one of my most memorable trips. The Rochester Winter Mountaineering Society was on a marathon-long weekend, trying to grab a number of peaks. The first night we camped near Lake Tear of the Clouds at 4,350'. Some of us had discussed a night climb of Marcy; after dinner, only three of us were still game. We donned our headlamps and snowshoes, grabbed our ice axes, and started out.

Soon we switched off our headlamps and climbed by the light of the moon. The night was so still and peaceful. Friends waved their lights from the lake and we continued up to the summit. At the top it was absolutely awesome. We could see shadows of other peaks in the moonlight. Stars were sprinkling the sky. And in spite of myself, I fell in love with Mt. Marcy. When I climbed her the next day, in the daylight, she already had me in her grasp.

Haystack, February 25, 1984—46th peak:

An experience that surpassed my hike of Mt. Marcy was my final peak, Haystack. I decided that I wanted to finish on a peak that had a spectacular view. The Society would finally have their first woman Winter 46er. We brought champagne to toast the summit. I had begun to feel my Winter 46 would be both their accomplishment and mine, if I achieved that goal. We had established relationships—necessary for working together to climb in some of the tougher conditions.

They wanted me to succeed and I wished the same for them.

We had planned another marathon-long weekend trip where we would do the Wolf Jaws, Gothics, Saddleback, Basin, and end with Haystack. On the final day the wind picked up and it was bitterly cold. We climbed to Little Haystack where I was almost literally blown off the mountain. A fellow hiker grabbed me and pulled me to an outcropping of rocks. As we clung there the trip leader came over. He had inspected the decline to the col between Little Haystack and Haystack and felt it was unsafe to proceed because of the wind. I respected his judgment but was disappointed and not sure that I, in the fever of reaching a goal, would have made the same sensible decision.

The following weekend promised sun and blue skies. Tom and I decided to approach Haystack from the backside. We hiked up Panther Gorge. After we set up camp we debated whether to hike to the top that night, as we would have to descend in the dark. I didn't want to wait. We dropped our packs and hiked to the top of Haystack just in time to see the sunset. The view was incredible! From Haystack's summit, twenty-seven peaks are discernible. As I looked around I felt that I was reliving the past few years, remembering a piece of every mountain and every experience. We skied down the mountain on our snowshoes in the dusk and hiked the trail in the dark. No champagne this time, but a wonderful feeling of accomplishment! Twenty years later I can still remember the evening vividly. As we sat on Haystack, watching the sun go down, having memories mingled with both pain and elation, I thought, "Never have I felt so at peace with myself and the world around me."

Jeanne started the Winter 46 at age 30 and finished at age 35.

BETTY MAURY HEALD

46er #1667W

I did not discover hiking until my children were in their mid-teens. When I did, it changed my life. Family vacations until I was six were two week visits with my mother's family in Indiana and my father's family in Kentucky. Beginning with my seventh summer we began to have real vacations. My father was a YMCA executive at Brooklyn's Ninth Street Y and my parents rented a cottage above a YMCA conference center on the western shore of Lake George, NY. We joined supervised day hikes and later went on over-nights, carrying bed-rolls and food in paper sacks; campfire meals were simple.

World War II ended these idyllic vacations. After the war and high school graduation, I graduated from Vanderbilt University, married a year later, spent several years as an Air Force wife, and bore three beautiful children. When my children were eight, six, and five, my husband left. I became the bread winner. Seven years later, I found a way to get us out of town for the summer. I was employed by the New York City YMCA as the Nature Director at a girls' camp near Port Jervis, NY. I loved my duties and being in the woods.

Fate had something special in store for me. In 1970, the camp director invited me to be the female leader of a group of ten co-ed campers on a three-day trek from Madison Hut to Lake of the Clouds Hut in the White Mountains. It was then that I discovered there were hiking clubs. It took me a year to locate one in northern New Jersey, the North Jersey Chapter of the Adirondack Mountain Club (ADK).

At first I day-hiked only on summer weekends; in 1975 I became interested in backpacking. I wanted to experience the isolated areas and alpine zones of North America and test my stamina for longer treks. I signed up for the Appalachian Mountain Club Presidential Range Hike, fifty-plus miles, hut-to-hut, in New Hampshire's White Mountains. I did every side hike that was offered, loved the isolated areas, and was challenged by the topography. The following December, I attended the AMC/ADK weeklong Winter School held in Littleton, NH. That training gave me all the skills I would need for my winter hiking quests in New York and New England. I learned how to use my new winter equipment: Iverson Bearpaw snowshoes and a pair of ten-point crampons. Now I felt prepared to join my fellow North Jersey ADK Club members on winter Catskill hikes.

Leaders screen hikers before permitting them to join a hike. We had lots of snow the winter of 1976. In January, I called the leader of a scheduled Catskill hike to sign up for a climb of Doubletop Mountain. He was reluctant to give permission for me to come along; he was afraid I couldn't keep up with the group. He required that I have my own transportation to and from the hike. If unable to keep up, I would have to return to my car and get myself back to New Jersey on my own. I assured him I would not hinder the groups' progress and I would have a companion. We would arrive and depart independently from the rest of the party.

It was a picture perfect winter day. The sky was blue, the air crisp and cold, the sun bright, little wind, and snow several feet deep. It was a large group—all males—except for me and my friend; we hung to the rear so as not to interfere with the regulars. Soon those in front started breaking through the snow's crust. My companion and I were lighter and we moved easily past them and reached the top ahead of everyone. Most of the men were panting, perspiring, and complaining of the difficult conditions. I was exhilarated! I soon became one of the regulars on the weekly winter hikes. I loved the beautiful snow-covered trees and trails, the challenge of each trip, and the camaraderie of the group. In spite of teaching all week I had no trouble getting up at 5:30 A.M. on a Saturday morning to meet the carpool for the one-and-a-half to two-hour drive to the Catskills. I received my Catskill 3,500 Club-winter number, #102, at the March, 1979 annual club dinner.

During the summer of 1976, I participated in a week-long Sierra Club strenuous backpack in the Mt. Zirkel Wilderness, 10,000' above Steamboat Springs, Colorado. The size of the group was limited to fifteen; again my ability to keep up with the group was questioned. I was not accepted until the last minute when no one else applied for the one open spot. I was the eldest in the group at forty-nine years old. I flew out to Colorado Springs two weeks early to visit friends and become acclimated to the elevation. I borrowed a bicycle and biked many miles daily up and down the steep hills. I contacted the local hiking club in advance, and leaders took me on ascents of several local 14,000-footers. I joined a weekend backpack to the Weiminuche Wilderness in southwest Colorado where we camped at 12,000' and climbed several 14,000-footers.

After completing the Catskill 3,500 Club winter requirements, I began to make winter trips to the Adirondacks. In December 1980, I received a call from Phil Heald whom I'd met on a weeklong backpack in Baxter State Park. Phil wanted me to help him meet the requirements of the Winter Catskill 3,500 Club. We had both taken up hiking in middle age. In just one season, Phil earned the 3,500 Club Winter patch and we joined friends for winter Adirondack ascents. We climbed Mt. Hood in Oregon and Mt. Shasta in California. In 1982, Phil and I were asked to take on the leadership of the Annual Presidential Range Hike for the Worcester Chapter of AMC and soon after that, we married. We continued our winter ascents of 4,000-footers in the Adirondacks and in New England. Thirty summit attempts in the Adirondacks were unsuccessful, some requiring several return trips before reaching a summit. Only Esther Mt. in the Adirondacks was easier than anticipated!

I am constantly aware of the physical danger of winter mountain hiking. We usually hike in groups of four to six, minimum. A bright sunny morning can end up with a snowstorm eager to cover tracks that are helpful in the descent; you can rarely rely on visual markings and must have map and compass skills. Assessing weather conditions, direction, trails, time of day—these take careful judgment all along the line. We trained by climbing nearby Monadnock Mt. weekly from Thanksgiving weekend to the official start of winter.

In March 1985, on Phelps Mt., I completed my forty-sixth Adirondack High Peak—#46 on the Winter 46er list! This qualified me as a "Winter Northeast 111er," the second woman on record to have achieved this goal, the first finishing just two weeks previously. Phil and I are the first married couple to touch the tops of 113 peaks in the Northeast over 4,000 feet in winter—at ages fifty-seven and fifty-eight!

Climbing the Winter 46 was great, building self-confidence and gaining valuable experience. Hiking changed my life in many ways. It made me fit. I used to think by the time I was forty, I'd be down the tubes! This sport makes every day an exciting experience. It gives you perspective, provides time for thinking matters through. I continue to make good friends. Unexpectedly, I found someone who became my best friend as well as hiking companion.

Recent excursions include a spectacular camping and hiking trip in Big Bend National Park and rafting down the Rio Grande, hiking in the beautiful Parc de la Gaspesie on the Gaspe Peninsula of Quebec, a wonderful hiking trip in the canyon lands of Utah, and two weeks hiking Glacier International Park. In February 1999, our group hiked the Milford, Greenstone-Routeburn, and Hollyford Tracks in New Zealand. In March 2001, I was thrilled not only to be able to hike down to Phantom Ranch in the Grand Canyon but also to hike up the following day—5,000 feet of elevation change each way. I did not want either day to end! Since then, I've climbed Guadalupe Peak, the highest mountain in Texas; Harney Peak, tallest in South Dakota; and White Bluff, North Dakota's tallest point. Trips included beautiful treks in the Black Hills and exploring the barren, arid Badlands; Montana's Custer State Park, Little Bighorn National Monument, and the Bozeman Trail. Hiking in Wyoming's Big Horn Mountains was beautiful.

The adventures have not ended! I hike regularly and have had the joy of introducing my four grandchildren to hiking. When I can steal them away from organized sports, I take them to Harriman State Park. For the five past summers we've spent a week in the Kittatinny Mountains of western New Jersey and I've introduced them to New Hampshire's White Mountains. I hope to get them to the Adirondacks soon!

Marshall, January 16, 1982:

It was just getting light when Phil and I arrived at the Heart Lake trailhead. We could barely see the dark tall evergreens against the snow. I had tried to talk Phil out of attempting this so early in January. The days then are short and temperatures the coldest. But, no! the others said this would be a good weekend.

The plan for Saturday was to hike the seven miles into the lean-tos at Lake Colden and set up our tents. We'd get up early Sunday and follow the herd path to this trailless peak. After summitting and signing the register we'd hightail it back to the campsite, break camp and hike out. This was the first winter backpack for either of us. Phil provided a two-man tent and I had my reliable alcohol backpack stove.

My jacket thermometer read -14°. After signing in the register, Phil suggested we start hiking toward the lake. The others were stronger hikers and would easily catch up. Within a short time four young people passed us. They said they, too, planned on hiking into Lake Colden to camp. No, they hadn't seen anyone else coming along the trail. Their tracks compacted the trail for us. The day gradually brightened but with no sunshine or wind. The silence was broken only by chirping chickadees and the soft shush of our snowshoes. The boughs of the evergreens were laden with six inches of light, fluffy snow. It was a fairyland all around. The exertion kept us warm. The trail ascends about nine hundred feet to Avalanche Lake. We made good time for a pair of fifty-ish adventurers.

In the summer, the trail to Lake Colden involves climbing ladders and traversing boardwalks along the north side of Avalanche Lake, hugging the side of Avalanche Mountain that drops vertically into the lake. But at this time of year I was delighted to see that we could cross on the frozen lake! No one else passed us going either way. Where could our friends be? By mid-afternoon we sighted the DEC Interior

Outpost. Smoke was spiraling from the chimney. We stopped in to pay our respects to the ranger and enjoyed cups of hot tea and had our canteens refilled with water. He followed us partway to the lean-tos, stopping to break a hole in the thick ice of the lake with his hatchet. It would make it easier for us to re-break the ice for collecting water later that night and in the morning.

Daylight was fading fast. We set to work putting the tent up. No matter where we looked the land sloped toward the lake. After settling on an area with the least slope, I got the stove lit and started heating water for dinner. In addition to the water needed for supper, we would each need two quarts for the night. One canteen would go in each boot to keep them from freezing. The boots would also insulate the water and keep it thawed for starting breakfast. While I kept an eye on the heating water, Phil zipped up the sleeping bags and arranged our gear inside the tent. There was no sign of the four young folk who had passed us the previous day. Where were they camping? Where were our friends?

By first light next morning we were up. It was very cold—even colder than Saturday! Later that afternoon the ranger would tell us his thermometer had read -27° that morning. We quickly downed hot chocolate and instant oatmeal before starting on our way.

The ranger had told us that a group of Rensselaer Polytechnic Institute students from the Outing Club had camped at the lake the week before and climbed Mt. Marshall. As there had been little new snow, he expected we'd have no trouble following their tracks. We soon found them leading into a valley between high ridges. Soon the climb became steeper and we were kicking steps in the deep snow. It was close to 11 o'clock as we worked our way between short, thick scrub trees when I looked up to see a small open area with short, branchless tree trunks. One had the canister with "Mt. Marshall—4,363'" printed in large letters. Hurrah! We were there. After signing the register we quickly downed some food. It was then that I noticed the white skin on several fingers on my right hand and their lack of feeling—frostbite! As much as we'd like to enjoy the views, we needed to get back to our tent and pack up.

We made a hurried retreat following our tracks back to Lake Colden. After packing up our equipment, we stopped by to thank the ranger. He kindly gave us cups of hot tea to help us stay warm. After 3 o'clock we began our six-mile return hike to civilization. The sun that had shone brightly all day was already dropping low in the southwest. It was very cold! We put our heads down and headed out. It was quite dark by 6 P.M. and there was no moon. Though we had headlamps, we found our eyes quickly adapted to the darkness. We could just barely see the trail through the trees under the clear, starlight night. I felt frozen and decided the time had come to put on the heavy fisherman-knit sweater I carried for an emergency, but I could not unzip my 60/40 jacket to put the sweater under it; perspiration had frozen the zipper. The sweater wasn't large enough to go over my jacket, so there was nothing to do but keep putting one snowshoe in front of the other as fast as possible to generate heat. We got back to the trailhead at 9 P.M. Oh, to get to the motel for a warm shower and a real bed. There was one more problem to face. Phil's diesel engine car would not start because it had not been plugged in!

The Seward Range, February 23-25, 1985:

We did the Seward Range during a winter warm spell, this was the first time I'd had to camp in a steady drizzle of rain; the temperature was just above freezing—these were prime hypothermia conditions. This weather lasted for the three days and two nights we were at the Duck Hole Lean-to. My feet stayed cold and wet except when inside my sleeping bag. The seams of the new tent hadn't been sealed and water seeped through and formed puddles that saturated our sleeping bags. I was amazed that they kept us warm.

The poor weather didn't dampen our spirits, though. The navigational skills of Mike Bromberg finally led us to Seymour. Above 3,500' the fog was so thick we could see just a few feet ahead, so foggy we almost didn't find the canister on Seward Mt! The streams that had been ice when we hiked in were roaring torrents by the time we hiked out carrying heavy, wet sleeping bags and gear. A bitter cold front moved in as we hiked out.

The Santanoni Range, March 1983 to March 1, 1985:

Our last winter trip of the 1983 season was the first of six to the

Santanoni Range. On most trips, we set up camp at the Bradley Pond Lean-to. Winter camping at this site is frustrating. The spring is buried in snow, so we spent a lot of time watching a pot of snow slowly melt. In the cold it seemed an interminable job with four canteens to be filled. In addition, water had to be heated for supper and breakfast. I had a devil of a time keeping my fingers warm because of the frostbite that I suffered on the backpack to climb Marshall.

The first trip, we followed Panther Brook to Times Square and climbed Panther Mountain. We hoped to go on to Couchie but couldn't find the herd path and aborted further climbing plans that time. We made two more unsuccessful attempts hoping to get Couchie in the winter of 1984 and another failed attempt in February 1985, with ten strong hikers! We gave up in frustration because visibility was so poor and the snow so deep. I think we were on the wrong ridge.

Our success to Couchie finally came a week later, when four of us followed our broken trail of the previous week to Times Square on the ridge before setting up our tents at 4,200'. It took us hours to make our way to the canister on Couchie; as usual, there was no visibility. Soon after returning to the tents, it began to snow and that night a snowstorm dumped eight inches on us! Santanoni had been our goal for the next day—but I was too wet and cold to feel like I could handle the challenge, so down Panther Brook and out we went.

When we returned to climb Santanoni on March 1, 1985, we experienced our first good weather there ever! For the very first time the sun shone on us. What a fine day for Phil to complete his winter Adirondacks, with time to sit and bask in the sun while we enjoyed a leisurely lunch!

Basin, Haystack, Gothics, and Saddleback, March 8-10, 1981:

This was my very best winter hiking experience! Phil Heald, Norman Smith, Howard Adriance, Sam Steen, Neil Zimmerman, and I hiked into Grace Camp. In teams of two, we prepared the dinner for each of the three nights. The menus were varied and deliciously creative. I packed in a hearty, pre-cooked casserole of lentils and sausage. Phil lounged on the porch amidst snowdrifts, admiring bowls of pudding that were cooling on the railing.

The first hiking day we climbed Basin and then on to Haystack; the following day Gothics and Saddleback. Everywhere there was more snow than I had ever seen in my life! The evergreen branches had hoar frost extending six inches beyond their tips and were weighed down with fluffy snow. It was a fairyland, a fun weekend.

Betty began the Winter 46 at age 49 and finished at age 58.

8

CHAI-KYOU MALLINSON

46er #1171W

My first hike, mountain climb, and backpack was a trip to Mt. Marcy organized by my future husband, for the express purpose of making a hiker of me. I am probably the first native Korean to complete the Winter 46. I have also hiked and climbed in the Needle Mountains' subsection of Colorado's San Juan Mountains with my husband, as well as in the majority of the White Mountains, and I am a member of the Catskill 3500 Club.

The Winter 46 quest began as an answer to the "Now what?" letdown at the end of the all-season 46. There were some quasi-winter trips as we were climbing the first round of the 46, at Thanksgiving and in April, which gave us a good idea of what to expect. The big push to go to Winter School, where we really got started, was meeting Wally Herrod, a winter school instructor, at the Fall 1975 meeting. Our first six true winter camping experiences were from a tent camp at Marcy Dam. We climbed parts of the Great Range and Big Slide with Grace Camp as our base.

Since it is such a long drive from Binghamton to the High Peaks, once we were there we made the drive count—that meant backpack with tent. We did only a few day trips. We stopped whenever night-fall forced us to stop hiking, although we attempted to plan for the tent to be somewhere convenient. The most beautiful place we have tented was on the top of Allen, which is not permissible outside the winter months. The snow was so deep and dry that it felt like a feather bed under our sleeping bags. Usually I felt cold overnight, even after a warm supper and with extra clothes in a warm winter bag. Hence, even when I was dead tired, I had a hard time falling asleep—but the night on Allen I slept like I was in heaven!

We always adhered to the instruction by the Winter Mountain-eering School that a party should share carrying a sleeping bag, a thermos with a sweetened hot drink, and a tent or emergency shel-ter, in case someone has an immobilizing injury or begins to devel-op hypothermia. Dick and I shared carrying this backup, after being unable to persuade the MacNaughton trip leader that this was neces-sary. We especially appreciated the school's prudent advice because Dick is insulin dependent; increasing exercise requires tricky adjust-ments in insulin dose and food intake. He does well at this, but inevitably has times when blood sugar is too high or low. Corrective action works, but not immediately; low blood sugar goes hand-in-hand with hypothermia, so I worry about him. The hot Jell-O ther-mos is always in his pack.

In summer, you don't always have to be thinking ahead to outwit hypothermia or carry so much heavy gear or keep from sweating up your clothes. Except for descents, everything takes so much longer in winter; on the other hand, there are no bugs! Descents are eased by skiing the snowshoes or sitting and sliding instead of stumbling over rocks. Each season has its good and bad points; so enjoy both and rejoice in the positives! Other than a small scar on my eyelid from a branch, I had no injuries; my husband has had three (not in winter). That's another advantage of winter; you walk on top of all the cripplebush, instead of pushing through it.

Our first climb up Mt. Colden was with the Adirondack Mt. Club/Appalachian Mt. Club winter school leader Dick Barnett and others. We had climbed thirty-nine peaks by January 1980, but I con-vinced my husband to take a break for a home-building project. In 1988, he was impatient to finish the Winter 46 and we did that year.

However, after an eight year break, everyone we had been climbing with had finished. In 1988, we did most of the rest by ourselves.

Climbing the Winter 46 was exciting, exhilarating, beautiful, but hard, hard work—a lot of preparation for each climb, and those long drives in sometimes hair-raising conditions might pose a greater risk than the mountains! The experience taught me that perseverance, patience, and good planning, combined with love for what you are doing, can get you to the top in any area of life.

I am a professional pianist who teaches at the State University of New York at Binghamton, now called Binghamton University. Until I met Dick while I was a graduate student in music there, I had never climbed a mountain. As a child in Korea, I was always busy practicing piano—or participating in musical activities. During my student days at École Normale de Musique de Paris and at the Juilliard School, I never paid too much attention to physical activities. I got drawn to hiking by Dick's enthusiasm, thorough knowledge about the Adirondacks and love for outdoors. I began climbing with Dick and his friends. Quite often, I felt I couldn't afford the time and energy because of my career, but the attraction to vigorous physical activity and moments of living in an enchanted world were too strong to ignore. I think I am a happier and healthier person since I climbed all forty-six mountains in winter.

Colden, December 28, 1975:

One of the most vivid memories of my winter climbs is of the first mountain Dick and I climbed with the Winter Mountaineering School in 1975. Two days before, we had driven to the North Country School, where we registered and received a helpful lecture on hypothermia by a local Lake Placid doctor. After a night sleeping in our bags on the gymnasium floor, we were assigned to cook groups, each with a leader from the school; had our equipment checked by the group leader; made a foray into Lake Placid for last-minute equipment purchases and rentals; and then were driven to Adirondack Loj. From there we dragged all our gear two miles in to Marcy Dam, where we set up base camp for a five-day stay.

This first morning at Marcy Dam, we woke up at 4:30 A.M. to find a crisp -20°. After dressing, putting on our cold boots, breaking ice to get water, firing up the stove, and having oatmeal, cheese, and hot cocoa, we considered the several trip options. We chose a Mt. Colden trip led by instructor Dick Barnett, leaving camp at 6:45 just as it was getting light enough to see our boots. The snow was deep, pristine, and the air was filled with light snow. I was getting comfortably warm and invigorated. It was my first time on a snow-covered mountain on December 28, 1975, my birthday, and the view from the top was a worthy gift for the occasion. Looking to surrounding mountains was like looking at the unending white waves of an enchanted ocean! So the mountain magic was cast unto me.

Haystack, February 3, 1979:

The severest weather conditions we encountered were on Haystack, with the wind velocity close to 45 mph. The rocks on Little Haystack were covered with a thick crust of ice. While we had begun our day at the Garden parking lot, friends of ours had camped halfway in at Johns Brook Lodge. We met them returning after they turned around at Little Haystack; they considered the conditions impossible.

However, we were equipped! All four in our party had brought crampons, which we swapped for our snowshoes at Little Haystack. We had to claw our way very slowly, stooping down as low as we could. There was a short stretch of soft snow in the col between Little Haystack and Haystack where, without snowshoes, we swam. It was a bracing and very brief summit celebration, even with leather facemasks, with just enough time to measure the wind velocity and temperature (2°). The view of Mt. Marcy from the ice-covered top of Haystack was imposing and majestic. We camped between Haystack and Basin near the junction with the trail to Upper Ausable Lake, and climbed Basin the next day—calm, sunny, and anticlimactic.

We had planned to climb Basin previously, over Saddleback, with a group staying at Grace Camp. Dick spoke of the precipitous cliffs west of Saddleback and the necessity of bringing crampons and rope for the descent. On Saddleback we put on our crampons; the trip leader took one amazed look down the cliffs and ordered a turnabout. He remembered these cliffs as being on the west side of Basin! He and everyone else had reneged on their promise to bring crampons, so we turned back. There was still time for a very enjoyable climb of Big Slide.

Whiteface and Esther, February 28, 1988:

Although Dick considers the Haystack trip with its wind and ice the most dramatic of all, for me that honor goes to the climb of Whiteface in the dark and blistering cold. The full moon was casting its cool beams on the desolate white landscape, and we went up the icy steps gripping onto the rails to the top. We were the only people on the mountain that night. What an eerie looking landscape!

We had gotten a late start that day, parking the car below the gate of the toll road closed for the season. We had then skied up the road to where the Wilmington Trail intersects it below Whiteface, stashed our skis, and descended the trail on snowshoes to pick up the herd path to Esther. After climbing Esther we got back to the Wilmington Trail just as the light was getting too dim to be off trail. By the time we had climbed back to the junction with the road, it was quite dark.

After a hasty round trip from there to Whiteface's summit, we switched back to skis and headed down in the dark. The good part was the easy shuffle down the ideal grade of the road, but the worst part was that we felt frozen to death by the time we got down to the car.

Seymour, March 11, 1988—46th Peak:

The longest hike was to Seymour in 1988, which was my last climb of the Winter 46. We decided to make it a day trip and it was a very long day! Leaving our motel in Tupper Lake early that morning, we drove past Corey's to the end of the plowing at the Stony Creek Bridge, just past Axton Landing. Since it was an extra 3.3 miles to the summer parking lot, we again used sleds with our heavy backpacks to save energy and make better time. We left the car at 4:30 A.M. and reached the lot just as it was starting to get light. We pulled our sleds all the way on the flat and almost entirely open trail to Ward Brook Lean-to.

We then put on snowshoes and began the bushwhack up Seymour with our packs on our backs in a recent heavy snow that made traction difficult. Our snowshoes kept coming off because the bindings kept icing up. At the slide, which is a popular way in the summer, we had to make our way through the bushes rather than going up the sheer ice-covered slide. I wasn't feeling very perky that day, so I was happy to turn back after signing the register for the last time in my winter climbs. Coming back was as hard as going up since I was exhausted and feeling a bit off, and the snow conditions had gotten worse.

A weld on the hinge-rod of one of my snowshoes broke just as we got within a hundred yards of the lean-to, where, fortunately they were no longer needed. By the time we got to the car it was 8:30 P.M.; we had walked for sixteen hours non-stop—literally without stopping for a few moments of rest on this almost twenty-mile trek. Was I discouraged by this kind of exhausting experience? No. I was proud of myself for being able to manage hardship and, in retrospect, I felt exhilarated mentally and physically.

Chai-Kyou began the Winter 46 in 1975 and finished in 1988.

CINDIE LOVELACE

46er #2585W

I had a job at Putnam Camp in Keene Valley when I was in eleventh grade. We got to hike on our days off and I was hooked. I went on an Outward Bound excursion between college and law school in the San Juan Mountains in Colorado—hiking with all our rations and tents on our backs! I enjoyed hut-to-hut hiking in the White Mountains in New Hampshire. I gave my all to law school, made Law Review, was published, and from my post on the board, edited the work of others. I plunged into Wall Street, the very picture of the dedicated attorney working eighteen-hour days. I lasted two years and, realizing I didn't want to die with nothing but "ship financings" written on my tombstone, quit to become an actress. For eight years I studied, explored, auditioned, rehearsed, performed, lived and breathed theater. I was happy! I became an actress; my first New York Times review was glowing.

Then I discovered love for the first time—felled like a tree at age thirty-two. Revelation: Nothing else mattered. CB was a starving actor and I was hungry myself, so I began to take legal jobs to support the love habit; soon I was at it full-time. After much sturm und drang, my blond Midwestern beau went back homeward. I buried my sorrows in the world of rock-climbing, winter mountaineering, and ice climbing. I went to Winter Mountaineering School in Bethlehem, New Hampshire, and loved it; I learned to use snowshoes, crampons and an ice ax; met Gene Prater, Guy and Laura Waterman, and hiked the Whites in winter—what a thrill. The next winter I went again for the advanced "B" School and camped out in a snow cave at minus thirty degrees on the Presidential Range.

At age forty, I attended the National Outdoor Leadership School, a month-long course in which we ice-climbed, slept on glaciers, jumped over crevasses on Mt. Rainier wearing seventy-pound packs, and practiced crevasse rescue. I ice-climbed on the glaciers of Alaska. My best buddy, Jo Applebaum, and I climbed Mt. Hood; she also went to the Winter Mountaineering School to climb with me my second winter, and although she is under five feet tall, she is mighty! Also, she knew how to get those little stoves to light!

But there are so many other things to try. I pursued tennis, rediscovered downhill skiing and yoga, took windsurfing lessons, became a devotee of Pilates and an avid kayaker. Other sports I like include squash, sculling, sailing, roller-blading, and mountain biking. I've been weight lifting on a regular basis for years. I bought a 100-year-old apartment on Carnegie Hill in New York City, restoring all the old details, and interned at Sotheby's; I found great joy in being part of that rarefied art world and took the Graduate Record Exam to return to grad school in the field—although I didn't want to move from my beloved apartment.

I seem to have come full-circle now, preparing for this book. I'm reminded that I was at my happiest two times in my life: when I was in theater, and when I was climbing. All the sports I'm involved in are nowhere near as scary and demanding as hiking and camping in the snow. I never felt as passionate about summer hiking as I did about winter hiking. It took my mind off everything else, required full concentration and commitment. And there are no bugs! Fewer people are out there. I love the magic of the clean snow and how the sun sparkles on it. I love all the gear! Backpacking is fun because for some weird reason it's cozy to be snuggled into a sleeping bag in a tent with total strangers after a huge dinner.

I had written to Guy and Laura Waterman: "Mountain climbing is for me what methadone is for a drug addict—it may not cure what ails me, but it does keep me off the street. The 'exercise-in-the-outdoors' satisfies something in me that gets miserable when I'm 'unexercised-in-the-indoors'!"

Saddleback, Basin, and Gothics, January 30-31, 1988:

The first four hours with the Rochester Winter Mountaineering Society, leaving late and then rushing, were sheer hell. Those guys are real amazons and I was last except for our poor leader/sweep. Why race like mad, leaving me and luckily one other relatively slow guy in the dust, feeling inadequate, miserable, and pushing ourselves to the limit trying to keep up (and failing)?—because they'll just have to stand around waiting for us to catch up!

The next hours were scary. The route down Saddleback was icy rock and sixty mph gusts. Two climbers were actually blown off Haystack within recent memory. By 3:20 P.M. the last hurdle to Basin's summit looked too far given only two more hours of light. On the way back up Saddleback, the wind was whipping the words out of our mouths—it blew a snowshoe off the top of the mountain, which whizzed by and nicked me on the shoulder! I put on crampons and was having a problem with the bales that don't like to stay in the welt; meanwhile everyone was gone off the ledge.

Jack was acting as sweep and instructed me to climb a steep rock area using his feet as a handhold; the drop-off below was impressive. Being 5'4" tall, I couldn't reach his ankles; after scary attempts to reach his feet I tried front pointing up a steep gully filled with pure ice—only to reach a point twelve feet up where the gully narrowed to a foot jam; an attempt to put a leg over onto rock seemed foolhardy without a belay. Clinging precariously to the hold I had with my ice ax, wondering how long my hamstrings could take the pain of holding the front point position, I waited for Jack to advise me. After what seemed like a long time, a lonely time indeed, he did appear—and said "yes," he thought my planned route would "go," but if I were nervous without a belay there was a way up with snowshoes. So, gingerly, down I went to my ledge, off came the crampons—wind still whipping wildly—to try the snowshoe route. Those on top took an interest in my progress; no one would get dinner if I didn't somehow get over the top! Darkness was closing in, as well.

The snowshoe route was impressive. Deep, unpredictable snow, following the side of the rock face all the way up—literally standing on trees for footholds—squirming up a very narrow, extremely steep man-made shaft, each step an act of sheer will: "I will my foot to go this high and reach that branch." The cold group above was cheering me on. I willed myself not to think about the final obstacle, knowing that I must face the rock once more. I never lost my cool, which in retrospect amazes me. There was another very high step for me to take; they had a human chain set up which gave me more confidence; Jack extended a snowshoe for me to grab. He insisted on taking my ice ax, which I still think was a mistake, as there was a place to dig it in over my head—and no handholds. But I deferred to his seniority. The first one-two-three did not go, as—deprived of my ice ax—my right hand grabbed onto a bit of dead tree branch. What a yell was heard as I slid back down to a precarious perch good for one foot only. The second try had it—by mostly sheer will. I used my knees. A few more icy steps… summit… and down to camp on my rear end.

Donaldson, Emmons, and Seward, February 14, 1988:

I had one of the greatest trips ever into the Sewards. The drive up was gruesome—big snowstorm, cars off the road. I met the guys from the Rochester Winter Mountaineering Society in Tupper Lake with butterflies in my stomach—they looked serious and mean (as in "the lean, mean climbing machine"). We followed the Calkins Brook route to within ten minutes of Donaldson's summit at a humane pace because of deep snow, bushwhacking, and route finding. Also, the leader called for regular food/water breaks, which no other Rochester leader is known to do! I broke trail along the unplowed road for an eternity—whew—hard work! And did a lot of second place. By the time we found ourselves a camping spot it was dark. My two tentmates froze their hands and feet putting up the tent; my chore was to gather snow for the cook.

The next day dawned gorgeous and clear! After summitting Donaldson and Emmons, we decided to gain the summit of Seward via some exciting rock climbing and then a magical ridge walk with the sun glistening on the snow, blue sky, and breathtaking views in all directions. Such a perfect "top-of-the-world" feeling that afternoon! Back at camp by 3:30, everyone in our tent napped until dinner! I was so out cold they had to shake me to wake me up. Jerry and I chatted the whole way out next day—he's a very open fellow, although a little too talkative for my taste, believe it or not. I had a great time and felt as if I had finally come into my own with the Rochester group—partly because Jerry likes women so much and is such a humane-type leader.

Dix, February 27, 1988:

We skied the first six and a half miles of our twenty-mile round-trip. What a treat! Nearing the summit of Dix, though, I thought I'd had it—total fatigue, slight lightheadedness, and nausea. The fellow behind me said, "Just go your own pace, that's the key." I started to climb again and began singing to dispel the fright of running out of energy. The trail breaking had been intense, hard, and steep, and we'd been at it without any real rest for three hours. I always took my turn breaking trail when it came up but noticed that Sue Eilers, a stronger and faster climber than I, had taken a rest break instead of rotating into the lead trailbreaker position. Better that than to drop dead of fatigue if you are near your limit. I didn't break trail the rest of the way, but it wasn't far.

We still had to scale the Beckhorn before we could walk the ridge to the summit—involving some pretty fancy ice ax and foot work over several scary, icy rock cliffs! Despite near total exhaustion, up I went. Where the adrenaline came from, I'll never know. Descending, as my old self began to inhabit my body once more, I realized just how near the "edge" I'd been.

Lower and Upper Wolf Jaw, March 19-20, 1988:

I hiked this one alone—Amy, my hiking partner, couldn't make it—this long, lonely trip all by myself where my young life will probably come to an end as a frozen corpse in the snow. As it turned out, I had the most rewarding two days. I had the luxury of setting my own pace without feeling that if I slowed down (or stopped!), I'd ruin somebody else's trip. I could pee without getting left behind—men can't seem to understand that for us the process is more complex.... I, for example, am partial to fallen trees for optimum comfort; I also appreciate the privacy that can only be obtained after the men have gone by; therefore each simple pee stop means I am, yet again, left behind. On this trek I could drink when I got thirsty, eat when I got hungry, take off or put on layers without asking anybody's permission. I could walk as slowly as I liked uphill and run as fast as I liked downhill. I could dawdle when the view struck me as particularly fine. A most satisfying experience.

Obvious drawbacks were, I had to do all the trail breaking and if I broke an ankle or had a concussion, Ranger Pete Fish wouldn't find me until the next day. The exertion on my solo days was far greater and cost me an additional peak each day. I lost the trail a few times on Upper Wolf Jaw and a companion's moral support would have been nice. And there were three scary drop-offs.

I got started an hour later than planned and guidebook directions were unclear in accessing the route from the Ausable Club Road. I reached the most dramatic footbridge, high over a gorge with a rail on one side only... on the other, empty space! There were several feet of snow piled up on it, untouched by human feet, so to get any support from the handrail I had to bend way over. The bridge was so narrow that I feared I might fall through a cornice! Once over the bridge I had to negotiate one bit of steep bank, a slip from which would precipitate a spectacular slide into the gorge far below. My adventure was off to a rousing start.

The walk along the edge of the river gorge was gorgeous! The snow conditions could be divided into three sections: along the gorge practically nonexistent; then like cement—on every step the snow balled up in my Tucker claws so that I was virtually walking on my heels. I shed the ball of snow every few steps by smashing the snowshoe down onto the tip of the other shoe. Then the fun part— deep new snow! High up it was a whole different world, serious trail breaking! I felt fine at the summit at two o'clock and thought I'd see how far up Upper Wolf Jaw I could get. I got misled by signs to a camping area and lost fifteen minutes. I turned around one hour from the summit; I would've been spooked cutting it so close to dark and I hate that feeling. Reaching a false summit on Upper the next day, the true summit looked horribly high. An enjoyable experiment certainly, worth it for all the discoveries I made about the joys of soloing.

Saddleback, January 21, 1989:

Jo's and my first winter backpack was after dark to the lean-to near Johns Brook Lodge; Providence gave us moonlight. What a lovely experience it was; we never used our headlamps on the trail. Saturday's trip was thrilling—two of my favorite guys from Albany came. At the Gothics-Saddleback col we were having doubts about the wisdom of attempting Gothics; the day was cold (-15°) with extreme wind chills! I hadn't realized how cold until, when I began putting on extra layers, I went through an agonizing few minutes with my hands. I had removed my over-mitts and pile mitts in order to manipulate my pack fasteners and get extra clothes. Although I wore silk glove liners, by the time I had all my extra layers on I had lost the use of my hands. I tried doing "windmills" to no avail. I was unable even to put my hands in my armpits as they were no longer dexterous enough to undo my jacket and the other layers. I finally managed to rip open a pair of chemical hand warmers and knead them until they began to produce warmth—but I was close to desperate before I solved the problem. The entire incident probably didn't take as long as it did for me to put words on paper—but each second felt endless.

We decided Saddleback was better for today because it is not nearly so exposed as Gothics. We had awesome views of Gothics the whole way up Saddleback and on the summit we were dazzled by the panoramic view of what seemed to be the whole world. It was a glorious, perfect blue-sky day, and to be up there was thrilling. On our return we stopped in at the warming hut; it was very seductive—the wood stove gave off a cozy glow and Neil Woodworth and Steve Brown, manning the hut, offered us cup after cup of hot water. I put one of my sandwiches in a frying pan on the stove where it thawed to a mushy but delightfully edible state. Neil and Steve invited us to spend the night in their two extra bunks, but we were determined not to take the easy way out; after an hour of basking in their good conversation and the luxurious warmth, the two of us donned all our layers and headed for our lean-to.

Algonquin and Iroquois, January 28, 1989:

I started over an hour ahead of the Albany guys; they caught up with me at the junction for Wright Peak at 10 o'clock. Algonquin was wild, with sixty mph winds. When I got to the summit, last as usual, only one guy was still there—the "Sweep," waiting for me. We plunged down to the col between Algonquin and Iroquois to get out of the gale-force winds. When we reached the col he wondered aloud what was keeping the rest of the group.

The trip back over Algonquin was a nightmare. I had the good sense to put on crampons in the col; the mountain was one big ice-skating rink. The wind buffeted me about like a bit of flotsam; when I finally staggered, exhausted, onto the summit of Algonquin, I realized to my horror that I was all alone—with no idea of the correct direction to get down, since tracks weren't visible on the ice in that fierce wind. My fingers would have frozen, retrieving and studying a map and compass in that gale. After endlessly long moments of fear, I glimpsed a small figure a third of the way down the face below me; it emerged briefly from behind a large boulder, gave a quick wave and vanished again.

On I struggled, grateful to the core of my being that someone had bothered to wait for me—agonizing as it must have been in that wind. The wind was so wild, I actually tried sitting down so as not to offer such a large surface area for the wind to attack. This was a mistake, as I easily could have slid all the way down the steep, icy mountainside. Whew!

Marshall, February 3-4, 1989:

We stayed at Calamity Lean-to the first night and in the morning crossed Flowed Lands, setting up our tent near Lake Colden while awaiting two last arrivals. Jeff Tishman wanted to approach Marshall from the Iroquois-Marshall col—although longer, he thought it easier with the bushwhack only half as far. Off we went with a late start but great conditions. At 1:30 P.M. we reached the col. It was 3 o'clock and Lauren decided to go back; Jeff guessed an hour to the summit. The conditions were super for a bushwhack—no more than fifteen spruce traps! The surface of the snow was stiff and crunchy. Where was the canister? We tromped around the top for ages with no success; now the impending darkness was worrying us. We finally made it back on the marked trail at 5:15, still light!

Our friends at Lake Colden had chosen a lovely, open meadow and we had set our tents up next to theirs. We made a great effort to make our nature calls as far from the campsite as possible. At 4 A.M., Jo went on such a foray; her headlamp conked out en route and she wandered off the beaten track. Not more than ten yards from the tent she fell in up to her waist! I was snuggled way down inside my sleeping bag and didn't hear her at first. Then, "Cindie." I groggily struggled out of the tent. "I fell in" was all she said as she walked toward me; we ripped her clothes off her lobster red body in the tent. She was incredibly brave and we both kept our heads. We left the clothes she'd been wearing outside and the next morning they were frozen into crazy shapes. I didn't sleep much the rest of the night; I kept envisioning our tent breaking through the ice, our struggling to no avail to open the zipper on the tent door as icy water poured in through the ventilation sleeve and the tent sinking to the bottom of the Opalescent River with us as unwilling ballast.

Macomb, South Dix, East Dix, and Hough, March 19, 1989—46th peak:

Dear Grace, It is with a tremendous sense of accomplishment and joy that I write to tell you that on March 19th, I climbed the last four peaks of my Adirondack 46. Bob Veino and his Albany gang were scheduled to come in; but when Jo and I woke up Saturday, it was pouring. The next day dawned beautiful! By 8:15 the guys were outside our tent and we were off. We never saw Bob Veino again, that's how fast those guys are!

We had a thrilling ascent of the Macomb slide in full crampons. If we had slipped, we would have gone all the way to the bottom! We reached the summit at 12:30. South Dix was a piece of cake, but East Dix seemed long. Back at South Dix by four o'clock, Jo said, "Hough is only three-fourths of a mile from here." At 4:40 we reached the col between the hogback and Hough and at 5:30 we summitted Hough, with the sun setting and the moon rising. I've never seen anything more spectacular in all my days!

We cried, laughed, and cried and laughed again! I wasn't expecting anything special on Hough after forty-five other winter ascents, remembering that Hough in the fall was nothing special in terms of views. But in winter, we were perched on top of the world. No view anywhere could have surpassed the beauty and drama of the landscape around and below us.

Cindie started the Winter 46 at age 38 and finished at age 40.

MARY CONNOLLY RABIDEAU

46er #2051W

I started hiking in 1983, in the Adirondacks and in the White Mountains, but only winter-hiked in the Adirondacks. I prefer warmer temperatures and non-winter hiking, but was inspired to set the goal of Winter 46ing to experience the challenge and the beauty of the Adirondacks in its wildest and purest form. We had camped in winter previously in the lower foothills of the Adirondacks and began the Winter 46 by a combination of day-trips and overnights; we started getting away from overnight camping through better planning and experience. It was more physically demanding to pack in overnight equipment and to withstand the night cold.

The most frightening thing that happened, on an overnight trip during our first attempt at Seward, was when we almost caught the tent on fire while we were inside it in zero-degree weather!

I rated each hike according to difficulty, from A+++ to C, with A+++ meaning "to the limit of endurance," and C, "easier than in summertime." The most difficult trip involved breaking trail to Couchsachraga, navigating by compass through a snowstorm that dumped eight inches of new snow on us—and we carried full packs to camp overnight. So that peak rated A+++, as did Donaldson and Emmons where only Duane and I broke trail all the way, carrying full packs to the top of Donaldson. It was the only time I considered quitting the quest for the Winter 46.

Completing the Winter 46 on Cascade with no snowshoes on a sunny, spring-like day provided a fine contrast! Three peaks received an A+, fourteen an A, seven A-, eight B+, eight B, Phelps B-, and Cascade and Porter got a C!

The experience of climbing the Winter 46 was very demanding

physically, emotionally, and mentally. To experience the beauty of the Adirondacks at its greatest fury and also at its most serene is a great privilege, something that few people have experienced. The Winter 46 has had a calming effect on my mental outlook by refocusing myself on the real reasons why I am on this earth. This experience was a very special part of my life because of my love for the Adirondacks, and it was where I met and fell in love with my future husband, Duane.

SUE EILERS

46er #1965W

I started hiking and skiing with my children who were four and six at the time, as a way of getting them away from the T.V. When they grew older and wanted to spend time with their friends, I joined hiking groups and found information such as "The Walk Book," which had hikes in the New York City area where I live and in the Catskills. I also run, ski, bike, and work out at a health club. I've hiked the 770 peaks in the Northeast over 3,000' and finished the Winter 111s and Northeast Hundred Highest in winter. I'm a past president of the Catskill 3500 Club and was their representative on the New York-New Jersey Trail Conference. My daughter and her family moved only three miles away, so I'm busy with my three grandsons a lot lately!

Phelps, January 3, 1987:

We got fifteen inches of new snow last night. John Kennedy got sick, so I climbed Phelps alone. It was one of my harder hikes of the year. I was the first one on the trail at 7 o'clock, and so had this fluffy wonderful snow to push through. As I started up Phelps, it kept getting deeper and deeper. When I got to the top, it was up to my waist! I felt like I was swimming in this fluffy, frothy, cold surf! It took me until 1 o'clock to get to the top.

The Wolf Jaws and attempt on Armstrong, March 1, 1987:

I left alone at 7 o'clock to climb Lower and Upper Wolf Jaw and Armstrong. Approaching Armstrong, I got as far as the cliff at 4,000 feet. I just could not get up it. I was at the bottom at 11:30 and tried to get a foothold for over an hour before I gave up. The snow was very deep and soft and I could not kick in steps that would hold. I was quite frustrated.

Gothics, Saddleback, and Armstrong, March 15, 1987:

I started from the Garden at 6:30 A.M. and had coffee with friends at Winter Camp. I climbed Saddleback and then went up Gothics. This was the finest day you can imagine: clear and not cold, yet crisp. The view from Gothics was absolutely fantastic! You look back over Saddleback to Basin and Haystack and Marcy, snow-covered and the blue, blue sky beyond.... I was enthralled. Then I continued over Armstrong, where I met another solo hiker and we ate lunch together. This time, I was able to slide down the cliff on Armstrong. You could see how people got up, the same way I'd tried—it was just a matter of having snow that would hold steps. Not that it was easy, even then. That is a very tricky spot!

Giant, March 20, 1987:

I tried to go up the ridge trail on Giant, but it was very icy and I only got to 3,200 feet. At that point, my crampons did not hold and I slipped down about ten feet. I walked over and around that spot, but then got to an open place where, if I slipped, I would go about thirty feet before I hit enough vegetation to stop me. I didn't like that at all, turned around, and went home.

Sue began the Winter 46 at age 45 and finished at age 53.

MARY BUNCH

46er #2003W

Mike and I started hiking the High Peaks in winter and liked it, not thinking of completing all 46 peaks. I like hiking in all seasons, but especially the descents in winter, which are great fun! We liked staying at Grace Camp, a good base camp for climbs of the Great Range, Marcy, and Gray. Once, the Schenectady Chapter of ADK stayed at Grace Camp to hike these peaks and it was so cold that we all stayed in the same room, huddled near the wood stove. We had boiled five gallons of water by 11 P.M. and it was frozen solid in the morning! We took apart and reassembled the wood stove, to see if it was working. It was just that cold!

It was -30° on the hike to Saddleback; Mike got frostbite on his nose. But we experienced a real temperature inversion on Big Slide; we started at -10° and climbed to a warm summit! The Santanoni Range took us four or five tries. One day, Mike broke through Panther Brook and quickly changed his socks. We immediately descended, changed clothes, and hiked out.

Mike and I, with Bruce Wadsworth and the Schenectady Chapter of ADK, wrote ADK's first comprehensive guide to all the trails in the Catskill Forest Preserve, "Guide to Catskill Trails."

The Seward Range, March 19, 1988:

I talked with Elsie Chrenko about winter hikes but when I exclaimed, "Not the Sewards!" she replied, "Sure you want to, they're just a long day. You get up in the middle of the night, start hiking before dawn, you're out by dark or early evening, and it's only twenty hours including travel time." So we went up and tried it. We set off in snow flurries at 4 o'clock in the morning and actually topped Donaldson at 11. Wow. This isn't going to be so bad after all, we thought. Well, it took us four hours to get to Emmons. It was like a tunnel that we had to practically dig our way through! It wasn't a spruce trap problem, just a wall of white the whole way. Three years and thirteen peaks later, we tackled Seward and discovered a plane wreck not far from the summit.

Mary hiked the Winter 46 in her early thirties.

JACKIE PARKER

46er #2563W

While driving through the Adirondacks I would often see individuals going in on trails; and read articles in newspapers that advertised hikes led by various groups. I thought it would be fun to try hiking, providing I knew what to do and wear. In the spring of 1987, our school's adult education booklet listed a class, "Introduction to Hiking," and my husband very reluctantly decided to go with me. That was our beginning. Neil went from Mr. Couch Potato to Mr. Hiker.

Being a goal setter, Neil did not want to just walk in the woods, so our first endeavor was to do the Northville-Lake Placid Trail in sections. We started that in May 1988, doing a section a month. After our first section Neil asked if I would like to try one of those 46 High Peaks that was right off Route 73—Giant Mt. We became hooked on hiking and became 46ers on Haystack in October 1988. Receiving our 46er numbers was exciting, especially for me.

Aside from going to church, Bible study, and prayer, the most spiritual thing I do is hike. What a blessing it was to hear the Vesper service at the meeting and to sing "How Great Thou Art." I was in awe. In one of my letters to Grace I mentioned being at Skye Farm and she made comments about Methodists and our having something in common. Little did I realize the history of the 46ers and how it had been started by a small church group. It was then I understood the spirit of their service. It is my hope that it will never be lost.

When we began our hiking careers, Neil became involved with the Schenectady Chapter of the Adirondack Mountain Club. An outing listed in the Chapter's newsletter interested him and he went on his first trail work trip. During a week every summer, I volunteered as a counselor at Skye Farm, a church camp in Warrensburg, so he decided to do a four-day work weekend with ADK on the Northville-Lake Placid Trail. The following year I joined him on both the Chapter-led maintenance trip and an ADK-led trip to the Catskills. That began our second love—trail work. We have worked with the 46ers on their projects and as of 2002 have spent thirteen years with the ADK Trails program. We enjoyed hiking in the Adirondacks so much and knew that we had to do something to give back to this great natural resource.

Since our finish of the High Peaks in the fall seemed more like winter conditions, we decided to take a class at the Adirondack Loj in winter mountaineering. Neil had become a hike leader, and we wanted to be prepared for all hiking conditions while taking others on Adirondack Mountain Club hikes. We climbed Wright Peak in 1989 with the class and then Neil and I did Panther together. Instead of reaching up to the canister to sign in, we reached down into the snow. We had views in every direction and felt as though we were on top of the world. We went on to climb the 35 peaks in the Catskills over 3,500 feet in winter as well as summer.

While hiking the 46 High Peaks in summer, Neil learned about the White Mountains of New Hampshire from Frank Sorbero. It was then on to the 111, those peaks over 4,000 feet in New England and New York. Our first hiking vacation took us to Maine to hike its twelve High Peaks, and there we met a young Appalachian Trail through-hiker who "peaked" Neil's interest in the Appalachian Trail. This became his ultimate dream and consequently mine. Once he made the decision, the family knew what to get him as Christmas gifts—books and videos about the AT. He started planning for the hike that would take place when he retired from the FAA. Once he had made his itinerary, every year starting in March and throughout the summer he would ask, "Do you know where we would be today if we had started the AT?"

In the meantime, we did a through-hike of The Long Trail in Vermont. (While doing the trail we met section hikers and thru hikers and were impressed with how the hiking community took care of each other. Everyone we met was willing to share their knowledge and we asked a lot of questions.) The following summer we did the Northville-Lake Placid Trail, north to south, with our friend Sandra Tornga whom we had dubbed "Crazy Woman." She hiked with braces because she had no cartilage in her knees and was rubbing bone on bone.

Finally the time came to fulfill our dream! Neil retired in December 1998 and on March 10, 1999, Mud Puppy and Woodcutter (our trail names) started up the approach trail to Springer Mountain in Georgia. Neil again wanted to "give back" to trails, so offered our trip to the Adirondack Mountain Club as a fund-raiser. We asked for no support, paying our own way, and ADK created "All the Way for ADK," a pledge system for members of the club that raised over $16,000 for the trails program. On August 7, 1999, in 149 days, long-time ADK trail volunteers Jackie and Neil Parker completed all 2,160.2 miles of the Appalachian Trail. Five months, five million steps, and our fantastic journey was at an end. The difference for those who make it is focus. You can't have anything else on your mind. You must stay focused on what you're doing, mile after mile, day after day. Sometimes all I could think of out on the trail was a rotisserie chicken. Oh, what I wouldn't have given for that!

Gothics and Armstrong, February 18, 1990:

We headed for Saddleback and Basin, but because we were following a broken trail we continued up a stream leading to a bushwhack of Gothics. Was that ever impressive, all the ledges covered with ice! We went to the left of the icy ledges and bushwhacked up— straight up. The area was open and with its being so steep, the only thing to do was to plunge the ice ax into the hardened snow cover, take the two or three steps to pull ourselves up to it, lean forward, then follow the procedure again. I had a sense that if I let go of the ice ax it would be a very long slide down the area I had just covered with nothing around to stop the fall. Neil was using only a ski pole to steady himself, and I can only guess that his success moving forward was because of his strength. After awhile we managed to head into some brush and were able to use it for support while using the branches to pull ourselves to the next step upward.

We finally arrived at the northernmost crest of Gothics. We first went to the summit of Armstrong and then on to Gothics, planning to go down the cable. But we met Bob Grimm, with a party of five, who advised us not to descend that way since it was too dangerous— they had struggled to come up that open rock.

After summitting Gothics, we caught up with his group for a bushwhack down Armstrong to the Orebed Trail. We basically went down "going by the nose," taking the route that was most open, realizing that at some point we would come upon the marked trail. A couple of times we had to traverse across an area. As some in the party had modified bear paw snowshoes, I was in the lead at those times and had to pack a trail wide enough with my Sherpas so they would have an easier time of it. With most of it going downhill, packing a trail was easy. A word of wisdom from Kathleen Gill was the reason we traded our modified bear paws for the Sherpas. As she said, "No matter where you are in line, if you have modified bear paws you are always breaking trail."

Marcy and Gray, March 10, 1990:

A warm day and soft snow; sounds like heaven but it wasn't. No matter how many layers came off, it was just too warm and the heat sapped my strength. With the soft snow clumping up under the claws of my snowshoes, it felt as though I was hiking with a cement block on each foot. This was a trail that skiers used and snowshoes were a must, but since noticing that more damage was being done to the trail by the snowshoes than by my Sorel boots, I decided to take the snowshoes off and continued up Marcy. After reaching the summit and resting, a decision was made to continue on to Gray.

I had finally hit the point where I was exhausted. Although my mind wanted to hike, the rest of my body was in rebellion! But with the thought of how easy the bushwhack to Gray would be from Mt. Marcy, I continued on knowing that the hike back up to Marcy's summit would be a slow one!

Hough, February 2, 1991:

What a toughie this was! Never made it to the summit until 3:45, with Neil, Ray Held, and Dave McPherson. (Ray is an extremely strong hiker; we never would have made it without his help. Actually, he did most of the trail breaking. Ray is more like a sleek race car, while our pace is more in the Model T line.) Our trek started at the winter parking lot two miles from the trailhead. We hiked the trail about three miles before finding what we felt sure was the cairn marking the route to Hough.

The going wasn't too bad until we started the steeper ascent. The snow was deep and soft. To go even a foot, the leader had to kick out the snow several times just to make a step since one could not raise their leg high enough to do it in one fell swoop. We were getting fairly close to the summit when we met up with a group planning an overnight. Ray was getting tired and put me in the lead and was urging me on. As usual, when fast hikers were behind me I was embarrassed by my turtle pace and tried to go too fast, managing to get out of breath in a short time. Knowing that the time was late, we pushed on as quickly as possible and soon were at the summit.

What I remember most was the camaraderie that developed with the individuals we hiked with. We owe our winter "peak bagging" to many of our hiking companions as we certainly would not have had success without their help. The biggest problem in the larger groups was that we were generally slower than many we were hiking with, and felt that we did not do our share of breaking trail. My best advice would be to hike with individuals who are similar in strength and pace—or with those who are fast but can be comfortable with those who have a slower pace.

Jackie began the Winter 46 at age 44 and finished at age 46.

CHERYL ESPER

46er #1603W

My hiking career began during my college days at the age of twenty. I attended a three-week Colorado Outward Bound course to catch the attention and gain the respect of an avid mountain-loving, blonde-haired young man. Chip would become my husband two years later, and in the process I became a mountain climber—a strange concept for my parents to accept. I did not come from a hiking family.

For our honeymoon we took a five-week camping trip through western National Parks. I brought him to my beloved Rockies and we returned regularly to climb more of the "14ers," peaks exceeding 14,000 feet. After Johnathan was born we carried him up to those lofty heights. Chip introduced me to the Adirondack Mountains. While he attended medical school we went to the mountains for renewal; I became an Adirondack 46er in June 1980.

From August 1988 to May 1989, we three traveled to all fifty states on a Trek Across America; we hiked extensively in mountain ranges and national parks. We learned to camp and hike in the Rocky Mountain States in the dead of winter. We ignored the impulse to stay in motels and learned how to stay comfortable while cooking, eating, sleeping, getting up, and dressing in frozen clothes in below-zero weather. This experience prepared us to tackle the 46 High Peaks in winter when our son turned seven.

After Johnathan had climbed a few winter peaks Grace wrote, "If you continue to climb at that rate perhaps you will become the youngest Winter 46er!" We became committed to help him reach that goal; he had shown us his ability to endure and persevere for long, difficult climbs. Some climbs were day trips and for the longer approaches we camped, heading for a lean-to after Chip had worked for twelve hours in the Emergency Room.

Our hiking attire was in stark contrast to others who looked like "real mountaineers" in their colorful new Gore-Tex layers, ice axes, plastic boots, and all the newest technology. We used down parkas, nylon ski pants (when ripped bushwhacking we were glad they weren't Gore-Tex), Gore-Tex shells, Sorel pack boots with wool liners, leather ski gloves (mittens for me), wool hats and scarves, and older external frame packs. Wicking under-layers were too expensive so we settled for the traditional cotton-polyester long johns! Johnathan and Chip wore wool pants under their outer bib pants and I—yellow corduroy pants! Finally we bought Sherpas with built-in crampons, which saved us tremendous time and effort and made ascents a bit safer. We had to work together and rely on God for our success. We exercised extreme caution, minimized risks, and tried to plan realistically.

Before we began seriously climbing the Winter 46, with God's strength, I tackled the unconquered peak of infertility in my life. We had a dear baby girl named Hannah Mary who was born prematurely and only lived three-and-a-half hours in 1990. After climbing Mt. Kilimanjaro in Africa and rafting the entire Grand Canyon, a new season blossomed in our lives. We were blessed with a cherished twin pregnancy. In and out of the hospital, trying desperately to keep them from being born too soon with thirteen weeks on strict bed rest, I'd think of our mountain sojourns and how often I'd be so tired, just wanting to sit and rest! Now I longed to get up and walk. Twin boys, Brecken and Josiah, were born though a natural delivery, healthy and well, at full-term. Chip and I joked that the only vertical feet we gained was by running up and down the stairs changing diapers all day and night! After four years a fourth son, Galen Jeremiah, was born on May 1, 1998. I became pregnant again and gave birth to our fifth son, Hansel Katahdin, in a pine forest alongside the Hudson River.

Marcy, Skylight, and Gray, February 23, 1992:

There was a curious track coming from the Lake Arnold trail, apparently made by a snowshoe, but a very narrow one compared to our wide wooden ones and there were marks as if crampons were attached! This was my first introduction to the new concept of crampon snowshoes! Our woes with our snowshoes continued; I was literally climbing Marcy on my hands and knees. At tree line we had to switch from snowshoes to crampons. My hands were numb soon after being taken out of my mittens; Chip patiently changed us all. The cloud ceiling had dropped, snow was beginning to fall, the wind was picking up, and soon there was little visibility. Suddenly a group of four men appeared, heading to Gray but unsure of the route. I examined their snowshoe crampons. "Wouldn't it be nice to have something like that," I queried while noting my husband's frozen hands. "Not just nice but perhaps necessary for our safety," he answered. By compass we headed up Marcy, careful not to spiral around the other side as we ascended. The wind was blowing a steady forty mph; we had on all our clothes and goggles.

Back at tree line, we took off our crampons and put on snowshoes again. Using map and compass we headed for Gray; Johnathan needed assurance that there really was a mountain where we were headed. I emphasized how important it is to develop accurate orienteering skills; one's survival depends on them. We dug out the canister from deep snow and decided to head for Skylight. We reclimbed Marcy to tree line to retrace our steps back down. Where were our footprints? Where were the rock cairns? We couldn't find the trail; we would have to tear our way through the vegetation. Chip called back to us that we had intercepted our packed trail! We left our wooden snowshoes at the junction to Skylight and climbed in crampons. We thanked God for safe and successful climbing and prayed for safety back to our lean-to.

Colden, February 24, 1992:

We'd planned a leisurely hike out because Chip was to work at the emergency room that night. Now he was proposing a hike up Colden first! I mildly protested, thinking about the time. I agreed to go if: we'd go light, move fast and not take many breaks, go only with crampons, and no complaining. "OK, let's go!" The snowstorm had left six inches of beautiful fluff on top of a well-packed trail. We had good grip with crampons. On the summit of Colden, we had a moment of grandeur closed suddenly by a veil of clouds. Then we experienced a thrilling slide down the mountain; there was enough snow to cover most of the rocks and stumps. Chip and I took turns going first to "smooth the way" so our young son could have the best conditions. We slid down the trail in twenty minutes! Hikers coming up jumped out of the way as we whizzed by with the word, "Wow!"

Wright, February 28, 1992:

One of our most frightening experiences occurred on Wright Peak, known for windy conditions. The jet stream was moving at the fastest rate it had been measured in the past year, we later learned. Below in the birch forest I could hear the howling wind way up on top; it was quiet. My husband and I exchanged glances. "Let's hope it's not as bad as it sounds," I whispered. Should we wait for another day? We put on all our clothing and our goggles to protect our eyes.

Above tree line we tried to find the leeward side of the mountain but the wind seemed to be coming from all directions. It was a steady sixty to seventy mile-per-hour with gusts up to eighty. Ice particles were flying at us like bullets, stinging even through all our layers of clothes! During the worst gusts we could only press our bodies flat against the rock and wait it out. I dug in the ice layer with my ice ax to get a more secure hold. Chip and Johnathan were a little ahead and I felt so alone; I was terrified. Crawling, as we had to, it took a long time to reach the summit. At times Johnathan feared he would blow off the mountain. At the summit we had to shout due to the wind's loud roar. We crawled back to tree line; it was even more difficult due to extremely poor visibility, tearing eyes, and foggy goggles. I have a new respect for windy conditions on mountaintops now.

Macomb, South Dix, East Dix, and Hough, March 3, 1992:

After a comfortable night's sleep in Slide Brook Lean-to, we climbed the slide right to the summit by mid-morning. The climb was steep and deep after six to eight inches of fresh snow. We appreciated immensely the packed track of Phil Corell's group. Off to South Dix; we lost the herd path, but never spent much time looking for it. We would set our compass and push our way through the underbrush no matter how foreboding it looked. The sun, beautiful in the blue sky, had begun to soften the snow and the thick balsam and spruce dumped their heavy loads of snow on us. This would later create a grave concern for our safety.

On South Dix and East Dix we signed the log books in our own unique manner: "Praise God for safe and successful climbing!" and usually included a Biblical verse. I was content to head down. I saw Chip, however, glancing over to Hough. "Its only 2 o'clock and we've gained all this elevation. Why don't we take a compass bearing and start angling over there?"

The climb to Hough proved to be more difficult and energy consuming than we had imagined. We took the most direct route and that left us trying to scale a southern face of the mountain. It was incredibly steep! Johnathan and I would push Chip and secure his footing until he could reach a well-rooted handhold; then I would assist my son to that level, and finally the two of them would pull me up. The steep angle and avalanching snow made it extremely difficult to get a secure foothold with our snowshoe crampons. Much time was consumed by this inefficient method of gaining altitude. I felt discouraged and knew that we were really pushing ourselves to the limit this time! We summitted at 4:15 and began our descent immediately after signing the log. There was no time to celebrate; just a tone of seriousness and concern that lay heavy in our hearts.

If ever we raced down a mountain, it was here. We followed the stream down in the col between South Dix and Hough. Chip seemed to fly over the uneven terrain, trying to find the best route; Johnathan and I followed in quiet pursuit. As twilight edged upon us, I knew my young son was getting cold from the wet clothing he had on, and that he was very tired and hungry. We could not stop; we had only minutes left before total darkness enveloped us.

The stream-banks became too steep to maneuver; we veered away, hoping to intercept the Dix Trail. The problem was that the marked trail was unpacked and the land had leveled off. I pondered what our chances were of recognizing the trail—we could easily cross right over it! Thoughts of hypothermia flooded my brain as I visualized us wandering around checking every possible opening that might suggest a trail. The prospect of spending a winter's night outside without warm, dry gear spoke of disaster. Tears welled in my eyes and I began to cry. We had pushed too much this time. There was no help nearby. I prayed for God's divine intervention.

Chip called a halt to our search. We needed to study the map, eat, drink, rest, and determine if any clothing was dry in the soaking wet pack. He and I would have to wear our wet down parkas. Thankfully Johnathan's had been protected, and it gave me much comfort to be able to provide a warm dry jacket to my shivering son. I also rewarded his lack of complaining with a bag of jelly beans. I looked up at the moon, which was beginning to shine brightly. And then I noticed it! We were sitting in the middle of the Dix Trail! I cried for joy and we all hugged each other. We thanked God for His care of us.

We feasted back at camp by a roaring fire and slept peacefully with thankful hearts. Awakening at 9 A.M., we attempted to defrost our stiffly frozen boot liners enough to get our feet into them. They felt like ice blocks as we headed off to climb Dix. The "up" was difficult with our tired legs and the unpacked trail, but the "down" was fun, sliding on our bottoms.

The Seward Range, March 17, 1992:

We began our hike to the lean-to near Seward at dusk. Tracks had been obliterated by a foot of new snow. We began our climb at 6 A.M. and it was already snowing. At the summit the snowstorm was raging, with visibility only a few feet; the canister was just barely above the snow. Since it was still early we pushed on to Donaldson. We followed our compass right up cliffs between the two mountains and lost over an hour trying to negotiate around the drop-offs; the summit of Donaldson seemed to elude us.

We had never been forced to forfeit a summit attempt before, but this time we were not making progress and the weather was worrisome. Just as I resolved that we had to turn back, Chip discovered a barely-visible depression from a snowshoe; we pushed on to both Donaldson and Emmons, route-finding as we went. Not wanting to follow our tracks back over those cliffs, we took a different compass bearing and found ourselves in a difficult blow-down. More time was lost. As we neared the summit of Seward again, our previous tracks were gone; that meant route-finding yet again. Surely we would be on this trailless mountain after dark. Fortunately we came across our tracks farther down, almost covered with new snow. The sun glistened on the one-and-a-half feet of new snow the next morning, a beautiful day to climb Seymour in wintry conditions. We hiked out that night.

Haystack, December 21, 1992:

With the anticipation of a new winter climbing season, we left home at 4 A.M. I had rested for a few hours but sleep had eluded me. The more we hiked the wearier I became. For the first time, Johnathan took weight off me when we took a break five miles later at Bushnell Falls to put on snowshoes. After struggling another mile to Slant Rock, I was totally exhausted from lack of sleep. I just wanted to curl up in my sleeping bag and let Chip and Johnathan continue climbing; no way would they let me sleep! As we neared Little Haystack my adrenaline surged. I had literally been falling asleep while I was hiking. Now I was worried about that steep, icy summit cone.

We cautiously made our way up to the summit with the use of our crampons. There was hardly a trace of wind! I looked back down at Little Haystack and wondered how we could possibly make our way back down again. Those colossal features look formidable when viewing up close. Chip coached both Johnathan and me as we re-climbed that steep side of Little Haystack with the precipitous drop-off. We made haste back to the lean-to as nighttime enveloped us. Johnathan was so tired he fell asleep with food in his mouth!

Allen, December 24, 1992:

The canister tree on Allen had snapped and the canister was on the ground. Grace was worried that it would be buried all winter under the heavy snowfalls. She contacted us and we promised to correct the problem when we attempted Allen. With wire, nails, and hammer on our essential equipment list, we trudged into the former lean-to site at Twin Brooks. We had to pack the entire trail of five miles in the dark; it seemed an awfully long way! I reminisced about our previous hike to Haystack and Basin two days earlier, covering nearly twenty miles of unpacked terrain. Having just dried our clothing and equipment last night, we were back on the trail in less than twenty-four hours. No wonder I felt so tired! We made a fire, set up our tent, and ate. I felt apprehensive about the next day's climb and slept fitfully.

We awoke to a bitter cold day; temperatures fell below zero overnight. We laid the first tracks in winter up Allen Brook to the summit. I began digging with my snowshoe to find the canister; it was still attached to the broken tree. Chip and Johnathan decided to leave the canister on the tree since it was so firmly nailed. We wired the whole thing to another tree. To test its sturdiness, Johnathan hung his entire body weight on it and it didn't move. We knew Grace would be happy that it was permanently fixed! That night, in below-zero weather, we built a nice fire, starting it with birch bark. On Christmas Day, we awoke to find that "Santa" had left our supposedly lost lens cap at the entrance of our tent!

Flowed Lands, December 26, 1992:

As cautious as we were in crossing Flowed Lands, I made a careless mistake that could have cost us the final goal of our Winter 46 quest before the year ended. We had spread out to locate the lean-to across Flowed Lands. I came across a small brook in a three-foot ravine, made a quick assessment, and leaped like a gazelle—or at least I thought.

As soon as I had launched myself I knew I had made a grave mistake. My full pack was heavier than I realized, so I just went down. Ice broke and freezing cold water saturated my clothing from my knees down. It could have been worse, except for the fact that I grabbed an evergreen tree and held on tightly to keep me from sinking further. I hollered for Chip's help. It took the strength of both him and Johnathan to grab hold of my pack and pull me out of that little ravine. How heavy my boots felt—the wool liners had soaked up the water. We were near the lean-to, so I was able to get out of my wet things and into our down bag. I watched my husband make a fire and attempt to dry my boots, liners, pants, and gaiters—until one o'clock in the morning! He stood there like a clothesline, hovering over the fire with wet clothing draped on his arms and shoulders. He accidentally burned a hole and melted the zipper in one of my gaiters. I fell asleep feeling upset with myself for using poor judgment.

Cliff and Redfield, December 27-28, 1992:

The boots were so frozen the next morning that I could not even get them on my feet. Chip thawed them a little over his camp stove and they became usable, but it was like putting feet in blocks of ice. I put on the rest of my frozen clothes and felt miserable. Chip's solution was to hike me real hard. As long as I kept moving I could tolerate the wet items.

We climbed Cliff the first day and prepared for our final summit of Redfield. On 12:55 P.M. on the 28th of December, we finished our 46th Winter High Peak. Johnathan had become the youngest recorded Winter 46er at barely age ten. We also had become the first family to finish their Winter 46 together. We began a three-hour celebration on the summit of Redfield. Johnathan signed in on the canister log with blue, green, and purple pencils. Chip noted, "Without Cheryl's wisdom, patience and endurance, and Johnathan's strength, enthusiasm, and encouragement, none of these climbs would have been possible. We have withstood high winds, no visibility, extreme cold, deep snow, uncertain orientation, wetness, darkness, dense bushwhacks, steep climbing, and exhaustion. With God's help, each sojourn has led to a safe and successful climb."

We went back to Uphill Lean-to and built an eight-foot snowman for all to enjoy who might pass by. It had been a special day in the lives of a small Adirondack family.

Cheryl began the Winter 46 at age 33 and finished at age 36.

MARTA BOLTON

46er #2971W

I was born December 4, 1962, in Plattsburgh, New York, the fourth of five children. I was married for seventeen years until my divorce in December 1998, and have not remarried. My former husband, John, and I started hiking August 26, 1990, on Pokomoon-shine Mt. near Plattsburgh on I-87. There, we decided to climb the highest mountain in New York State, Mt. Marcy. One year later we completed our quest for the Adirondack 46 on Dix Mt. and started another round with our daughters, Jennifer, then ten, and Renee, then eight; they completed their 46 on Dix two years later.

John and I had no intention of climbing the 46 High Peaks in winter. One December, we climbed 3,556-foot Noonmark Mt. and the beauty was so breathtaking that we were curious about what the

High Peaks would be like. So on January 12, 1992, we started a winter adventure up 4,714-foot Mt. Colden via Lake Arnold. Our intentions were to climb only trailed peaks in winter. However, Grace Hudowalski had other plans for us, asking us to please put a fresh summit log on Tabletop Mt. in winter. Grace was a very special person! Anything Grace asked for, she got. She started us on the trailless summits in winter. Bless her heart!

At the time, I had worked for twelve-and-a-half years as a customer service clerk, and for four years during that time worked two jobs, putting in ten-hour days, in order to get Wednesdays and weekends off. In 2002, I became a factory worker full-time. I normally set aside one to two days a week, year round, just to go to the mountains, whether it be to climb, bushwhack, downhill ski, or snowshoe. They give me a sense of relief from the stress of everyday life. Spending time in the mountains every week is as natural a lifestyle for me as work, shopping, housekeeping.

I've completed almost eleven rounds of the 46 High Peaks and, in 1995, became the first woman to climb all 46 peaks in each season of the year. I spent a couple of summers climbing a dozen High Peak slides; the most challenging and exhilarating ones were Eagle Slide on Giant and the Nippletop Slide from Elk Pass. I've nearly completed my fifth winter round of the High Peaks. I've also rock-climbed and was an avid cyclist for eight years, biking up to thirty miles a day. Through the mountains I met my best friend and hiking companion, Mike Bush. We climb in Vermont, New Hampshire, Maine, and the Catskills in non-winter periods.

Even years after first finishing the Winter 46, I still feel the pride of achieving that goal. It gave me a new view of myself, gave me more confidence and self-esteem. I will always hold the memories and challenges of winter climbing in my heart. My love for the Adirondacks inspired me to have tattoos of wildlife painted on my body: a black bear, wolf, fox, and buck—symbolizing my love for the outdoors. I consider the High Peaks the "Heavens of Life." The mountains have taught me a lot about life and myself; I need them to function in everyday living. For years I battled eating disorders that almost destroyed my life; the climbing of the 46 in every season has given me the desire to live.

In May 2002, I was involved in a car accident in which I sustained serious injuries. My doctor claimed that I may never climb the High Peaks again. Thinking about life without mountains, which have enriched me in so many ways, is devastating. Yet the love and memories I feel for the mountains have given me the encouragement I need—along with family and friends—not to give up. Mountains got me through tough times before, so I know they'll get me through this one, too! I write poetry about mountains and how they have enriched my life. Most recently, I've become a correspondent with aspiring 46ers with the Forty-Sixer Office of the Historian.

Lower Wolf Jaw, Upper Wolf Jaw, and Armstrong, February 29, 1992:

From the beginning, everything was going wrong that day. After getting up late we lost a precious hour trying to unthaw the frozen car doors. I kept going into our daughters' bedroom to kiss them that morning and to tell them that I loved them. Did I have some kind of premonition? Thick fog slowed down our drive to the trailhead. Stepping out into what felt like a 50 mph wind, I wanted to get back in the car. Sparse trail-markers on the unbroken West River Trail caused us to lose our way. Breaking trail in knee-deep snow up the Wedge Brook Trail took us five-and-a-half hours to reach the col; the last steep 500' wasn't bad.

Standing on Lower Wolf Jaw's summit, John said, "Since we've already gained all this ascent, why not go for Upper Wolf Jaw and Armstrong? It's only a mile and a half." The going was getting tougher on Upper Wolf Jaw and the snow deeper. We finally reached the vertical cliff up Armstrong; a large ladder is bolted to the lower half of the cliff and a metal cable hangs halfway down to a ledge to hold and help maneuver up to the top. It was all buried in deep snow. I couldn't get a secure foothold; John scaled the cliff and lowered a rope. As we kept losing the trail, John decided that we should bushwhack straight to the summit and stop wasting time searching. I took my turn breaking trail. He kept us on course with map and compass; but suddenly we reached the cliffs in deep snow. In sudden panic I yelled, "I don't want to die!"

Four long hours after leaving Lower Wolf Jaw, sometimes in

waist-deep snow, we reached the summit of Armstrong and found the trail; it was 4 o'clock. We were home free; it would be fairly easy sailing downhill. We agreed that we would at least reach Lake Road before dark. We lost the trail again at the col between Armstrong and Gothics, but then found a clearing to begin bushwhacking down the mountain. That was fine with me! That narrow trail along the cliff-face scares me—it always seems that one wrong step and you'll fall off.

John said that we were heading for the lakes; every streambed leads to a bigger body of water and we were on a tributary of Beaver Meadow Falls. Suddenly one of John's snowshoes went through the ice and got lodged; it seemed a long time before hammering the ice released it. Now it was dusk and we knew we weren't going to make it out, so John immediately started gathering firewood and tried to start a fire. I began searching for a blown-over tree stump or large boulder or thick clump of trees to protect us—the temperature was to be -20° overnight!

"Don't ever be afraid of the woods." I could hear Grace saying these words to me and it helped. "I can't get it started!" John yelled. "We're just going to freeze to death!" "Bull!" I said, tossing my map over to him, "We won't need that if we freeze to death, will we!" It worked. We huddled together and I practically put my feet into the fire. We were well dug into the snow under a clump of spruce trees, protected from the wind. Looking at the falling snow scared me, so I kept my eyes closed. The night passed quickly.

At daybreak we found the trail in about ten minutes—we had been so close! We met a search party organizing in Keene Valley and knew they were looking for us. They said that a ranger and local care-taker had searched around the Ausable Lakes for two hours after my sister notified state police that we weren't back. Wind-chill was -40°.

Street, March 8, 1992:

Everything was falling into place—crossing Indian Pass Brook, going in the right direction, finding the beaver ponds—we saw places where the beavers had slid down banks, and made fresh cuttings and channels. It was still early; we had started at 5:20 A.M. by flash-light. We could see the top of Street...we were almost there! But the snow was extremely deep and soft from drizzle and mild weather.

We started falling through, our snowshoes wedged under snow and were hard to move; we tugged, pulled, and yanked to get them out. It was annoying, for every time we pulled them out and took another step, the whole process repeated itself. The thick forest of spruce created holes many feet deep under the branches. Looking ahead and seeing only John's head, I yelled, "John, are you standing up?" It was funny—the snow had eaten up the rest of his body! He was in a spruce trap; conditions were getting worse, not better. We decided to abort the trip; John remembered what Grace once wrote: "It's not important if you reach the top, it's how you make the climb."

Eleven months later we climbed Street again, this time in subzero temperature; we barely ate because stopping caused loss of body heat. The freezing air penetrated the five layers I had on. We couldn't stay on top of the snow and kept crashing down up to our waists. It was a horrible bushwhack but with our aborted climb of Street last year, we went through all possible pains to get it. "I'm at the can!" John finally yelled.

Panther and Santanoni, January 10, 1993:

This was one of the best winters for good conditions. Judy and Ellsworth King met John and me in Keeseville at 3:30 A.M. I was really excited about this trip, hyperventilating for three days in anticipation. It was a chilly -2° at the trailhead in Tahawus at 5 A.M. I always layer-up for fear of freezing to death, but I was sweating by the time we got to Bradley Pond. The beautiful pre-dawn moonlight lit up the trail, with minimal use of a flashlight. Reaching the pond at 7:30, we had our reward of sunrise over Santanoni. It was so fiery red it looked like a ball of fire ready to explode, breathtaking beauty.

The walk up Panther Brook seemed icier than the week before and, even with crampons, every step needed attention. Beautiful views of Marcy, Algonquin, Iroquois, and Colden made the trip even more enjoyable. I ripped my gaiter and lost my watch on the way to Santanoni. The forest was so dense, it was tough getting my pack through and I got stuck a dozen times and kept falling into spruce holes. I was getting irritated and wondered why I was even climbing Santanoni in winter. Reaching the canister I knew why—for the satisfaction, the pride, and the beauty of it all. I couldn't wait for

Panther. Being tired of pulling my way out of trees seems unimportant and forgotten. No one had been to Santanoni.

Panther's summit of open rocks and ice-covered, caked snow was awesome, the views spectacular. The feeling of accomplishment was overwhelming. Panther looked like an entirely different world, a combination of Iceland and Graceland—a heavenly work of art.

Haystack, January 2, 1994 and March 9, 1996:

The winds on Little Haystack were so fierce! Their force blew us all around, at times so strongly that a gust would hold us down and not let us go; blowing snow and pieces of ice stung our faces. John was on his stomach and grabbed my hand; I rolled my body across the rock to get off Little Haystack. The climb up Haystack itself was thrilling—winds ferocious but views awesome. It took two hours to maneuver our way across Little Haystack, up Haystack and back.

Two years later with Mike Bush, Haystack looked like one big mass of ice! The temperature was five below zero and the winds were howling. Even with crampons, going down Little Haystack toward Haystack was tricky, very icy. On the summit, the winds were fifty mph and Mike estimated wind-chill at forty below! No pictures—the wind would take the camera anyway. My legs were numb. It was a complete challenge, but what a way to complete winter round #2!

Nippletop, January 15, 1994:

Today was twenty below zero with the wind blowing. Winter season is too short to miss a weekend of climbing, so on Saturday morning I called in sick to work. John and I figured that a day's pay is nothing compared to becoming a Winter 46er! We broke a foot of snow up the Gill Brook Trail, making it slow going. The snow felt like cement on our snowshoes. The winds were picking up, blowing snow off the trees and whipping it off the ground. The trail was broken to Nippletop! Beautiful views of the Wolf Jaws.

Because of the steepness of the last 1.1 miles it took us two hours to climb! We finally reached the 0.2-mile-away sign, and summitted six hours after leaving the car. The winds were severe; the view of Dix awesome. "No summit pictures today, it's too cold to take off mittens," John said. But I take a picture no matter what! Nippletop was a hard hike.

Dial (and Nippletop Again?), February 2, 1994:

Since we already did Nippletop, Dial would be done by way of Bear Den Mt. I'd never forgotten how steep Bear Den is and was not looking forward to the climb. But we had the whole day to do Dial and would go slow and easy to make it more enjoyable. John put on his snowshoes with Tucker bindings; I didn't—they make the going slower and hurt my feet. This was a big mistake. I kept sailing down steep slippery pitches and broke through crust to my knees, hurting them. Even John took a few good spills. I reluctantly put on my snowshoes After an eternity of steep pitches, groaning, complaining, we reached Dial's rock viewpoint. John said that it wasn't the official peak. I told him I wasn't going any farther. "If you don't, you can't count Dial," he persisted. I went right behind him. "We aren't going back over Bear Den, though!" I insisted. John agreed that it would be just as easy to go back through Elk Pass.

After an hour and fifty minutes we reached the Elk Pass Junction, thankful for Ed Bunk's broken trail; I can't imagine breaking trail through there! Going down the 1.1 miles was very tricky and dangerous. To prevent falling we had to grab trees and try to brake, getting a foot above a tree. I was scared—conditions were not good to sit and slide—because you'd sit and fly, hoping not to slam uncontrollably into a tree. John flipped over once, rolling and stopping himself with his feet against a tree. I was really nervous that he had gotten hurt but he was OK. Dial is rated #1 Most Hated Hike I've done in winter. Nippletop's descent was the Most Dangerous winter hike I've ever done.

Marcy, Skylight and Gray, January 30, 1994:

Today Judy and Ellsie King, John and I climbed Marcy, Skylight, and Gray in twelve hours! I always believed that this was an incredibly long hike for winter in one day, but knowing Marcy's trail was always broken we could make good time going up. It was -2° at Marcy Dam and sunny, in spite of the temperature. None of us needed to climb Marcy (for our 46), but John and I had never seen a winter view from Marcy! Going up Marcy above tree line there was very little wind and clear skies. We paused to savor the spectacular views. The rocks were ice-caked and beautiful and the heavy crust allowed us to stay on top of the snow.

Descending to Four Corners and reading the sign "Skylight .5 miles," I couldn't believe it. I never thought I would see that in winter! I asked Judy what to carry to add to Skylight's famous cairn in winter—maybe a snowball? There is a legend that says a rock prevents rain, so does a snowball prevent snow? We were treated with beautiful views and could even see the Tahawus Ironworks. On the herd path to Gray we were still on crust—easy going. It all seemed too good to be true.

We searched for the canister; after half an hour, I decided to take photos of us on top as proof of being there. "I'm at the can," John yelled the magic words. We saw why we hadn't seen it before—it is white, blending with snow under balsam branches and just barely visible! The snow was as hard as cement, making it impossible to dig for the canister, if we'd had to. Standing on six feet of snow, the views on Gray in winter are one hundred percent better than in summer. It was 2 o'clock and John wanted to go over Gray's ridge to Marcy. Judy fell into a spruce trap to her waist and then slowly started falling down more and more until it went to her neck! It was one of my absolute favorite hikes.

Seymour, February 27, 1994:

We walked the road to Corey's trailhead at 3:20 A.M.—it was snowing and 2°. Frost was forming on us and you could feel ice in your eyes. No one had climbed Seymour since Jan. 1. I was tired from work and only four hours of sleep. John was way ahead; I don't like that because I feel I'm hiking alone and I want him close in case I fall—especially in darkness. It took four-and-a-half hours to Blueberry Lean-to. John had cooked chicken the day before for the hike—now frozen. We had plenty of other food and I felt a spur of energy. But I wanted that chicken! John figured we'd be at the summit by 11; we set a one o'clock turn-around time.

The slide was very beautiful in winter. We climbed it until a huge ledge full of ice made us decide to get off. We grabbed trees to get up; on steeper sections, John pulled me up with a ski pole. I felt we'd have to turn back but John said "No." We kept going up and up and the route got harder. We reached a real thick section where there was nowhere to go but through it. John scaled a small cliff and threw down a rope, but I was determined to do it myself; I maneuvered my way up with my legs spread apart on tree roots and branches, pulling and grabbing to get up. He was surprised that I did it alone. After eight-and-a-half hours, John yells, "I see it!"

What a feeling of excitement and accomplishment to get that mountain in winter! John did most of the nine-and-a-half miles of trail breaking; I felt pride in him for such a feat to get us there. Seymour was the roughest, hardest hike I ever did in winter! We were back after a grueling day of fifteen hours. To help the Kings on Seymour they'd each have to pay me $1,000 up front in cold cash.

Seward, March 13, 1994—46th Peak:

Everyone got together at 3 A.M. It was snowing hard; if it weren't such a special day I would've gone home. It got worse as the day progressed. A nice crust underneath made a super base, so breaking trail wasn't bad. Judy was worried about how we were going to get to Seward and I was, too. Conditions were blinding for the 46th peak. I trusted John to get me there; he set the compass at 76°. I never remembered the descent off Donaldson as being that steep.

As we neared Sewards' cliffs some sections looked unclimbable. The ascent was extremely steep, we had to get on hands and knees and literally grab what few trees there were for handholds. It was very challenging, incredible, just like a dream or something out of a movie—I never experienced anything like it before! I worried about Judy in steep sections because she gets scared. At the top, the trees were covered with ice balls; they reminded us of Christmas trees. They sounded like door chimes. Totally awesome. We were in another world. We looked for over an hour for the canister before we gave up, with much mental anguish. I cried—I had always envisioned my 46th peak: seeing the canister...screaming and hugging John for our accomplishment. Not what I got—a lost canister and a snowstorm.

Redfield, February 17, 1996:

It makes me nervous to posthole in a brook but Tom Pinkerton convinced me it was safe. Test every step to assure safety before taking the next; I'm in the lead and trying to be cautious. We come upon a waterfall, completely frozen. I get to the base and crack—snapple—pop! I'm floating on a sheet of ice. Tom reaches out to grab me and somehow I slide off the sheet of ice and go down into the freezing water, screaming for help, and I'm up to my waist in water, not even touching bottom. Tom tries to pull me out but can't; Mike Lonegan and Joe Ryan come running to help. It takes them all to rescue me from the icy waters.

We bushwhack up the bank, get dry socks on and put plastic bags over them before putting my boots back on. But within ten minutes my feet are starting to feel like two iceboxes. I cry silently to myself, my feet are so frozen and I worry. I lie down in the lean-to while Tom and Joe remove my frozen snowshoes, boots, and wet-again socks, and rest my frozen feet on their chests. Mike gathers wood for an unsuccessful fire. I go into a shiver and fear hypothermia, even though I'm wrapped in a space blanket to keep heat in my body. It takes twenty minutes before my feet feel better. The men put dry socks on my feet; our only concern was to get out the seven-and-a-half miles as quickly as possible. Luckily I run into a friend at Marcy Dam and didn't hesitate to ask for dry socks, which she had. Now I always carry extra pairs of wool socks with me. I received mild frostbite to my toes.

Marta began the Winter 46 at age 29 and finished
her first round at age 31.

JUDY KING

46er #2660W

While I was in high school I began hiking on the smaller peaks, but didn't pursue climbing with my husband Ellsworth, "Ellsie," until our two boys, Jeff and Jamie, began hiking. As a young mother I was busy caring for them and our home when they were in school all day. Then I enrolled in a two-year program at Clinton Community College and graduated with a management degree, soon getting a job as a receptionist at the *Press Republican* newspaper office.

We learned about the 46er Club one day on a hike to Whiteface. Writing to Grace and her response to us gave us the drive we needed to complete our first 46 on Tabletop. We were touched by our youngest son asking to be there with us, along with a friend. Doing the 46 in winter was the furthest idea from my mind; I feared winter in the mountains. Friends kept talking about doing the High Peaks in winter and my husband wanted us to try; so we bought equipment and began our trek. But my work schedule was Tuesday through Saturday and my husband worked Monday through Saturday—so we were limited to Sundays to do our hikes. Many planned climbs had to be postponed or aborted due to bad weather.

We met John and Marta Bolton and became instant friends and hiking buddies. We reached all our peaks as day-trips. The Boltons' drive and determination kept us going. We've completed seven full rounds of the 46, two in winter. The mountains have done so much for me. I always feel closeness to God out there and a deep sharing experience with my husband. This was "our" time together, away from it all, doing what we enjoyed, working for a common goal. Without my partner, my husband and best friend, I wouldn't have accomplished this feat; we will never forget our success and pride at doing these climbs.

Words don't easily describe the feeling I have about hiking. I wasn't really good at sports in school, but with hiking, I felt good—I could do it—and I was good at it! It did wonders for my self-esteem. Climbing the Winter 46 proved to me that if I want something bad enough, I will do everything possible to reach that goal.

In July 1998, our company downsized and I was offered full retirement after twenty-one years of employment. This was perfect timing; my husband was also retired from his mill job and would be closing his part-time business the following fall. I had lots of time on my hands, so I joined the YMCA and began aerobic classes three times weekly. I also swim laps daily in the early morning. During the summer months my husband and I bike; the first season after we were both retired we went over 1,600 miles. We also took up kayaking.

In winter we cross-country ski and continue the second round of the Winter 46, helping friends finish. Our latest goal is to climb the fire tower peaks in the Adirondacks and the Catskills. Somehow it's more exciting striving for a goal. I always feel a little let down after we've completed one. We've hiked the highest peaks in northern New England—Mt. Washington, Mt. Mansfield, and Katahdin—but still prefer our own Adirondacks. We have so much beauty in our area and thank God that we are able to enjoy it.

Marcy, March 15, 1992:

Anticipation followed me all the way, wondering what awaits us above tree line—will those winds hold us back again? With determination that we'd give it all we've got, we hiked. As we reached the final climb above tree line we took off our snowshoes, put on crampons and facemasks to protect us from those bitter and strong Marcy winds. With the Lord's Prayer on my lips, I soon saw the plaque and knew we had made it. Emotions were heavy up there; I cried and we all hugged and took quick snapshots. What a gorgeous hike and finally the summit. This was an eventful way to end our 1992 winter hiking season.

We'll put away our hiking gear for a while to catch up on chores. Not for long though. I'm already getting the fever to go back to the Adirondacks. I love the good-all-over feeling I get, in spite of all the sweat, the pain, and anguish—it's the greatest thing that ever happened to us. You can never replace the togetherness and freedom I feel when I hike with my husband. The Adirondacks and our love for them have drawn us closer together.

Dix and Hough, January 1, 1993:

I think this hike was my most horrific. I prayed all night prior to this climb; I was really afraid of the winds on Dix. We hiked in with flashlights beginning at 6:30 A.M., still in darkness. Approaching the lean-to at 9 o'clock, we saw the rushing waters of the Bouquet River that we must cross. There was a thaw; we'd never encountered such a gushing flow of water. There was no way we could cross this river. I felt defeated and discouraged—how would we complete our climb? The trusty guys got together; luckily Ellsie carries a folding saw in his pack, so for an hour the men cut trees and Marta and I helped drag branches to make a bridge. Finally it was ready and one-by-one we crossed over. I was petrified. Even if we're able to cross in daylight, what about conditions later on—returning in darkness? I worried all day about that, among other things like: Can we make this climb of two mountains? Will Hough be broken out? Will we find the canister?

I have a lot of faith in God and always carry a cross in my pack. Once we were hiking Hough, helping a friend complete the 46; I didn't realize that my cross had been missing. As we reached the summit of Hough she said, "Look, there's a cross hanging on the branch here." "That's my cross, the one I've carried for so long. Someone must have hung it here hoping the owner would find it." What an uplifting day that was.

Faith can move mountains, they say: Why can't faith help one climb them? By noon we'd reached the summit of Dix. What a gorgeous mountain with such magnificent views. We voted to go on to Hough although we had to break trail all the way. Snowshoes and determination were in order—you must go way down, 800', and then way up to get to Hough. This takes us two hours today. Oh, that beautiful canister. Seeing the canister on Hough is so much more rewarding in winter after so much effort to get there.

The most gorgeous sunset is awaiting us as we climb back up to the summit of Dix by 4 o'clock. The views are still magnificent, sky so clear and the moon shining brightly as we head down. We use crampons on the now-icy trail. I keep worrying about that bridge of branches and sticks we must cross. Finally we reach the rushing waters of the Bouquet, scary in the darkness. The guys help us back over our makeshift bridge. At 9:15 P.M. we reach the car, totally wiped out, but proud. We did it! Fourteen hours, forty-five minutes of hiking. Two days later I can't believe we are talking about attempting Couchsachraga.

Couchsachraga, January 3, 1993:

I prayed all night prior to this climb. I was afraid that I would not have the energy to climb Couchi—it's so far away. Night wasn't long; we set our alarms for 2 A.M. to meet the Boltons in Keeseville at 3:30. Reaching "Times Square" on the Santanoni-Panther Ridge, a storm is brewing; the winds are heavy. Marta's Gatorade leaks out, forming a red path on the way to Couchi. That summit is such a long way from the Panther-Santanoni Ridge. There is a view from Couchi. When the trees are bare you can see for a long way; it was a neat experience seeing views from this isolated peak. The weather stayed pretty clear until we were heading back to Times Square. The return trip, eight hundred feet back up to the ridge, seemed endless and you think you're never going to get back there. A storm was pending and the winds were howling, visibility almost zero, as we were approaching Times Square. Then we saw the Gatorade path guiding us on our way—a pleasant sight in the snow. Couchsachraga took twelve hours.

God blessed us once again with a safe climb and a strong group of determined friends. Grace, you join us on all our hikes—you are there in spirit. We always talk about you and how much you help us all. You keep that desire, that dream, of another peak alive in us. Thanks for being there for all of us. We share that common love of the peaks... one climb at a time... one day at a time.

Marcy, Skylight, and Gray, January 30, 1994:

We completed our planned hike of Marcy, Skylight, and Gray. I still have a hard time believing that we were able to climb over Marcy, then climb two more peaks then climb back over Marcy and survive. This was the most memorable hike—I'll be on a high for days. What a reward we shared!

Over Marcy and down the south side to Four Corners. Skylight needed to be broken and John led. Just after noon we sat on the summit cairn and hugged. The view is spectacular! We could see Gray, but will we make it today? Down Skylight and on to Lake Tear of the Clouds and Gray. Upward. John's strength leads us once again up this steep stretch. We finally reach the top, but where is that canister? We search, search, and fret. Must we tie a bag with our names to the highest tree? Later, seemed like hours—probably fifteen minutes—John hollers, "I'm at the can!" Ellsie puts survey tape on the branches to help future climbers. After hiking this peak, one should be able to find the canister!

To our surprise we were the first to sign in this season. Marta and I yell, hug, take pictures, rejoice—we finally did it. Someday we'll be Winter 46ers, but we've got lots of work left, and lots of hope. I will always climb as long as my health holds out. I love those mountains and the memories they hold, the friendships we enjoy and the good times yet to come.

Seward, March 13, 1994:

Has it been a year? First it was a cold one, so many sub-zero days and the snowfall just never seemed to end. The weatherman said we'd had sixteen storms so far. In February and March, Ellsie and I both suffered from flu bugs that kept us from the peaks. March 13 was our first trip to the Sewards—oh, how I've dreaded this trip, worried for three years about these peaks. But today was a special day, John and Marta's 46th peak in winter. We were so happy. We awoke at 12:45 A.M., leaving at 1:45 and reaching our beginning point at 3:15; Mike Bush and Victor Pomerville were also there. Off we went to Corey's trailhead on snowmobiles, saving walking an extra six round-trip miles. We signed in at 4 o'clock.

It snowed all day but we headed upward, John in the lead—always up there, way ahead, breaking trail and finding our way; I don't know how he does it and never seems to tire. Ellsie was always there for me; I feel so close while we climb. With every climb, I talk to God and thank him for my many blessings and often say, "If I can ask just a bit more: could this be a successful climb, please?" We reached the Donaldson summit at 9 o'clock. Boy, this was steep at our final climb up; so much snow up here and more kept coming down. Thank goodness John had taken compass readings the week before, because with the snow and fog it was difficult.

I was so excited for the Boltons until Seward's summit—the canister was nowhere to be found. We all searched for an hour or more all over the ridge, poking holes in trees; finally we had to leave. We were wet and exhausted; it would be a long haul out and the snow kept coming down, covering our trail. I felt devastated—Marta and I cried. John was so upset and discouraged. It wasn't until we reached a lower elevation that they finally would accept congratulations and enjoy our wine and hold up a banner for pictures. I'd read articles in *Peeks* magazine about hikers leaving plastic bags in tree tops on the summits in such a case—and have always kept a bag, paper, and pencil in my backpack. We used it and Grace reports to Marta that a Canadian hiker finds our bag and that we were on target.

Macomb and South Dix, December 26, 1994:

Chris Dresser and John Wheeler join us for the Dix Range. We must walk the Elk Lake Road today and so begin early at 5:40. No one has been here yet; we must break trail all the way. Macomb's slide is beautiful, no ice, seems easier than in summer when sand moves under our feet. Elk Lake views are continuous in the clear air. In the upper reaches, the herd path is hard to find and we can't find the canister. We search up and down the ridge; I'm getting discouraged because we must find this canister in order to go on to South Dix and East Dix. Much climbing remains and will we be able to find those canisters? Darkness comes quickly in winter and we don't want to be up here bushwhacking then!

Finally Ellsie finds the canister. It's noon and we vote to go on to South Dix, but that herd path is hard to find. We use snowshoes when the snow is deep, but on icy rock we have to put on crampons; we put on snowshoes and take them off so often that I lose count! Finally summiting South Dix at 1:10 and at 1:55 seeing East Dix, it seems only a few minutes away. I want to go on, but know deep inside we'd better go back because our return route via Lillian Brook may be hard to follow in darkness, and the marked trail, if unbroken, might be difficult to spot.

My trusty husband did his job well. By 2:45 we reached Lillian Brook, but this is a tough bushwhack. As darkness set in it was scary. We feared we'd be spending the night, but I began praying as I always do to help with my doubts. Full darkness had set in by 5:15. Then we find the cairn on the Dix Trail at the end of the Lillian Brook bushwhack—oh, that rock cairn looked so great! At 7:45 P.M. we reach the car, fourteen hours and nineteen miles after beginning. Our snowshoes are frozen on and I can't get my boots off.

The Wolf Jaws, February 19, 1995:

We began the ascent at 5:05 A.M. from the Garden trailhead with Marta and John Bolton. In the pre-dawn darkness, we could hear wolves or coy dogs howling back and forth in conversation as we were climbing the Wolf Jaws. It's 40° and sunny, with views as far as Mt. Mansfield in Vermont. Trails are broken; we meet lots of hikers today who have spent the weekend in the mountains. We meet a group from Virginia Beach—amazing—our friends head south for warmth and these folks come north to our Adirondacks. Marta and I were pleased that we were the only women climbers. The Wolf Jaw climb is steep but the summits are always rewarding.

Colden, February 26, 1995—46th Peak:

IT'S OFFICIAL! Ellsworth, #2659, and Judith, #2660, today at noon on Colden's Summit became Winter 46ers! Rejoice! Grace was right—if we stuck to it, someday, on some summit it would happen. I'm still on a "high." It was wonderful, every step of the way. We couldn't have chosen a nicer day and a more perfect mountain for our finish. Along with us were our dearest friends. John and Marta were so happy this day you'd think it was their celebration. This has been a six-year dream for us.

At 7:05 A.M. at Adirondack Loj, Marta hugs and hands us a bottle of wine to celebrate. It's ten below zero but the sun should be out soon. This is the first winter hike this season that we began and ended in daylight. We break at Avalanche Lean-to and then up to the lake; it's fun "walking on water" again. John, Marta, Ellsie, and I hold hands to make our last grade to the summit together. I fight back tears and then we're there. I pray in gratitude and happiness.

Marta pins us with our Winter Rocker and has cupcakes with two candles, one with a four and another with a six. Ellsie finds an area out of the wind for our celebration. We spend fifty minutes celebrating, eating, hugging, sharing, and drinking—Chris Dresser has a bottle of champagne and we carry wine on celebrations like this. It was wonderful, the happiness on top of this summit. Oh, the views on this bright and sunny day. The memories of this day will last a lifetime.

We are so grateful for the mountains that brought all of us together; grateful for the happy times, the struggles, the dreams that come true, these lasting friendships that only hikers know. God has truly blessed us—the mountains brought a husband and wife closer, working together for a common goal; the tenderness and caring that Ellsie shows me in these mountains will always remain in my heart, and the memories of the hikes we friends share will always be there.

Judy began the Winter 46 at age 46 and finished at age 53.

WENDE GRUBBS HOKIRK

46er #2542W

I started hiking with a "Y" camp outing when I was sixteen years old. A friend mentioned the 46er Club and my father and I decided to try a few High Peaks. We got bitten by the hiking bug! I like to hike in all seasons—they each have their own special ambience. After we finished our summer round we decided to do the Winter 46, starting on Cascade and Porter in 1988 and finishing on Seymour in 1995. We also climbed MacNaughton, making three separate attempts until we finally made it. We would pack in on a Friday, set up camp and climb if there was time. When we first started we were not well-equipped; we learned by trial and error.

Dad and I went on a camping trip with a YMCA group in 1989, our first year of hiking a lot of the mountains in winter. Six of the ten of us climbed Marcy on a beautiful day. Usually it's so cold and windy that you can't stay on the summit for very long. But that day there wasn't any wind—we stayed on the summit for one and a half hours! Dad and I had a real blast on this trip and wished it didn't have to end. In December 1993, Dad and I were volunteer instructors for the AMC Winter School and led a group into the Dix wilderness for four days. Unfortunately Dad got sick and had to go home. It was snowing all day when we climbed Dix, and at the summit a 40-50 knot wind was blowing. It was fun. One of the guys did push-ups on the summit.

There are so many great memories: starting out at -12° and finding the wind on Wright's summit just a breeze—we stayed for a long time enjoying the wonderful views to Lake Placid and the Great Range; being able to linger on a summit is rare in winter! On the trip to Sawteeth, Rainbow Falls was frozen, just a little water still flowing—beautiful. At the summit on that very clear day we could see Marcy, Haystack, Basin, Saddleback, Gothics, Pyramid—it was such a wonderful sight! On Colden, I remember seeing skiers on that warm sunny day with beautiful views. At Marcy Dam, chickadees sat on my legs and hat—so cute.

I was married on June 15, 2000, to a wonderful man. We met going on trail-crew outings with the Forty Sixers; until recently Larry was the trail Crew Master for the club and I was on the Board of Directors for a term. He's a fitter for a steel company in Rotterdam, NY; I work at a hospital in Schenectady as a financial advisor. Other than hiking and snowshoeing, we enjoy cross-country skiing and canoeing.

I appreciate those who first hiked these mountains thousands of years ago—to imagine what they must have gone through! Sometimes out there, all you can do is survive. I know I'm a survivor and use my knowledge to help me do that. Climbing the Winter 46 was a wonderful experience. Even if you had a horrible climb, you forget about it once you've gotten to the top and see the views. I don't think there is any better high.

Giant, February 4, 1989:

Dad and I were at it again. We started out early to conquer Giant, a third attempt. It was tough going. Good thing we had crampons for our boots—we had enough problems just starting out, but later in the climb we really needed them! It was very cold. We had to keep making adjustments to our crampons and our hands nearly froze off.

It amazes me that you can keep climbing a mountain over and over again, but yet it never seems the same. It took us forever to reach the top. Our drinks froze and so did our sandwiches! The views were spectacular but we couldn't enjoy them for more than five or ten minutes since it was so cold. We tried to go over to Rocky Peak Ridge, but didn't make it. We weren't sure where the trail went. Dad and I didn't want to risk our lives, so we turned back. I remember Dad seemed a little tired that day, so I talked his ear off! In the car we put our sandwiches over the heat vents to defrost them.

Saddleback, Gothics, Armstrong, and Upper Wolf Jaw, March 11, 1989:

Dad and I hiked into the Johns Brook area and set up camp. We took the Orebed Trail and had a fairly easy time climbing Saddleback because it wasn't too icy. Gothics was harder, quite icy, and one of my crampons broke. I had a tough time on the icy sections. The snow was crusty on the the climb to Gothics and on the way over to Armstrong. Descending the other side of Gothics, I lost my footing because of the broken crampon and ended up falling on my butt and sliding down Gothics out of control, seemingly toward my demise! Luckily my father was able to grab my hand as he ran down the side of Gothics, trying to stop me. Was he going to fall too, trying to keep up with me? I finally ran into a small alpine tree using my other crampon, and with the help of my father my fall was arrested.

Dad and I tried to find a way to bushwhack down between Gothics and Armstrong, but no luck. We ended up traveling over Armstrong and Upper Wolf Jaw again, which we had just climbed the week before. At least we didn't have to go back down the cables! I don't recommend hiking with "one crampon and one cramp-off!"

Street and Nye, February 17, 1992:

Dad and I climbed these peaks with the Albany ADK Chapter. We started on the trail at 8 A.M. and then the fun began. We had to find a way across Rocky Falls Brook—and luckily found a snow bridge we could cross safely in snowshoes. From there on to the summit it was straight up, no gradual incline. Dad kept saying, "I think we're almost there," every time he saw an opening. He was wrong. After fighting through and over bushes we finally made it; we had to dig the canister out of the snow.

After an hour over to Nye, we all decided to bushwhack down from Nye instead of climbing all the way back up Street to descend in our tracks. We kept descending into the valley, but after awhile some thought we were one valley too far north. We were too far down to turn back and climbing over the ridge to the south didn't appeal to anyone, so we continued down. Needless to say, we walked and walked for what seemed forever.

It was near dark, 5:45 by the time we came out farther down the brook. We looked for a place to cross, but there was open water as far as we could see, except for what we thought was an ice bridge. Bob Wilcox went first; it was slushy but he kept on until his other foot sank lower and the ice gave way. He fell sideways into the brook up to his chest in water! We fished him out quickly and took out extra polypro so he'd be dry. The temperature was zero.

With the last light rapidly fading we found a safe crossing to the north. Bob had lost his ice ax, now somewhere on the bottom of Indian Pass Brook. He was having problems with his feet. We walked for what seemed like ten hours along the brook until we found the trail. My dad and another guy were going by compass and their sense of direction—it was pitch black. Finally we signed out at 8:41 P.M.

Donaldson, Emmons, and Seward, March 9, 1992:

We pulled our packs in on sleds to the Calkins Brook area. I never thought anything could be so easy—it sure took a lot of pressure off the bones. We followed Calkins Brook to Donaldson's summit. It was a very warm day and that last two and a half miles seemed to go on forever! We hiked to Emmons after pitching camp below Donaldson's summit, not a bad walk at all. We spent a long time melting snow for supper.

That night it rained; there were frozen raindrops on our tent. Sunday we woke up to a spectacular sunrise from the mountaintop!

What an absolutely beautiful day, so very sunny and warm for our hike over to Seward. After returning and breaking camp, it was a long descent and walk out—seemed we were never going to see our car.

We had a great group; the trio Bob Veino, Bob Wilcox, and Ray Held kept us amused. I remember one of the men playing on the ice-falls. I enjoyed Bob Veino's stories, but Bob Wilcox was disappointing because he wouldn't fall into Calkins Brook for us on that long walk out.

Iroquois and Algonquin, February 17, 1994:

Dad, Dave Hudda, Greg Bachinsky, and I climbed Iroquois first. Although the temperature was in the 20s, I actually had to strip a layer of clothing off when descending to the col. The ice on Algonquin was something else! It was definitely a full-crampon day.

At least three of us had a spill. Coming off Algonquin toward Wright, my father fell and one of the men helped him—I think that scared him. The wind was so strong that it was difficult to stand still. We had beautiful views the whole day. We also fell into spruce traps up to our knees—always fun, especially when you find yourself hip deep, have to dig out your snowshoes, and you've already expended much of your energy!

Hough, South Dix, Macomb, and East Dix, February 21, 1994:

What an absolutely beautiful weekend for climbing in the Dix Range! We started the bushwhack from Route 73 and soon shed a layer of clothing. We'd planned to climb East Dix before setting up camp, but one of the guys started having trouble with his boots—he wears plastic ones and could barely walk, which slowed the pace. We set up camp when we came to a water source. The sky was beautiful and clear; there was a half-moon that glowed so prettily. We tried to pick out constellations; we all need a little work on our astronomy.

The next day we bushwhacked up the ridge to Hough first. The snow was heavy and stuck to our snowshoes; that makes a couple of extra pounds you're lifting with each step! We took turns breaking trail every five minutes up to the ridge. On the summit the wind felt so very good. The views over to Dix were just fantastic! There isn't anything better than being on top of the world, looking down and seeing mountain after mountain.

Over to South Dix it was "spruce-trap city!" Everyone went into a spruce trap. Dad took a picture of Dave Hudda after he fell into one up to his chest; Dave is six feet tall! The climb up Macomb was tougher—higher, and our third peak. One guy was really tired and decided to go back to South Dix and fill up water bottles from a source he'd seen. Even Dad was running low on steam, probably because he was a bit dehydrated.

Then off to East Dix, definitely the easiest, thank goodness. Again, the views were terrific and we spent a lot of time on the summit. We headed down to the valley; this was the toughest part of the route! We didn't need our headlamps hiking back to camp; the moon gave enough light. The best sight at day's end was the lantern at camp. Greg had started the stoves and had water ready. How very nice. Dad could hardly stand up. He and Dave did a lot of the trail breaking. Dave is a true hiking animal!

Santanoni, Panther, and Couchsachraga, March 21, 1994:

This weekend, Dad and I banged away at the Santanonis. We packed into the lean-to on Friday. Luckily a couple of guys went in yesterday so the trail was broken. We ran into Sam Jones, one of Dad's fellow climbers, near Santanoni's summit. The day was cold and overcast. You couldn't stand around for long. I almost gave up looking for the canister on Panther. I poked down into one spot where no one had searched yet. "No, it couldn't be there," I thought, but dug and sure enough, I found it! I was everyone's best friend. Some guys saw a weasel in the col.

Couchie seemed to take forever, as if we were climbing to the ends of the earth. A guy who shared the lean-to with us had had enough and turned around. Too bad, because it wasn't all that difficult and he had already lost all that elevation. On our way out I ask Dad if he wanted to head over to Allen since we still had three hours and twenty-eight minutes until Spring. He gracefully declined.

Allen, February 27, 1995:

It was a very nice hike in along the Opalescent River on a broken trail; the sky was clear. Some of the group located a water source so we didn't have to boil snow, which can take awhile. The rest are making a snow kitchen, piling snow up to make snow benches and a table to use while cooking and eating. After setting up our camp and snow kitchen, the toughest part was standing around—we were there at 2:30 P.M. As we were cooking our dinner we saw some guys coming back. They'd broken trail all day and they had to turn around—they never made the summit of Allen.

We woke to a very cold morning. It was hard keeping feet warm, in spite of sleeping with boots in your bag so they wouldn't freeze. It was a great sunny day. Even from where we camped about five miles in, it was a hard, long slog. Rob, Bob, and Dave did a lot of the trail breaking; usually I don't do too much; it takes all my energy just to climb. Two of our group didn't summit—they had had enough.

It got real tough toward the top. We made it, though—I was so happy; number 45! The views were spectacular! We had a great time coming down Allen. There were some pitches where you just sat down and slid—I loved that part. It was quite a slog back to camp. Thank goodness for warm clothes—after dinner a couple of us went for a walk to warm up.

Seymour, March 21, 1995—46th Peak:

Cutting this climb close to the end of the winter season makes it that much more fun and exciting. We ended up tenting it, as the Blueberry Lean-to was occupied. The next morning, I woke up before Dad—that was a first! We had breakfast in our packs and headed up Seymour. We had a wonderful sunny day. Of course, it wasn't an easy hike. There were a few tricky spots where I had trouble maneuvering; being five-foot-three, climbing over a downed tree was not easy. But all went well. They let me lead to the summit in the honor spot. Dad presented me with the Winter 46 rocker; Dave had made Winter 46er cupcakes in honor of me. I was very happy.

Wende began the Winter 46 at age 18 and finished at age 24.

HOLLY SULLIVAN

46er #3177W

I grew up in New York City and spent all my vacation time at the ocean. I could never understand why anyone would want to hike up a mountain on a hot summer day when they could be immersed in cool, refreshing water. I did some hiking in the Rockies and Yosemite in my early twenties, but it was not until I was around forty that I started hiking on a regular basis.

I have a Masters Degree in Urban and Environmental Studies from Rensselaer Polytechnic Institute in Troy, NY, and I am a Senior Planner at the Hudson River Valley Greenway. The Greenway is a New York State agency established to promote development by 259 municipalities that is consistent with environmental and cultural protection, sound planning, education about and access to the area's resources.

My job is to provide both financial and technical assistance and to educate on issues such as waterfront and main street revitalization, natural resource and agricultural protection, and guidelines on Open Space Planning for municipalities, and to represent the Greenway in many formats.

This is a career change. Previously I worked in agencies that provided services to people in need. My last position was as Executive Director of a domestic violence and rape crisis agency; I enjoyed this but was ready for a change.

My undergraduate degree is in Studio Art; for many years I concentrated on developing as an artist even while working and raising a family. When a studio I rented with a group of artists was rehabbed for office space, I just stopped my artwork. It was hard to work on my art on a part-time basis; sometimes the vision, the energy, would be lost. Someday I hope to get back into my art again. I remember when I'd be lost in a piece, time wouldn't matter—self and work became one. That connection is similar to what I feel in the mountains and woods. Maybe that's why I started hiking and climbing about the same time I gave up my art.

I began working on completing all 46 peaks; then I had to complete the 46 in winter. Winter hiking is less crowded and, I think, more fun. I love the peace and quiet of winter as well as the stark beauty. I also like having to find your own way, as trails are often hard to follow. Half my Winter 46 peaks were climbed with the Rochester Winter Mountaineering Society; a trip with them usually involves one or two overnights in the woods. The other peaks were daytrips, mostly with my husband, John Wimbush, and our friend Howard Stoner. Hiking the Winter 46 helped me to be confident in the backcountry in cold weather. It was good training for the higher mountains I eventually climbed. The whole experience was, well, simply fun, and I became friends with wonderful people.

Sleeping out in the woods on a cold winter night is one of the great joys of being in the backcountry. My sleeping bag is rated to -15° and is toasty, usually, except for the night on Haystack when the temperature plummeted to -32° and one night on a hike up the Opalescent to Marcy when it dropped to -36°; even then I was never uncomfortably cold, kind of lukewarm. My pack averaged between forty and fifty pounds; as I grew more experienced, I was able to get it down to between thirty-five to forty pounds for an overnight. Less weight, even by a few pounds, makes a big difference. It is a fine line between carrying too much and having just enough. In summer it isn't as critical to go without a piece of equipment or clothing, but in winter consequences can be serious.

I enjoy challenge in general and I do like pushing myself to the limit physically. Whether it's training for a marathon, hiking the whole Great Range in one day, or biking until my legs are like jelly, intense physical exercise is exhilarating. Maybe it's the endorphins or the sense of accomplishment, but there is such great satisfaction pushing yourself to the limit of endurance and reaching your objective. That is why I love running marathons or doing marathon equivalent hikes, like twenty-four-hour-plus mega hikes. I have hiked in the Western Highlands of Scotland, Mount Whitney in winter, and several peaks up to 20,000' in the Andes.

I also like challenge in other areas of my life, such as my work. Achieving a goal that initially scares me, and doing a good job, is intensely satisfying. As long as the apprehension is not too great it can be invigorating and very motivating. I found this to be especially true in my art. There is always a phase where you are not sure if you will really be able to capture what you are striving for, whether the piece will pull itself together and be "good." That is the most energizing place to be. Even more so than when you reach the point when you say "Ah-ha, this is it, it is working." That feeling is wonderful but from there, it is simply a matter of completion. The period of uncertainty is what makes the completion so satisfying.

Marcy in February

The trip was up Marcy by a route that is far from any trail—up the Opalescent River and ice falls of its tributary that my husband dubbed, Holly's Brook. We bushwhacked through thick spruce and balsam to tree line at the northwest flank of Marcy. Howard Stoner and I were an advance party on Friday, breaking trail as far as we could; others would follow our route on Saturday and we'd take turns breaking trail through the deeper snow and spruce traps until we were out on the rocks.

Howard and I made quicker progress than we thought we would. By Saturday morning we were just about at tree line when we heard shouting in the distance. Howard and I shouted back, while very, very slowly working our way towards the voices; the snow was chest-deep in spots! One shouted, "Are you on the trail?" We yelled, "There isn't a trail on this side of Marcy!"

We saw two young guys, totally disoriented and so relieved to see us; it was miles from the trail. These guys had hiked from the Loj up to the summit of Marcy. The wind was strong and they had whiteout conditions, so they wanted to get off the summit; they started walking straight down the mountain without orienting themselves to the trail they had come up on!

When they reached tree line they couldn't find the trail; they were going to keep hiking down the mountain until they came to it. They never would have found one. They didn't have a map; we showed them how far they were from any trail. They did have warm clothes, food and water, and one flashlight. We drew a rudimentary map on the back of a candy bar wrapper, gave them extra batteries for the flashlight, and they followed our trail back. Had we not been in this isolated spot at this specific time, they would have been in big trouble with an unplanned overnight for which they were not equipped. The temperature that night dropped below zero.

Skylight and Gray, January 7-8, 1995:

Fifteen hikers were on this trip, organized by the Rochester Winter Mountaineering Society. This was an introductory trip where new, potential members were paired up with an experienced member. The objective was to insure that recruits get the skills and have the strength and stamina needed to successfully complete a winter trip that includes summitting one or more peaks with overnight camping.

Due to the illness of our experienced tenting partner, John and I were asked to bring our own tent and cook for ourselves. We were glad this to do because we had just bought a great, bomb proof Wild Country "Mountain" tent and were looking forward to trying it out. We took great pleasure in cooking in the large vestibule and hunkering down in our warm sleeping bags and cozy new shelter. We felt that life doesn't get much better than this.

By the time we arrived at Lake Colden from Tahawus trailhead, it was obvious that two of the new recruits would not be strong enough to pack up to Lake Tear of the Clouds at 4,350'. Others stayed below with them. An experienced member was designated leader to take the rest of us up the Opalescent Brook to Lake Tear. We arrived there at 3:30 P.M., set up our tents, and hiked up Skylight at dusk on this short winter day; it was completely dark by the time we got back to the tents. We were very tired, having carried too much weight up to Lake Tear—my pack weighed fifty pounds. Our new tent was waiting and we were thrilled to crawl inside, slide our thermarests into their chair frames, and light the stove for hot soup.

We hiked up Gray first thing in the morning, breaking trail all the way. Then we packed up and headed back 9.2 miles to the trailhead. The leader observed all my gear and stuff sacks and said, "Your pack must weigh a ton!" I learned the art of paring down but still having all critical items. By the end of that winter I'd lightened my pack by fifteen pounds!

Allen, January 28, 1995:

Allen was a trip that I will always remember—where my stove malfunctioned and another camper's tent caught fire. It was my second hike with the Rochester Winter Mountaineering Society. We packed everything for many miles to the area near Allen Brook that would fit all four tents, a long way with forty-five pounds on my back; after setting up tents we went on to the summit. I cooked dinner for four of us and then melted snow to fill water bottles. The stove worked beautifully, the food was delicious, and all seemed well with the world. Except for another tentmate's snoring that woke me up occasionally, I slept fairly well.

The next morning I scraped the ice off my shirt and put on my frozen jacket. Putting on frozen gear is sometimes a necessity when camping out in the winter. If you sweat heavily or your clothes get wet, sometimes they do not dry out; I always put my socks, water bottle, gloves into the sleeping bag with me and a damp shirt in the bottom of the bag, but I do not put my shell in. There is only so much room, and sleeping with a wet Gore-Tex shell is not especially comfy. A person's body heat will dry out the clothes within a half hour.

After putting on warm clothing I lit the stove and proceeded to make breakfast. The standard breakfast for winter camping is instant oatmeal with raisins and other dried fruit, nuts, breakfast bars, hot chocolate and/or coffee. After heating up the last course of breakfast, which went very smoothly and my stove worked beautifully, I started to shut the stove down. I turned the stove off but the burner still had a light flame due to pressure in the fuel line; this usually takes a minute to totally burn off. About fifteen seconds after the stove was turned off and before the flame on the burner had died out, a fine arch of liquid white gas began to shoot out of the valve on the stove to the roof of the vestibule. Within seconds, flames from the burner began to dance up this arch and immediately the roof of the vestibule caught fire. The fire began to spread quickly as the white gas continued to spray from the stove. I began to put the flames out but a spray hit my jacket. I had to get out of the tent immediately or go up in flames!

The tent was set up against a snow bank by the rear door so there was no exit from the rear. I immediately crawled out of the tent and my husband dove in, threw the stove out the rear window and managed to beat out the flames. What a hero! I was unhurt but smelled strongly of white gas. The tent and a few stuff sacks had damage.

Everyone was stunned; we all hiked out in shock. Nothing like this had happened before. Ultimately the outcome was good. The hiker whose tent was damaged (we shared tents) got a new, much better tent from MSR, the maker of my stove that malfunctioned; I got a new stove and fuel bottle from MSR. Three years later while I was on a hike up Nippletop Slide, a hiker began to tell me about a RWMS hike up Allen Mountain. He said that a tent caught on fire and the woman who was cooking was severely burned and could not walk, and had to be carried down on a stretcher. I had to finally confess that I was the woman, that I did not get burned but walked out on my own two feet.

The Santanoni Range, February 26 and March 4, 1995:

Howard Stoner, John, and I left the trailhead at 6:30 A.M. It was 15°. At 10 o'clock, we arrived at a grove of pines on level ground beyond a line of cliffs and set up camp; we followed the frozen, drifted, beautiful streambed of Panther Brook to Times Square, summitted Couch by 1:45, and headed back to Panther at a leisurely pace; breaking trail to Santanoni would be more than we should sensibly attempt.

At camp, hot soup "set us all to rights" as we watched the snow fall gently; times like this make camping out in winter such a wonderful experience. The sparkle of snow in sub-zero temperatures, the absence of sound except for trees cracking, are meditative and nourishing to the soul. This beauty has a hard side that is humbling, for the sub-zero air that creates such a magnificent environment can also create suffering and death. We humans are irrelevant in these circumstances yet we exist as part of such magnificence. It is liberating to feel this and understand that the earth and the universe do not need us—yet if we work in harmony with these forces we are greatly nourished—physically, emotionally, and spiritually.

The following week we were climbing only Santanoni, but decided to camp because it's so wonderful to be in the backcountry. We reached the summit at 1:30 in brilliant sunshine, no wind, and 28° —allowing us to bask in the warm air for a long time. Most of the way down, John realized that he had left his thermometer on the summit! Back up the mountain he trudged while Howard Stoner and I waited. Howard slept in his bivy sack under the stars while John and I had the lean-to. It is difficult for me to leave the woods when it's time to get back to civilization.

Haystack and Basin, February 3-4, 1996:

This trip could not have been better. We packed in eight-plus miles on a cold but sunny day. After climbing Haystack we camped right under Little Haystack at 4,500' with a clear view of both Marcy and Haystack. There was only the slightest breeze and the ambient air temperature was -32°. The sky was luminescent with stars and the snow sparkled as it does on those cold winter nights.

When it gets that cold, cooking becomes a new experience. The condensation from hot water in the cooking pot is so thick that basically one is cooking blind. You cannot see the pot! I had to cautiously feel for it with my hands to refill it with snow. Pouring soup or spooning dinner into a bowl is also tricky; finding the bowl so that hands are not scalded is a complex, delicate procedure. Filling a water bottle is even more delicate; pouring is out of the question and using a cup to pour is almost as bad but at least doable. Simple tasks become much more difficult at extreme temperatures.

No one but Howard Stoner and I wanted to hike to Basin the next morning. I put another layer on and we decided to hike on; our decision was the right one. The section with the ladder was completely covered with thick layers of ice. We needed ice axes and to front point with our crampons to get up a fifteen-foot stretch; sections like this make winter hiking so great. Clear skies allowed fantastic views; it was -11° on the summit. We met no one all day; it was wonderful.

Algonquin and Wright, February 19, 1996:

John, his niece Theresa Gubbins, who was visiting us from London, and I set out to climb Algonquin, Iroquois, and Wright from the Adirondack Loj. Theresa did orienteering over in England, but had not done any winter hiking and was not used to the snowy weather and cold temperatures of the Adirondacks. It was in the single digits, but there was no wind in the woods so it was very pleasant until we broke out of tree line. Then it was brutal. The wind must have been blowing at least fifty miles an hour.

We managed to half walk, half crawl to the top of Algonquin. Every now and then there would be an especially fierce blast of wind that would cause us to stop and get as low to the ground as possible so that we would not be blown off the mountain. At the summit we hunkered down between the rocks and debated about trying to get over to Iroquois—but going on would have meant crawling. We decided to attempt Wright instead.

When we reached the junction there was little wind, as we were still down in the trees. Half way up Wright we met two young men who had turned around because they were almost blown off and it was all they could do to stay on the rocks. We had a little discussion, keeping in mind that Theresa had never hiked a mountain in winter and wasn't used to these conditions. But she really wanted to give it a try. To her, this was fun. Our kind of woman!

When we broke out from tree line we were immediately blown over, but we continued on with great big smiles plastered on our faces. We crawled the last twenty-five feet to the summit, stayed in a crouched position and then worked our way slowly off the open rock. We all had a great time and Theresa thought it was fantastic; this would be one of her most memorable experiences and she meant that as a positive statement.

Colvin and Blake, March 17, 1996:

This was another beautiful day. Almost every day is a beautiful day when I'm in the mountains. The beauty of nature from the smallest plant to a majestic summit view nourishes most of us who come here. We wouldn't make the effort if we didn't know that. Although we struggle through deep snow, go over slippery ice-encrusted rocks, sweat up a storm, freeze when we stop struggling, have winds rip at our clothing and turn our noses white, we gain far more than the effort we have put out. We get spiritually nourished, our bodies grow stronger, our sense of accomplishment and humility at the force and beauty of nature is reinforced. Unfortunately, as a species, we take much more than we give.

The hike up Colvin and Blake was sunny, in the low twenties. Comfortable was the word of the day. A lone hiker from Albany was having trouble ascending the icy section near the summit of Colvin; we suggested he replace his snowshoes with crampons. He asked us to stay with him during the tricky, icy stretches. We had an uneventful hike over to Blake and back. Perhaps it's just my perception, but the path back to the trailhead on Lake Road actually seems to lengthen on the walk out. This is also true for the stretch from Marcy Dam to the Loj and the stretch from John's Brook Lodge to the Garden.

Porter, March 19, 1996—46th Peak:

I left Porter for my final peak knowing that, except for Cascade, it was the easiest one to obtain. Flooding, wind, heavy rain, mud, late snow, none of it would interfere with finishing my Winter 46, if I left Porter for last. This final winter peak was a leisurely day trip for Howard Stoner, John, and me on a beautiful day in the high twenties with bright sunshine. We reached the summit at noon and opened champagne to mark the occasion, thinking "What next?" Lying on the rock in the warmth, we lazed awhile, inspecting the north face of Gothics through binoculars. It was covered in snow and ice and we searched for a route up—perhaps our next winter adventure! These mountains offer so much variety, so many possibilities. The more I get to know them, the more I find to love about them.

Holly began the Winter 46 at age 46 and finished at age 48.

CAROL STONE WHITE

46er # 2879W

I grew up in Florida, which is why I love mountains and winter. I worked in New York City after college, met my husband, Dave, and we moved to central New York after our daughter was born. When the children were young, we hiked and swam in the Finger Lakes region; we'd never heard of "the 46."

For twenty-five years, I had as many adventures in politics as I did later on the frozen mountains of northern New York. When our son was two, I was writing a weekly column for Utica's newspaper on congressional reform. I chaired the Clinton Planning Board for six years, was elected to the Village Board, and was congressional coordinator for Common Cause. I edited "Corn Hill Speaks," a journal of inner-city issues, was active in "A Better Chance," an education program for minority youths; worked with legislators and city officials for low-income neighborhood improvement; and received a Department of Housing and Urban Development (HUD) grant to work with the Greater Utica Board of Realtors to eliminate discrimination in the marketing of houses. For many years, I've been a tour guide for the Oneida Community Mansion House.

After work in the Peace Movement, the local United Nations Association selected me—among nineteen other activists and journalists in the United States—to study nuclear proliferation at the International Atomic Energy Agency (IAEA) in Vienna; while we were there the Chernobyl nuclear power plant tragedy occurred. When military base closings began, I coordinated a county task force on economic conversion to study defense spending and possible alternative uses for bases. I was president of Utica's Food Bank and the League of Women Voters. Then everything changed.

In 1988, I quit smoking. A year later, Martha Precheur, now a 46er Club correspondent, asked Dave and I if we'd like to climb Mt. Marcy. On the summit of Marcy, I felt an overwhelming desire to know this vast wilderness, to climb all these beautiful mountains. Dave and I climbed all 46 High Peaks in the next year, and learned that the Catskill 3500 Club offers the same kind of challenge. That club requires climbing four of those thirty-five high peaks in winter! We bought snowshoes and full crampons, required on 3500 Club hikes. After finishing that list, we re-climbed all of them in winter. Now hooked, we returned to our first love, the 46 High Peaks. We think that winter is perhaps the best season of all to hike.

The year of the transforming Marcy climb, I learned about Cornell's environmental project, the Global Walk for a Livable World. I decided not to run for reelection to the village board in order to walk 550 miles from Santa Monica to Flagstaff, learning and teaching about the environment. Navajo and Hopi walkers wrote an Iroquois principle on our support bus: "In our every decision, we must consider its impact on the next seven generations." Dave met me in Flagstaff and we hiked eight miles down to the Grand Canyon's Havasupai Village—down travertine cliffs to the base of a 150' waterfall; trekked through many national parks: Zion, Bryce Canyon, Capitol Reef, Arches, Natural Bridges, and Monument

Valley; and rafted down the rapids of the Colorado River.

I wrote ADK's "Catskill Day Hikes for All Seasons" and am editor of their "Guide to Catskill Trails." I serve as Recording Secretary for the Adirondack Forty-Sixers and am Conservation Chair for the Catskill 3500 Club. Dave and I are Northeast 111ers and have nearly completed the winter climbs of New Hampshire's forty-eight 4,000-footers. We've climbed eight of Colorado's 14,000-footers. Hiking in the mountains gives us a feeling of "re-creation." We return at every opportunity.

Marcy, Christmas Day, 1994:

We decide to go for "The Big One" on Christmas Day, our third High Peak in winter. Sitting on a ledge across from the summit dome, we contemplate this colossus—its scale and grandeur such a contrast with the fragile human life that challenges it. A young couple passes us, descending. Above tree line the wind hits so strongly that I can barely hang onto my poles. We're nearly blown over in gusts, but the temperature is mild and we want to stay on this summit as long as possible. The wind abates for intervals; we eat lunch and savor these precious fleeting moments on New York's highest mountain. Under the summit boulder, a fresh red rose and white carnation with a spray of baby's breath are wedged between two icy rocks! The young couple must have left this lovely bouquet to celebrate a momentous occasion.

Algonquin and Iroquois, January 1, 1995:

We decide to approach via Lake Colden, it's longer but we can walk on frozen lakes and avoid the climb over Algonquin. The tremendous west wind hits with such ferocity when we reach the Algonquin-Boundary col that it's difficult to remain upright. We'll have to traverse the range to Iroquois and retrace to mighty Algonquin in this howling wind. I stash my pack under scrub. At the summit cairn we can't see anything. A lone hiker emerges out of the fog. "How is Algonquin?" I inquire, nervously. "Fine—can't see much—windy!" he smiles, eyelashes and mustache white.

On Algonquin the wind is steady, no sudden gusts; the grade is easy with crampons. My fear evaporates into total enjoyment of the rime ice wrapped in fog—unearthly beauty. On the summit we're jerked back into reality—how do we find the trail far below? We're in a whiteout! Starting down, the compass says we're ninety degrees off course, heading to the precipitous northeast slope. Correcting to the left, a yellow blaze appears—we're on the trail!

Below tree line, steep sections are tremendous fun sliding down. Hikers are descending from Wright at the junction; we share adventures and then Dave says, "We'd better get going or we'll be going out by flashlight!" "No, we won't," says the father of the teenage girl. "How is that?" Dave prompts. "Because," he exclaims, "I don't have a flashlight!" Before the final ascent to the trailhead we see a white snowshoe hare near us in the woods.

Attempt on Marshall, January 15, 1995:

During a January thaw we decided to climb remote Mt. Marshall, a fourteen-mile round trip and partial bushwhack. Off we go to Scott Clearing. We can cross the first tributary on rocks; the second one is deep and swift. Two young men are descending a steep bank. "There's blow-down upsteam," they report. "We're packin' out; conditions aren't good."

"Why don't we pack it in today, too," I suggest. Dave, undeterred, shimmies across the log; the water roaring inches below our boots is unnerving. It's still early—let's go for Marshall. From the high-water trail we decide to bushwhack over to Iroquois Pass Trail. Steep descents to get over there persuade us to keep bushwhacking. Slabbing the steep bank, at times we must go up or down to find terrain where staying vertical is possible. We skirt rock ledges and push through thick evergreen; snow seeps down our necks. Dave jumps off a fallen tree into deep snow. I'm beat and discouraged; we won't get to Marshall at this rate. What retreat means persuades us to continue, and the Interior Outpost is on the other side if needed.

Dave yells, "I'm on the trail! It's good news and bad news—it's under a foot of water." Well, we're soaked, but warm, we're generating tremendous heat. "Let's plow through it and get down," is my thought. After slipping off a submerged rock into knee-deep water I realize, with a sinking heart, that progress will be slow. Now I'm frightened. If we have to bushwhack it'll take hours; the evergreen is thick. We move carefully through the slush, occasionally going in up to our hips. I realize I can't feel my feet and jump out of the water, fighting off panic. Now we're in real trouble! Thoughts of permanent consequences, even survival, flit through my mind. I imagine bushwhacking 1,000 feet down and reaching an icy cliff that cannot be traversed, impenetrable forest, post-holing and breaking an ankle.

"We've got to eat something," Dave says, slinging his heavy pack to the ground. "We have only two and a half hours more of daylight," I calculate, but realize that not eating or drinking enough will make us exhausted and dehydrated. It's hard to choke down a sandwich with a churning stomach. Suddenly—I can feel my feet! We realize with tremendous relief that the outside temperature is warm enough—a murky 50°, if we stay out of the slush we can keep our feet warm. The trail veers downward and the slush is gone!

At 3:15 the ranger lets us into the Interior Outpost to finish our lunch. Can we safely walk across Avalanche Lake? "It's probably safer now to go over the trail," he advises. Six miles later, we arrive back at the trailhead. To splurge for our thirtieth wedding anniversary we stay at a motel with a hot tub and walk comfortably across the parking lot in bathing suits.

Colden, February 11, 1995:

The broken trail stops at Avalanche Lean-to; the snow is very deep and breaking trail is slow; we're losing body heat. We finally emerge at the foggy summit where a boulder tips forty-five degrees at the brink of the slide. It's probably best that we can't see anything, for the view is straight down—a little unnerving even in summer. We hurry across the blustery summit, down steepening slopes. I try not to look at the drop on our right; it seems like you could go into a slide off the mountain. Dave goes crashing down on an icy downward slope. Although he gets right up, I'm near panic. How are we going to find the trail? Get safely down the huge ledge? What is the steep trail down to the lake like? What if we get partway down and have to retrace? A dozen catastrophes flood through my mind.

I yell above the wind, "We've got to go back up over the summit!" Dave scowls, "After we've come this far? Up and down the north summit again? This way down is shorter and then all we have to do is walk across the lakes. C'mon, this way will be better!" Hands are freezing, time is wasting, and we haven't eaten. "We have to go into the trees to our left," Dave points, and we soon arrive at the huge ledge. Dave jumps into deep, soft snow. "I'll catch you," he yells up. It looks horrendously far down—I sit and jump off; he breaks my fall and isn't even knocked over. Like other descents I've feared, this is tremendous fun sliding 1,700 feet down to Lake Colden. The trek across the snowy lakes is exhilarating; we're in that "natural high" one feels out here. The human brain must have evolved to generate this euphoric state after living and surviving in nature for millions of years.

Wright, New Year's Day, 1996:

Ascending on a gloomy day, suddenly near tree line brilliant blue sky appears. Scrambling up the first lookout, Dave calls, "You won't believe this!" He pulls me onto the ledge. It's a vista we've never experienced. A rippled ocean of clouds spreads out below us to the horizon, the white dome of Whiteface thrusting above it. The air is utterly still, warmed in sunlight. Moments like these transport the spirit into another state—an enormous welling up of love of creation. We stand on top of the world on this first morning of the New Year as though transported to a bright new realm of magical possibility. Don't let a cloudy unwelcoming day from the ground deter a climb—Ole Man Winter has a bagful of delightful surprises up the mountain for Mother Nature!

Above tree line I stop to catch my breath and marvel at the quiet. Wright's usual raging winds are obvious from the wildly whipped snow clinging to the granite in jagged iciness. Dave is way above me; I know he can't wait to see what the Great Range looks like. Snowy peaks pierce the cloud layer that is flowing below like a river through the narrow corridor of lakes between Mt. Colden and the MacIntyre Range. Ridges of snow-loaded evergreen downward at tree line disappear into the fluffy sea. As a half-moon rises we cook soup and then explore the large summit; we have this wondrous playground all to ourselves. Far above the sound and fury of the world, this incomparable beauty penetrates our souls and draws us back at every opportunity.

Skylight and Gray, January 14-16, 1996:

Our first backpack is five miles to Lake Colden to camp and climb Skylight and Gray with John and Susan Omohundro, Dick Mooers, Tom Wheeler, Armond and Ann Spencer, and Eileen Wheeler. After pitching tent we peel off sweaty clothes while we still have body-heat. Huddling in a lean-to, the roar of half a dozen stoves fills the dusk. The University of Vermont Outing Club is making an igloo and snow arch. Everyone is in sleeping bags soon after sundown. I lie awake and gradually realize we will be warm enough with foot-warmers. Sleep is fitful; my face is uncomfortable in the cold. I drink less water than I'd like so I won't have to get boots on and crawl out into the icy night.

I struggle out of the bag at 5 A.M. Frost on the tent walls is dispersing. I make my way to the outhouse through deep trails, following the tiny beam of my headlamp; the door is held open by snowdrifts. The wood is surprisingly mellow. Back in the lean-to, clouds of boiling water mix with the breath of mostly-silent bodies.

By 7 A.M., we cross the swinging bridge over the frozen Opalescent River and pass bluish ice-cliffs plunging to invisible depths. Backpacks knock heavy snow off bent-over evergreen branches onto our heads. Beyond Lake Tear of the Clouds something darts by—a pine marten circles widely around us. Above tree line on Skylight, forty-five mph gusts nearly blow us over and fog hides the enormous summit cairn until we're upon it.

Partway up Gray, at a snowy cliff several dozen feet high, Dick Mooers ascends and secures a rope for the rest of us. The canister is just above the snow. Back at the cliff, we inch down to reach the rope—alarming, trying to avoid going into a slide and dropping off. Body heat keeps us warm long enough to strip off wet clothing back in the tent. By morning the temperature is below zero, another gorgeous sunny day. Frost-nip injures John's fingers as he gets the stove going.

Allen, March 10, 1996:

We're on the trail at 6 A.M. for our nineteen-mile round trip. There's a big hole in the ice at Skylight Brook's tributary—yikes!—someone broke through. Is Skylight Brook impassable? The snow bridge holds. Allen Brook is a sparkling jeweled path up through icefalls. The very steep slide is difficult to ascend; hard crumbly snow texture isn't good for digging in. We haven't had to use our snowshoes and I find myself partway up, unable to sit to get them on at this angle. For desperate moments I imagine losing my grip and zooming down—at the rate we can climb it may become impossible to gain the summit.

The summit is within reach! We scramble off the slide, grab dwarfed trees up icy ledges, finally reaching a level lookout—what a panoramic vista! The terrain drops off steeply—most of the climb being in the last mile. I feel tremendous elation at this raven's-eye-view from an isolated mountain. We sit for forty minutes on the summit, reading hikers' comments and reveling in that special happiness granted by conquering a difficult mountain. Something flits across the snow; a pine marten is watching us near the canister. It darts away and then cautiously approaches; we slowly reach for the camera but it doesn't reappear for long. A captivating finalé to the climb.

Icy pitches off the summit require care, holding a tree with one hand and stretching down to tree-holds. We have our snowshoes on. Soon the fun begins—letting go on the steep slide; level areas break the fast slide and as the way narrows into the brook, it's easy to slow down. What was agony going up is hilarious fun going down. It's only 2:15 at the base of the waterfall; we have four and a half more hours of light for the trek back to the Hudson River—luxurious amounts of time in late winter!

Dix, February 8, 1997:

Dix is one of my favorites. Dick Mooers, David Meeker, Dave, and I cross the ice on Round Pond and see a dead beaver near his lodge—skinned! This is a beautiful hike along the Boquet River, up through a birch forest to the huge slide, today sun-splashed with views of Rocky Peak and Giant against the bluest sky. Near the summit, dwarfed trees are encased in thick rime ice that looks like the wind made—an alien landscape of fantastic beauty. Rainbows shimmer on ice-coated branches. The open summit offers 360-degree views. Although it was 15° when we started and 15° is lost during the 3,200' ascent, it's warm in the sun—the air is completely still.

We have time to explore over to the Beckhorn on this enormous summit. At 2:10, we very reluctantly start down. Dave's old pack breaks; he duct-tapes deteriorating sections. A tiny crescent moon shimmers in the darkening sky at 5:40 P.M. as we reach our cars. We learned later that Dick got a stress fracture in his foot during the descent and are very disappointed that he can't hike Hough next week, where we'll "46."

Hough, February 15, 1997—46th Peak:

We meet Susan and John Omohundro, Eileen and Tom Wheeler, Ann and Armond Spencer, and David Meeker at Slide Brook Lean-to. They're heating water for their bottles to keep them liquid on below-zero days. As the terrain steepens dramatically, the pace sometimes stops completely as the lead trail breaker flounders in thigh-deep snow. John switchbacks right and then left, struggling to lift each step up the precipitous slope through many feet of powder. Dave walks over to a slide and kicks small steps in the crusty snow. "If he loses control he'll be unable to stop himself," Tom worries. As we struggle upwards Tom says, "I hate to think we may have another thousand vertical feet to climb; my altimeter reads 3,650' and it can be off by 250'. "We might have only 500 feet to go?" I ask hopefully. "Nope, it always means more ascent," Tom says with a slight grin. Is he joking?

At 2 o'clock I wonder, will we make it? Dave takes the lead; featureless gray-white sky appears above; it feels like a summit—raging wind, trees covered with rime ice. Dave yells down, "We're not at the summit—it still goes up." Trees disappear into fog above. "It's only another tenth of a mile—things look farther than they actually are," Tom offers encouragingly. Eileen and I manage a weak cheer. I'm energized, can feel that canister, our 46th winter peak. We'll stagger out in the dark, but as Winter 46ers! Tom is right. Soon a huge grin transforms Dave's haggard features. A tree on the edge of the precipice holds the magical canister, with HOUGH written vertically on it. It is 3 o'clock. Icicles hang down Dave's face and neck from his snow-crusted hair. We bring forty-six icy shrimp and sauce out of our packs to share.

Euphoria dissolves at the prospect of descending that precipitous mountainside. I sit, grasp evergreen branches and stretch down to wedge a snowshoe on trees below, or whiz down, digging elbows into snow and braking with snowshoes; but a caught arm or leg could be broken. Sometimes I poke ski poles into snow below to inch down. When the path veers I try not to continue straight down. Branches threaten to yank off my mittens; a small stump hurts my tailbone. Elbows bruise as they bump against trees in desperate attempts to moderate the slide. Dave says he bounced from tree to tree like a pinball. Enjoying the Omohundro's champagne around the fire, David Meeker says, "It was wonderful being with you when you 46ed; I can't believe this day." It's his first winter bushwhack. "I've got new respect for Winter 46ers," he shakes his head.

The snowy forest glows in magenta and orange on the four-mile walk back. We laugh at memories, like when a vole got in our tent with the food bag, or when, lacking a pen, we wrote our names with a chocolate bar on East Dix, or when we reached the cliffs of Seward after hiking the range and Bob Zayhowski exclaimed, "This is all right for guys, but women? They're not human!" We're euphoric at achieving that improbable goal set two years ago when we tested the Adirondack High Peaks in winter. Winter mountain climbing continues to give us tremendous enjoyment and excitement; I'm more accepting of its challenges and being at the mercy of nature's many moods.

Carol began the Winter 46 at age 54 and finished at age 56.

20

SUSAN OMOHUNDRO

46er # 2679W

I overcame long odds to become a hiker, let alone a Winter 46er. I grew up in a totally sedentary family in the flatlands of mid-Michigan. Perhaps one indication of my latent tendencies is that I liked to go for solitary walks in the land behind our house, before the birch trees and ferns gave way to suburban houses. In college, I continued to be a mildly anorexic, cigarette-smoking, couch-potato-bookworm. I did, however, begin spending summers outdoors in archeology field schools in northern Michigan, where I appreciated the attractive lands along Lake Michigan and enjoyed a temporary increase in physical fitness. After John and I married, we visited parks and camped in our Volkswagen bus, but it was a casual, unfocused activity.

In 1974, John and I moved to Potsdam, New York, which is located north of the Adirondack Park between the foothills of the Adirondacks and the St. Lawrence River. The first thing we did after unpacking the U-Haul was drive down to the Adirondacks, accompanied by my brother, for a short vacation. We were totally ignorant of the region. By happenstance, we arrived at the Adirondack Loj campground. The next morning, we decided to climb something. Marcy, the #1 mountain, was too far away, so we decided to go for #2, Algonquin. We were confident we could walk eight miles easily. Well, we did make the summit, but by the time we got back to camp our legs were so rubbery we could hardly walk. This first experience did not prompt a sudden decision to climb every mountain in sight. Over the next several years, we climbed a number of High Peaks, but felt the notion of climbing all 46 was foolish and unappealing.

John and I bought a sandstone house built in 1838 by the founder of Hannawa Falls, a hamlet a few miles south of Potsdam. We researched the house's history and had it listed on the National Register in 1985. Restoring its original stencils and other features has been an ongoing commitment. An interest in local history led to the writing of a multiple nomination of Potsdam sandstone buildings to the National Register, an eight-year undertaking. That year, I began serving on the board of the St. Lawrence County Museum; involvement with historic architecture and related issues will probably continue indefinitely.

Living on the Racquette River, we became interested in its social and natural history. We paddled the length of the river from its source at Blue Mt. Lake to the St. Lawrence River, a rewarding experience. A current project is the establishment of a walking trail along the Racquette River near Hannawa Falls. We are active ADK members and have a strong interest in conservation. In my spare time, I'm still a bookworm, and I love to swim.

Our friend Dick Mooers started us in the so-called "trailless" High Peaks, the Dixes, and we learned we didn't need to feel intimidated by them. Eventually, we realized we had climbed a lot of mountains and decided we might as well finish the list. We had come to see that every mountain, every hike, had its unique features. Also, the more hiking we did, the more we wanted to do.

We finished the 46 in 1989. Meanwhile, we had begun hiking the White Mountains of New Hampshire. Dick got us started there, too, plus we had hiking friends in Randolph to visit. Their house faces Mt. Adams, an inspiring sight. We loved hiking in the White Mountains because the trails and the summit views are so good. We were on a roll, and began to hike all the 4,000-foot summits in the northeast. Many we did with ADK friends and a few we did on our own.

In the process we managed to be at Mt. Katahdin in Maine for Hurricane Bob, yielding indelible memories if blurry photos. By choosing our moments wisely, we did manage to achieve the summits we needed there. Fortunately, we had a lean-to at Chimney Pond to bide our time in; we had a tremendous amount of rain. I'll never forget sloshing through several inches of water just to get to the outhouse. One time I looked up from my feet to see a moose standing just a few feet away. Fifteen ADK friends from the Laurentian Chapter originally signed up for this week-long trip, but by the end of the week, standing on North Brother, our "group" contained just the two of us, John and I; everyone else had bailed out for one reason or another. Of course, the weather improved just about the time we got back in the car to return home. We finished the Northeastern 111 in 1994 on Mt. Madison in NH, walking up from Randolph with our friend, David. It was a hot, hazy day; I fell and scraped the skin off the palm of my hand; finishing the 111 was disappointingly anti-climactic. We wondered what we could do next.

Hiking winter mountains was next. Actually, we had begun winter climbing in the late 1980s and loved it from the start. Two of the mountains in our "regular" 46 list, Sawteeth and Tabletop, were winter hikes. Our first winter mountains had been Cascade and Porter, giving us a taste of how rewarding and how easy winter climbs could be. Tabletop, however, was a genuine bushwhack, and far more challenging. I knew I liked winter climbing, but didn't think I had the capacity to climb all 46 High Peaks in winter. As I said in my first letter to Grace in 1995 about winter High Peaks: "We achieved a milestone of sorts...to become half of a Winter 46er by climbing Street and Nye. Since we may not have the ability to climb all 46—and even if we do, it may take years—why not say something now?" It was on the Street and Nye hike that we met Carol and

David White, collectively forced a way to the summits, quickly formed a friendship, and subsequently did many winter climbs together.

It was becoming clear to me that unless I wanted to put in some horrendously long days, I was going to have to learn to winter camp if I wanted to do all 46 peaks in winter, as I increasingly desired to do. We started gradually, with a November overnight at Marcy Dam and climb of a then unnamed high point, now named T. R. for Teddy Roosevelt. This gave us a chance to practice using winter gear and sleds, and it boosted our self-confidence. Among other things, we learned that it is virtually impossible to peel frozen hardboiled eggs, and hardly worth the effort when you do, because they taste so rubbery and awful. Before long, we were ready to try two nights at Flowed Lands. We climbed Skylight and Gray on that occasion, in January of 1996. We didn't much like camping at Flowed Lands, however, and never stayed there again. It was way too popular and looked like a dirty slum, with denuded trees and unusable latrines. The next month, we camped at the base of Calkins Brook, en route to the Sewards. We liked that much better, choosing a remote wilderness site with ample firewood.

We gradually accumulated winter camping gear in 1995-96— including a winter tent, more pads, more clothes, and zip-together overbags to fit over our individual sleeping bags (a very cozy, warm, and inexpensive solution). We ordinarily pulled this extra gear a few miles in on a modified plastic sled to base camp. We found winter camping easier than expected. However, when sub-zero temperatures move in, I find it's difficult to be inactive and yet keep my hands warm. A campfire helps! By the end of the following season, 1997, we achieved our goal. The Winter 46 goal may be elusive but it is attainable, even by those who are not born athletes—especially if they get an occasional boost from their friends and spouses. Overall, it was a positive, even inspiring set of experiences. Some days were not fun but many were, and I had a big feeling of accomplishment from meeting the challenge.

I remember that the Dix Range was our most difficult trailless group—we ended up climbing the five Dix peaks one at a time, and having a tough time of it, too, carving paths in deep snow to socked-in summits. On one of those days we celebrated the Whites' completion of their Winter 46 on Hough with cold shrimp cocktail, eaten in haste in blustery weather. Although the Seward Range was a long, tiring day, it was less difficult than I'd expected (we had unexpected help from a crew from Albany); also easier than expected was climbing Haystack, Basin, and Saddleback in one day, and climbing the well-used Van Hoevenberg trail up to Marcy. On the other hand, Colden, Giant, and Whiteface were more difficult than I expected, the first two because of unbroken snow, and the latter because I tried and failed more than once to ski up the wind-blasted road; we finally snowshoed up the trail from the Atmospheric Science Center. Favorite peaks were Haystack, Algonquin, Colden, Marcy, Rocky Peak, and the Great Range.

After a burst of enthusiasm in 1989 when I did seven winter peaks, I didn't resume serious winter climbing until 1993, when I did seven more. One hike that stands out is the traverse from Gothics to Upper Wolfjaw. A Laurentian ADK group filled Camp Peggy O'Brien for a long weekend in February. Six of us decided we wanted to do a moderately ambitious but fun hike, and we thought this one met our criteria. Our six included Ann and Armond Spencer, John and me, and Tim Davis and Stacie Stone. Tim and Stacie were new at this, but young and strong. We had fun.

We enjoyed going up the cable route on Gothics and were thrilled by the views from the summit. It got harder and slower as we moved toward Armstrong, because it was difficult at times to find the trail and the snow was deep. I remember we used a rope to help manage the steep drop coming off of Armstrong. We forged on over Upper Wolfjaw, bodies tiring but morale good.

Colden, February 27, 1993:

We began this twelve-mile jaunt on a beautiful, sunny February day. We began by skiing from South Meadow to Marcy Dam, which was pleasant, and then we stashed our skis in the woods and switched to snowshoes. We planned to make a loop, ascending the slide on the eastern side of Colden and returning on the Lake Arnold trail, and then ski back to the car and go out to dinner.

The trail from Marcy Dam to Lake Arnold was open and the lower part of the slide was easy and enjoyable. We marveled at the ski tracks on the slide and wished we could ski like that. As we got higher, the slide grew steeper, but the scenery steadily improved and the sun felt warm. The air was very clear, and Marcy, glittering, seemed almost close enough to touch. As we approached the top of the slide, progress slowed. The top of the slide is very steep, so John tied a rope to a tree trunk so that we could pull ourselves up over the last ledge. Once we got there, the rest of us realized that this "tree" was about as thick as a pencil—so the benefit was more psychological than real. Ann still ribs us about that.

By the time we reached the summit and admired Colden's splendid views of Marcy, the MacIntyre Range, and numerous other mountains, it was mid-afternoon—time to think about heading back. We soon realized no one had been on the Lake Arnold trail recently and we would have to break trail. Worse, we discovered we couldn't consistently stay on the trail. Trail markers were hidden by snow, and we kept falling into spruce holes, which is very tiring and renders forward progress almost nil. We began to fear we'd be spending the night out there. We had already descended below the north summit, so retracing back up to the summit would mean considerable reclimbing and then 7.4 miles back via the Lake Colden Trail. It was reluctantly, therefore, that we decided to retrace.

Earlier we had seen figures on the summit, so reasoned that the trail to Lake Colden must be open. We stood on the summit for a second time, just as the sun went behind the mountains. Fortunately our guess was correct and the trail down was open; a speedy descent brought us to the lake by dark. Walking out was relatively easy to do because of the moonlight. Once we saw campers at the Avalanche Lean-to, we realized we were no longer totally on our own and relaxed a little. It was still a long walk out, though, and we were tired and the temperature was dropping fast. We had no choice but to keep moving. We didn't want to try skiing in the dark so we kept walking and carried our skis.

We were thankful to see our car at 9:45 P.M. Even more thankful to sit down and bask under the car heater. As for going out to dinner, by the time we got to Saranac Lake on a Sunday evening all restaurants were closed. We had to settle for Burger King. We were too tired to care. Lessons we learned: Get an early start. Expect to finish in the dark (we soon learned not to be scared of that). Don't bother with skis unless you're a good skier; it's just that much more gear to deal with. Think twice about ascending and descending on different routes; it's much easier to stay with the trail that's open. Don't make elaborate dinner plans for a big-hike day.

Standing on a mountain like Colden on a clear, bright winter day puts you close to heaven. The reward is worth the effort.

Dial and Nippletop, January 15, 1995:

This Sunday was a freakishly warm day and we broke our rule about not climbing in bad weather—I guess because it didn't seem like winter—to do our nineteenth and twentieth winter High Peaks. We climbed with Dick Mooers and Tom Wheeler on what proved to be an amazing day. Ascending Dial wasn't too bad on an almost bare trail, in light drizzle. Moving from Dial to Nippletop was harder because I brashly didn't carry snowshoes and found myself post-holing in drifted snow. The real challenge began after we left the summit of Nippletop; hard rain set in.

Descending Elk Pass was not fun. Our crampons sank into a mishmash of ice, snow, roots, rocks, mud, and water. Eventually our feet and clothing were waterlogged. We temporarily lost the trail near Elk Pond, in the dusk, costing us precious time. Then we lost Tom in the dark; the noise of the wind, rain, and rushing water in the streams meant that we couldn't hear each other. We could barely see the trail even with lights. This was one of the days when I wished my eyeglasses had windshield wipers. Gill Brook was a raging torrent. I could hear it even if I couldn't see it, and feared it might take out the Lake Road bridge before we got there, or, even worse, while we were on it! But we survived our watery experience and didn't even get cold. It was an unforgettable "winter" hike.

Haystack, Basin, and Saddleback, March 19, 1995:

I know that many people have a difficult time on these mountains, but they were amazingly easy and pleasant on both of our winter trips there—which demonstrates how much weather and snow conditions influence the outcome of winter hikes. Our companions were Carol and David White, Dick Mooers, and Tom Wheeler.

Camping on a mild night at a lean-to near Johns Brook Lodge was easy.

We ate lunch on Haystack's summit, enjoying the windless warmth and unsurpassed views. It was so mild and such easy walking that we scrambled up Basin with no more effort than we would in the summer. We put on and took off crampons several times, but we carried our snowshoes the whole day and never used them. John carried a rope and never used that either, but Tom took a tumble on the descent of Basin, so maybe that was when we should have used the rope!

The cliffs on Saddleback were bare, fortunately—I had forgotten how big a reach is needed to climb up. John and I missed the turn back to camp in the dusk, so had the dubious pleasure of walking an extra mile in the mud and slush. We were rewarded when we reached Camp Peggy O'Brien, our home for the night, by discovering that Dave had carried in a box of wine to celebrate with!

Allen, March 2, 1997—46th peak:

Allen lived up to its forbodding reputation. Our first attempt with David and Carol White failed, for a number of reasons. The four of us camped near Twin Brook the night before our attempt. The weather was mild and we got a good start in the morning. Dick Mooers and Tom Wheeler were supposed to hike in and join our trailbreaking effort. But we never saw them. When they had gotten up at 3 A.M., they decided it was snowing too hard in Potsdam to drive down to the trailhead. Snow didn't begin at Allen until midday. Our biggest problem was that we strayed off course before Skylight Brook and eventually realized we couldn't reach the summit unless we spent a second night out, which no one wanted to do. So we turned back. The one bright spot of the day was discovering Dick walking up with a thermos of hot coffee when we got back to our tents to pack up. The worst part of the day was driving home in a blinding snowstorm and running into a deer near Long Lake (actually the deer, which we never saw, ran into the side of our Jeep). A dismal, sad conclusion to the day.

So, come March, we were ready for our second attempt. It was ill-fated as well. We were six hours late because of car trouble and then discovered at the trailhead at 7 P.M. that we were short a snowshoe because John, when packing the car the previous evening in the dark, picked up a bundle of three, not four, snowshoes from the floor of the garage. Groan. Disconsolate, we drove home.

The weather forecast for the next night was not good, but when we got up in the morning it didn't seem too bad. I couldn't let go of the idea of climbing Allen, so we invited Armond Spencer to join us. We walked in easily that afternoon, meeting our friends coming out after their successful climb. We made a comfortable camp, complete with snow kitchen and tarp lean-to and had a fine evening. I know no one better at kindling a campfire than Armond.

In the morning the trail was easy to follow, but it rained all the way to the summit and we got soaked. We had to circumvent streams beginning to open up. It was not a good day for hiking, but we did achieve our goal. When we got back to our campsite, the temperature was dropping and it was beginning to snow. Some daylight remained, so we decided we would rather pull our sleds out and go home than spend a second night. We were wet and tired but satisfied.

I declared that I was going to "retire" when I finished the Winter 46, but we were back in the mountains many times, helping everyone in our circle of friends finish their Winter 46 quests. This involved yet another climb of Allen to help Ann finish—reclimbing Allen is a sign of true friendship!

Susan began the Winter 46 at age 43 and finished at age 51.

BARB HARRIS

46er # 2824W

I was born in Oak Park, Illinois, and came to live in Plattsburgh, New York in 1962, when my US Air Force pilot father was transferred from Little Rock, Arkansas. We moved a lot and by the time I graduated from high school, I had attended nineteen different schools. I married Gary Harris and we have two boys, Michael and Dean. Michael and his lovely wife Carmen have given us two beautiful granddaughters, Amanda and Kristin. I can't wait to take them to the woods. My career is a Mary Kay Sales Director; my passion is climbing mountains.

I didn't discover the Adirondacks until 1988, when a friend, Linda LaMarche Harwood, invited me on a hike to Round Mountain. I was hooked, even though the day was rainy and foggy, and I could barely move off the couch for five days after! Another friend, Joanne Hagar, after hearing my excitement, loaned me her copy of "Peaks and People of the Adirondacks" by Russell Carson, which I devoured and immediately wanted to try for the Adirondack 46 High Peaks. I had never heard of the High Peaks and I only live an hour from Keene Valley! I think I lived too sheltered a life.

I said to Linda, "Why don't we try a High Peak?" She thought we were too old. I suggested we start with the easiest, Cascade and Porter, and see what happens. We thought it was a piece of cake and we were off on our quest to become 46ers. While climbing our first 46 we started talking about the "V" badge to earn for winter, climbing five peaks in solar winter. After completing that I knew I wanted to continue climbing in winter. I didn't even know there was a patch until, doing trail work at Feldspar Lean-to, I saw the Winter Rocker on Trailmaster Len Grubb's hat and I just had to have one too!

Winter climbing is physically the hardest thing I have tried to do. I thought I would have to quit because of foot problems but surgery helped somewhat. Even though problems continue, I love climbing too much to stop. Mentally, too, it's sometimes hard to keep yourself going when it would be so easy to turn around when it starts getting really tough. I did all the winter peaks as day trips—long day trips. But the challenge keeps you going for the summits—to open all those "cookie jars" at the top of the trailless peaks. I've never been one to worry, so I'll do just about anything. Just "go for it!" Winter climbing has showed me I have great determination that I didn't know I had. After becoming an Adirondack Forty-Sixer, I headed to the White Mountains with Sally Hoy, Katie Hoy, and Cathy Ament. They were among those with me when I finished the Northeast 111 on a beautiful day on Carrigain Mt. in New Hampshire.

Weather permitting, I climb every weekend. If I don't get out for awhile my disposition gets ugly. I found I love backpacking when Sally Hoy and I hiked the Northville-Placid Trail together; we're starting the Vermont Long Trail along with Ellen Ohnmacht. I've completed the Adirondack Hundred Highest after being introduced to bushwhacking by Kathleen Gill, as well as the 46 peaks in all four seasons—the first woman to complete both goals. I can't explain why I enjoy being beaten by spruce trees, bitten by black flies, and gouged and scratched by pine tree branches except that it is a challenge to find that summit...and get out alive!

With the Adirondack Forty-Sixers I was a Director, Vice-President, and President through May 25, 2003. I have made CD recordings with Grace Hudowalski, Ditt and Mary Dittmar, and Helen Menz to have the voices and stories preserved for all time about the beginning of the Adirondack Forty-Sixers and their early mountain memories.

Esther, February 3, 1991:

Judy and Ellsworth King and I climbed Esther on a picture-perfect day, a beautiful, sunny day with warm breezes. But I didn't think I'd ever reach the summit. I'd been sick and didn't realize what a lack of energy I'd have; I climbed at a snail's pace. I wanted to tell them I was turning back so they could make Esther and Whiteface, but they would get out of sight. I'd yell at myself for being so stupid to think I could ever be a Winter 46er. Who was I kidding? The next minute I'd be telling myself, "You can do it," and, "Grace says, 'those Plattsburgh women, nothing stops them'."

At the turnoff to Esther I told Judy I didn't think I could make it. Ellsie could build a fire and I'd wait for them. Judy laid on the encouragement that I could do it; the trail was packed well, the conditions were great. I forced myself to eat a little, took aspirin, prayed. The climb to the summit was gorgeous and wasn't hard at all. We saw people skiing up the road to Whiteface! The snow on the trees made the trail look like a long tunnel, so beautiful; treetops had no snow—from the wind—but the bottoms were covered. The next thing I knew, I recognized the summit! I almost cried when I saw the register. How my energy had changed in an hour was amazing. And the views were fabulous...we could see Vermont! Whiteface was so close we felt we could reach out and touch it. I wanted to stay forever. I gave them both extra hugs and kisses for their encouragements.

Colvin, December 28, 1995:

We skied Lake Road, hid our skis at the By-Pass, and started for Colvin. I worried about the very steep rock pitch just below the summit because I knew it would be covered with ice. I wasn't wrong. Sally took off her right snowshoe so she could get her foot in the crack and get some leverage. Then I pushed her up and she still wasn't far enough to catch the tree limb; I then put my hands under her boot and she used that for more leverage and got up. Now my turn! Suddenly she dropped her ski pole and it went sliding down off the crevice way below. No way was I going down there after it; but I got on my stomach, leaned over and got the tip of my ski pole through her ski pole basket and was just able to pull it up. Now my turn! I had a rope in my pack; Sally tied it around a tree and I pulled myself up. What a workout! The summit was ours!

Donaldson, Emmons, and Seward, February 6, 1996:

Seymour Ellis and I went in up Calkins Brook and got all three mountains! Phil Corell had just done it so I knew there was a good trail. We were on Emmons at noon! I couldn't believe it! Me, on Emmons in winter! It was actually an easy walk to the summit. It was another beautiful day with no wind and great views; the pure white snow against the bluest of blue skies was picture perfect. When we headed back to Donaldson I was smiling ear-to-ear; I bet my smile even went to the back of my head. Seymour put both of our snowshoes on his pack. "No use to both of us being pulled and tugged at," he smiled. I couldn't believe he would do that. I looked over to Seward and thought it looked so far away. Seymour said it was up to me, but I felt great! I wasn't even tired. "Let's go for it!" I laughed, and we were off for Seward.

There were three bad icy spots to climb; I never would have made it without Seymour. It seems like all day long he was saying, "Hand me your pole," as he'd pull me up. We were on Seward at 3:15. I had to lie on the ground to get my picture with the canister, just above the snow. When I looked back at the ridge we had climbed I was stunned—I couldn't believe I had done that in winter. Seymour looked for Sharp Swan's trail off the mountain and then decided we'd better go back over Donaldson and out Calkins Brook. I was in a controlled panic, not feeling so smug anymore about getting the three Sewards in winter—I just wanted the car! Soon, though, we did find the broken trail down; we gave each other the high five and were off. I had signed us in only to Donaldson and Emmons—it was fun to add a mountain! I'd never done that before.

Gothics and Armstrong, February 23, 1996:

Seymour Ellis, Sally Hoy, and I climbed Gothics over Pyramid and then Armstrong. It was a beautiful, sunny, 50° day! Seymour and I hiked in long johns with shorts over the long john bottoms—much cooler. The views on Pyramid were more than awesome; we stayed thirty minutes and enjoyed the warmth. On Gothics fog started coming in.

The trail was hard to find on the way to Armstrong. Seymour pointed out fleas in the snow! I'll never eat snow again. While Seymour set up the timing on the camera for our summit picture, Sally and I stripped down to our jog bras—he was a little shocked. The trail off Armstrong for a quarter-mile is dangerous; you have to lean into the mountain and dig in with your left snowshoe to stay on the mountain and not slide off! I was never so glad to get off that stretch—I remember saying in summer, "I'd never want to do this in the dark or in winter"—and here I am! Farther down Seymour post-holed thirty times! I got in a good one—down two feet. "Stand up and I'll help," called Seymour, coming back for me. "I am standing up!"

East Dix, March 14, 1996:

We started off Route 73 on the north side of the Bouquet River, which eliminates one big crossing. It was a very late start, 7:30, on a gorgeously warm and sunny day. I had never hiked with ADK trip leader Jim Schaad before, so was glad to discover he didn't mind stopping to drink in the views and take pictures. Ah, a man who doesn't race through the mountains. At 11:45 there was absolutely no wind on the slide. It was magnificent. The rocks to the summit looked so far away, though. When we hit ice below the snow, we switched to crampons; Jim helped pull me up on the really icy spots. I had to switch to my insteps since my crampons decided not to stay on. I felt like Sandy Pittman on Everest. When was the Ghirardelli chocolate bar going to kick in that Jim had given us? The last chimney up to the top I was afraid was really going to be awful; it was covered in ice, but I kept pulling myself up with the trees and staying off the ice. The views were so splendid; it was like standing on the edge of the world. It was three o'clock!

Jim wanted to return over Spotted Mt. We voted to go to the col and then decide. Soon we reached a bump between East Dix and Spotted and were blessed with magnificent views again. Because the light was fading we decided it would be better to be up on the ridge than down in the valley on this clear, warm evening. It was the most awesome ridge walk under an almost full moon! It was one of my low energy days and I was dreading each bump we had to go over, but it's an experience I'll never forget. Although we agreed it had become the hike from hell, sitting in a warm house rested and reminiscing, it gets better and better.

Couchsachraga, January 4, 1997:

Sally Hoy, John Wheeler, and I climbed Couchsachraga on another awesome day. The sky was blue, the air warm and still, and the best part…three guys passed us! I loved following their tracks. I've never seen the views we were rewarded with in winter before—all the mountains had clouds below them so just the summits were peeking though—an ocean of mountains. Henderson Mt. looked like an island. It was so exciting. Pictures don't do justice to the beauty we were so fortunate to see. I enjoyed this hike immensely.

Blake, February 4, 1997:

Seymour Ellis and I climbed Blake from the Carry Trail. I'd been dreading this climb for a year; it's a 1,995' climb in just 1.6 miles. I walked around the house the night before saying, "Oh my heavens, can I do this?" Seymour saved the day, as usual. We skied in and he brought his sled to put our hiking boots and snowshoes in. The ski across Lower Ausable Lake was not windy, so it was enjoyable; it was sunny and warm with great views of Indian Head that you only get in winter. At the Carry Trail we hid the sled and changed into hiking boots and snowshoes, and started up. Immediately, it was so steep my calves were burning. I thought, I can't do this for three hours. The good part was, it wasn't icy and it was a newly broken trail. The trail finally leveled out so you could breathe and talk at the same time. There was no wind, it was warm, and the views were stupendous. Skylight was a big white dome. The views got better and better, then it got steeper again. I could have kissed the sign when we arrived at the col.

Seymour had said that this was the only way to do Blake, and I had to admit this was faster than going over Colvin first and then Blake. The last half-mile was just as steep as I remembered, so I was mentally prepared. There were views of Giant I'd never seen from this angle—isn't winter climbing just the best for views? The view of Elk Lake from the summit was breathtaking. I didn't realize how many islands there are. I hated to leave but we started to get cold. What took three hours, twenty minutes to go up took one hour, fifteen minutes to go down. For me it was butt sliding—how one stays vertical on sections like this is beyond me. I looked like a snowman—just needed a pipe in my mouth! I always hated Blake before, but now I can honestly say I have wonderful memories of it.

Marcy and Gray, February 20, 1997:

Ellen Ohnmacht and I headed down the trail an hour ahead of Mike Bush, Marta Bolton, Connie Morrison, and Bill Johnson. The group caught up with us at Indian Falls but ate at the view; it took them two hours to catch up! There was no wind on the Haystack side of Marcy's summit and so we ate there and enjoyed views for twenty minutes. We had to put on crampons for the south side of Marcy; we all had just instep crampons except for Marta, and I was having a troublesome time. I made one of the worst decisions of my life and decided to butt slide...I almost went off the mountain into Panther Gorge! I was able to hit my feet against a small rock and stop myself from sliding over the edge. When you butt slide on ice, you can really pick up speed when you don't want to!

It was so neat—after I got off the ice—to see the ridge where we were going toward Gray. Almost immediately we started post-holeing and got into serious spruce traps; Ellen fell in to her shoulders and it took two of us to get her out. There was one fun place where we slid fifty feet down; in the middle of the slide was a mound of snow to give you a "lift," and at the bottom you slid over a tree limb; everyone now has a purple bruise on their left cheek! The canister was buried under two feet of snow.

We'd planned to climb Skylight also. "It's too late; we should reclimb Marcy and start back," Mike advises us. Marta and I talked him into going against his better judgment. "We'll just fall into more spruce traps up to our necks," he argued in vain. We started down Gray and Connie fell into the ultimate spruce trap! She's six feet tall and she was eight feet down and still not touching bottom; she was petrified and I didn't blame her. It took ten minutes to get her out. I hate it when Mike is right; we had to give it up and return over

Marcy. I dreaded the thought of the climb. Later Mike thought we could've gone down Marcy to Four Corners and up Skylight that way. At Marcy Dam I was thanking God that Mike didn't think of it sooner!

Allen, March 21, 1997:

This was the one I was dreading. Could I do it or not? I might have to camp this one. I didn't know if I had the stamina and my foot problems didn't help. Marta Bolton and Peggy MacKellar had already done Allen this year on Dec. 21, yet they said they were coming on this trip; I screamed with delight when I realized they meant it. I told Marta the little men in their white coats would be arriving soon. We meet at the trailhead at 4 o'clock with Seymour Ellis, Sally Hoy, and Tom Regan. No one had been in since March 1 and 2. The crusty snow was hard to break—very slow going. It took three hours to get to Twin Brook! We all broke trail for ten minutes and then went to the back of the line. Off the trail the group didn't let Sally and me break; can you believe this? They are angels from heaven. We tried to go second as much as possible.

During the climb I heard honking—three big Vs of geese. It was almost 30° and blue skies when we got to Allen Brook. Marta had told me that this last mile to the summit was real steep and would take two to three hours; I didn't remember that at all. Then we hit the slide! You couldn't go in the person's tracks ahead of you because the loose snow would slide you back down—and there was ice. Almost at the top, Tom, who is 6'2", was in snow to his waist when his snowshoe broke. When he took it off to fix it, he went in snow to his shoulders.

It had taken ten hours to the canister; we spent thirty minutes on the summit. We literally slid from the summit back down to the falls. What took three hours to come up took an hour to go down, laughing all the way. But we didn't stop to eat and drink on the way out as much and that caught up with me. The last two miles were a death march; it was one foot in front of the other, left, right, left, right. We got out at 9:30 P.M. I had been up for twenty-four hours and hiked for seventeen of those hours. BUT I GOT ALLEN! At the gas station I told the guy we'd been seventeen hours on a mountain, were wet and needed to change. He asked, "What happened, did you get stuck?"

Hough, December 21, 1997:

This mountain was a real bugger for me. It had turned me back twice last year from Elk Lake. I talked Seymour Ellis into trying it from Route 73 along the Boquet River. It was a beautiful starry night with a quarter moon when we started at 5 A.M. We had beautiful views and could see Hough. Woody was off course way ahead of us—we finally caught up with this trail-breaking machine for the final steep climb. As we got to the top of the ridge, Dave White looks right and says, "Oh, no." I followed his gaze and said, "Oh, @#^&*"!" We were between Hough and the Beckhorn, so we'd have to lose 400 feet of ascent and regain that to Hough. It's one o'clock. I was so crazed I didn't even ask people what they wanted to do. "I don't care what time it is, I've never been this close, we're going for it." We signed in at 2:15. We had awesome views and it wasn't windy—a wonderful Christmas present. Taking a different descent through a splendid hardwood forest, we then got in the thickest spruce forest I've ever seen. My face must have been swollen from being slapped so much with branches; Woody looked like he'd been in a fight with blood dripping down his moustache. Not fun except for one great big butt slide.

Haystack, January 15, 1998—46th Peak:

Seymour Ellis, Sally Hoy, and I started for my final winter peak with reports of a snowstorm and cold temperatures. We didn't need snowshoes at all! It was wonderful. Above Indian Falls, Marta Bolton, Mike Bush, and Vic Pomerville caught up with us. Little Haystack was very icy and windy, probably sleet with snow because it sure hurt the face. I turned my head to protect myself; had my neck gaiter pulled up so just my eyes were showing. We brought rope for the descent off Little Haystack but it turned out to be not so bad. The guys stayed in front and made sure we didn't go sliding off that one ledge.

Because Haystack is my 46th Winter Peak, Mike had me lead. I'd think I was there, and then a higher outcropping of rocks would loom above. As I headed for the summit many thoughts ran through my mind: I wouldn't be a Winter 46er without Seymour's help—he sort of "adopted" me a couple of years ago when he saw how I was struggling. Sally Hoy, whom I "hooked" for winter climbing, always had me select the mountain and which way to go. Sally would say, "I'm not going to be a Winter 46er; I'm just here to hike with you." I remembered how Mike and Vic had warmed my hands when they were so cold climbing Marcy—my thumb, frostbitten on an earlier climb, had been really hurting me. How Marta had done Allen with me on March 21 after already doing it on December 21 the previous year! I reached Haystack's summit at 1:30 and cried on Marta's shoulder; all the struggles and happiness came pouring out. On the other side of Little Haystack we stopped to eat and Seymour pulled out a bottle of champagne, but the cork wouldn't pop! Frozen to the bottle!

Barb began the Winter 46 at age 43 and finished at age 52.

EILEEN WHEELER

46er # 2543W

Few of my friends would believe that in another lifetime—1972—I climbed a high Adirondack peak and said "Never again!" I had signed on to a college outing club backpack up Marcy with no idea of what I was doing. I wore bell-bottom jeans and brand-new work boots, just out of the box. I found out a lot about blisters and mud and dense fog on a strange landscape. We didn't climb Marcy—as there was a bad storm. Instead we trudged through the spring mud and mist up into the clouds on Mt. Colden. I was more than exhausted; I made it up the last stretches by picking my legs up and putting them down with my hands. The leaders had not waited and I was afraid to rest and get left behind.

I began hiking in 1984, with an Adirondack Mountain Club climb of Lyon Mt. north of the High Peaks. But it was the following year, hiking Cascade and Porter with ADK, that I consider my mountain odyssey began—I knew I would someday climb them all. (I've completed three rounds.) Since then, I've climbed in Maine, New Hampshire, and Vermont, and after five years of summer climbing I began hiking the High Peaks in winter.

Winter 46ing, however, was not in my plans. I didn't think I was capable of it. Not only would I have to learn to winter camp, but I would need greater strength, endurance, new equipment, and other winter hikers with similar goals. It seemed a far-fetched scenario. Then along came a mild winter and friends were getting serious about bagging peaks. I tried it and my thinking shifted to "Well, maybe." The more winter peaks I did, the more I loved it and the more confidence I gained. I do love summer and fall because I can stay on the summits a long time, but I got so caught up in winter mountaineering, I hated to see winter end. Today the mountains are an integral part of me, a home away from home in any season.

Climbing the Winter 46 was an amazing adventure. Its rewards included increased physical strength and fitness (I was never healthier or stronger), incredible views (so clear and utterly beautiful!), satisfaction in personal accomplishment ("Wow, we really did it!"), and meeting great people who shared the winter mountain experience (or should I say obsession?). A like-minded group was what made my ultimate accomplishment possible. The members were not always the same, but the group always had the same commitment to teamwork and support for one another. I was part of a team and together we made it up and down these mountains.

I teach music full-time in a local elementary school, but worked part-time when my kids were young. I was eager to share my love of hiking and knowledge of nature with them and their scouting groups, and we took many short trips. By the time I was tackling peaks in winter, my family was accustomed to me heading to the Adirondacks on a Saturday or Sunday. There weren't that many overnights. They knew how important my mountain quest was to me and I hoped they didn't feel deserted. I involved my children as much as they were willing to be involved. My youngest, especially, agreed to hike with me—although it was never really her thing.

Unfortunately, as she was growing into her teens I took her on a couple of hikes that were too long and too much for her. Whenever I think about it I feel like apologizing all over again. Alas, my passion for hiking did not rub off on my children—at least not yet.

Then there were the usual testaments to the great time I'd had: aches, scrapes, bruises, and perhaps a blister or two. Maybe that wasn't the best advertisement. My family and non-hiking friends thought I was crazy to climb in the winter. My ex-husband would always ask, "What time shall I call the police if you're not back?" One evening I returned home while he was reading in his recliner. I entered the house with my gear on: balaclava, ski goggles, parka, ice ax, and pack. He looked up and quipped while feigning alarm, "Our leader's not here!"

After finishing my Winter 46, I couldn't wait to get into the mountains of Vermont, New Hampshire, and Maine to conclude what I'd started there. In August 1999, I finished my Northeast 111 on Flume Mt. in New Hampshire. My hiking appetite slowed after that, although I kept active in outdoor pursuits. The mountains had taken a toll on my knees. Further payment was exacted by a cross-country skiing accident in January 2001; I tore two ligaments and needed knee surgery. It took eight months to fully heal. I worked up to a solo hike up Marcy in October 2001. It was a wonderful trip even though I gave myself elbow tendonitis by over-using my poles to take weight off the knee. Moderation is not always the easiest thing to learn. My other hobbies, birding and nature study, keep me outdoors—things you can conveniently do while hiking and canoeing. Birding, especially, has become more and more captivating over time.

Winter 46ing is indeed a lesson in endurance and perseverance, pushing yourself even though you're exhausted and hurting. Through some of the toughest hiking I've ever done I learned a lot about my vulnerabilities, but mostly about my strengths. I leaned heavily on that strength and determination recently as I faced the challenge of breast cancer. I felt empowered by my experiences and tried to inject that into my getting through this new situation.

As of August 29, 2004, I started a new chapter in my life as Mrs. Wheeler. Tom and I couldn't think of a better place to get married than on top of a mountain. After all, the Adirondack Mountains are what brought us together; we'd met on an ADK winter trip up Algonquin and Iroquois. We chose Mt. Jo for its picturesque views and easy access for our guests, and because it it owned by the Adirondack Mountain Club of which Tom was now president. Weather, however, is unpredictable! Sure, we were used to being out in rain, but we couldn't ask our ministers—a husband and wife team—and our family and friends to put up with it. Not only did it rain, it periodically thundered and poured, so we settled for a ceremony by Heart Lake, at the foot of Mt. Jo. The spirit of the mountains was with us and will always be a part of us.

Skylight and Gray, January 14-16, 1996:

Fear of cold probably is the biggest reason more people don't climb or camp in winter. It certainly was the biggest reason why it took me so long to try winter camping. I have good reason to be wary—my circulation is poor; my hands and feet are often cold.

My first winter camping trip was across Flowed Lands to climb Gray and Skylight. We were to be out two nights and I hadn't even made it through the night in my backyard test run! It went down to zero the second night, 12° inside my three-season tent—which has since been replaced with one more suitable. Boiling the next day's water and putting the bottle in the foot of my sleeping bag/over-bag combo helped a lot. Sleeping in a hat, dry clothes, and socks that I'd wear the next day was critical. I also have come to use chemical heat packets quite a bit. On our Dix hike I even used them in my long johns to keep my buns warm! Investing in vapor-barrier socks and insulated over-boots further helped keep my feet warm on very cold days.

I learn something on every trip I take. A whiteout and thirty-five mph winds with higher gusts greeted us on Skylight. I took so long fussing with my hood above tree line that, by the time I was ready, the others were out of sight. Yelling got me nowhere because of the wind, so I waited. Eventually one of my companions came back to see where I was. A survival technique we learned is to plant our ski poles in the snow every so often to make holes to guide our return to tree line and trail. These holes get blown in more slowly than snowshoe tracks—though you have to scrutinize the ground to see them.

Esther, January 4, 1997:

This might have been my easiest trip of the Winter 46. There was not a lot of snow but we wore snowshoes for grip. Although we weren't in a hurry, keeping up with Dick Mooers was hard over the first two miles and 1,800 feet of ascent. The day was overcast so Dick, Tom Wheeler, and I didn't expect a view. At about 4,000 feet on the ridge, suddenly a magnificent view of Whiteface jumped out at us. We were above the clouds and the mountain looked huge! Totally unexpected. What made it even better was the cloud floating below and around it: a surreal vision. Untrailled Esther looked far away but was only forty-five minutes with a little blow-down to go under and over. Hoar frost and snow feathers on the trees looked so pretty: an added bonus to what we realized was becoming a magical trip. The views from Esther were incredible! We looked out at scores of island peaks, buoys in a soft sea of white. There was no wind; the air felt warm under blue skies. Dick, Tom, and I knew how privileged we were, each of us quietly taking in as much as possible. The mountain gods were smiling: an unforgettable day.

Dix, January 20, 1997:

You've got to have respect for Dix. No matter what the season—it's big. With a vertical ascent of 3,200 feet and a roundtrip distance of fourteen miles, it's a substantial day trip. Factor in ice, wind, precipitation, and deep snow, and you've got a pretty good challenge on your hands. John and Sue Omohundro, Tom Wheeler, and I started from Rt. 73 at 8 A.M. We were to catch up to friends who were ahead, breaking trail through six to eight inches of new snow. We caught them not far from the lean-to four and a half miles in; they expected us earlier. At least now there were more bodies to break trail. Beyond the slide at 5.8 miles, the terrain becomes steep and the real climbing begins, gaining 1,600 feet in the next mile. The narrow trail winds up the mountain over rocks, many of which were covered with ice under the deepening snow. I have a very physical memory of this section.

My turn in the lead often seemed to come in the steepest sections. The routine was: jam both poles ahead into the snow; take a step, kicking hard with the right snowshoe and then the left, hoping you got some purchase so you didn't slide back down; yank the poles out; lift them overhead and thrust them into the snow again. Unfortunately large quantities of ice meant lots of sliding back and very slow progress. An ice ax would have been helpful. People waiting behind the leader had a difficult time staying warm.

We put everything into it—we had to or we never would have made the top. On the socked-in summit ridge we laboriously worked our way through drifts up to four feet deep. Unbelievably, that last four tenths of a mile took us over an hour. The weather became more severe: tiny ice pellets flew by stinging our faces when we turned into the wind. On the summit Tom and I snapped quick pictures of each other and dashed for tree cover where the rest of our group was waiting.

It had taken us seven hours to reach the top, but would take a little more than four to get down. My preferred technique for descending is to sit down and slide where possible. It sure takes the stress off sore knee joints, not to mention that it's great fun. Quite a day! Probably my toughest trailed winter peak.

Blake and Colvin, February 9, 1997:

What a great day! We left at 5 A.M. with stars and -10°; then full sun. We're so lucky to have had such a day! Lake Road was icy— we walked half way before putting on our skis. Crossing the lake I was frustrated; my partner, Tom Wheeler, was out in front and I couldn't quite keep up with him. At the Carry Trail, we stashed our skis and put our boots in our packs so they wouldn't freeze. This took longer than expected as Tom's toes were bleeding from poorly fitting ski boots. No wonder he hadn't been waiting much for me— he wanted to cross the lake quickly so he could get those boots off. I wasn't going to see much of his usual cheery self that day. And he didn't need these peaks; he'd already done them in winter but wanted me to get them! I hoped he felt better in his hiking boots.

Up we went on one of the steepest trails in these mountains: 1,400 feet in a little over a mile. I thought with dread about coming down—much tougher for me. On top at 1 o'clock, we still had a long way to go and Tom wasn't feeling well; we cut back on our pace. Finally arriving on Colvin's summit at 2:40, I was elated! The views of the Great Range were gorgeous.

Our descent was not as bad as I feared, although I had to be vigilant and very careful to prevent sliding into trees or off the narrow, curving trail. Snow in the face and down the collar is unavoidable when you are grabbing onto trees to slow the effects of gravity. We were back at the car by 6:20. The stars and crescent moon were stunning; after dinner at the Noonmark Diner, the day was nicely capped off with an unexpected fireworks show in Saranac Lake.

Marshall, December 28, 1997:

First of all, we had a gorgeous day—couldn't have asked for better. Our group of five on this Laurentian Chapter ADK outing had the good fortune to catch up with a group from Albany ADK. Unlike hiking in the summer when we might not want to share the mountain, a few extra trailbreakers are a welcome sight in winter. Temperatures fell a bit as the sky cleared. After hiking from Tahawus to Flowed Lands, we crossed the frozen lake to save time, finding bitter cold winds sweeping over the openness. On the other side of a bridge we followed a stream to Herbert Brook and hiked in and out of the brook all the way up to the swamp and ridge above the slide. Here we took a bearing, but mostly followed leader Tom's advice to head straight into the woods before turning left.

The going was tough from here. I fell into a few spruce traps, including a good-sized one made much larger by my floundering around. I needed help getting out. It's exhausting to try untangling snowshoes from trees with all the snow that falls in on them, and then climb out of the hole you're in without finding another air pocket to swallow you. With my small Atlas snowshoes I was a magnet for finding these snow mines, though the shoes were great for climbing over packed surfaces. I'm not good at judging distances, but the last few hundred feet or so took about an hour through the thick forest. No one had signed the canister in more than a month.

A most satisfying memory stays with me from this trip. I have never seen crisper, clearer views from any peak in any season. The mountains stood out etched in stark relief against the deepest blue sky, while in the foreground dense snow-coated trees stood at attention in every direction. An exceptional day.

Saddleback, January 4, 1998:

Tom, Peter, and I barely made it up the icy road to the Garden parking lot on this overcast day. On the trail at 8:20 A.M., Tom and Peter were much more energetic than I—not unusual. It was 1.5 hours to the Interior Outpost. After the suspension bridge over John's Brook, the trail wasn't recently broken, but was softening due to several days of warm temperatures and rain. I kept sinking, so Peter led. About half a mile from the col we had a tricky crossing of Orebed Brook. Thankfully I had ski poles to help me negotiate the icy waters on a combination of rock, snow, and ice islands. Peter, unhappily, did not quite make it; he changed his wet socks when we reached the Gothics-Saddleback col. While we ate and I took pictures, Gothics dramatically appeared out of the clouds and mist. Impressive. Huge! And it's more impressive the higher up Saddleback one goes. "I can't believe I'm going to climb that one soon!" I exclaimed with lots of "Wows!" sprinkled in.

On top at 1:15 with glorious views, 30° temperatures, and no wind! Looking toward Whiteface, peaks were beautifully colored with pastel blues and violets. Some were ringed with cottony cloud-skirts. The three of us were thrilled and realized how privileged we were. "Nobody knows it's like this," Peter said quietly.

Basin, January 31, 1998—46th Peak:

Basin was memorable not only because it was the final hike of my Winter 46er quest, but because it had a greater than usual element of risk. Our approach was from Chicken Coop Brook, a new route for all eight of us—Tom Wheeler, Dick Mooers, Pete Hickey, David Meeker, Laurie Gooding, John Hartzell, Bob Juravich, and me. The going was not bad through an open woods, although as it got steeper I found my snowshoes slipping backwards in the loose snow; the steep slide above the brook made for slow progress as I had trouble holding a step without it collapsing under my weight.

After hiking for six hours, we gratefully reached the Saddleback-Basin col. Yay! Views were outstanding and kept getting better. The ascent up Basin was steep and more exposed than I remembered—my last trip was in 1992. When we came to the ledge that the High

Peaks' guidebook describes as "spectacular," I stopped in nervous disbelief. I didn't like the looks of it: a narrow path up a steep incline that traversed the edge of a long drop-off. I didn't trust the snow—there might have been ice under it so I tried to put a little more space between me and the drop-off, holding onto small trees. I knew coming down would be tough.

Soon I was standing on the rocky, open summit greeted by fabulous mountain views, bracing wind, and full sun such as it is at 3 o'clock in late January. Tom gave me a Winter 46er rocker patch. The celebration was too brief, but wind and cold could not be ignored. And we still had to get everyone down safely. I suddenly slipped near the edge of a drop-off. I couldn't get up. The snow was unconsolidated under me and there were no trees to hold on to. Dick carefully planted his snowshoes and extended his hand, while David had me grab the end of his ski pole with my other hand. I sure was glad to have friends nearby. In retrospect the ice ax I left in the car, because of its weight, would have been useful and should have been with me. The long, fast butt-slide above Chicken Coop Brook was fun! The hike took eleven hours, ten minutes. It was hard to believe I'd reached a goal that had once seemed so impossible. I'm very aware it was the team effort that made the Winter 46 possible. It was a great adventure!

Eileen began the Winter 46 at age 38 and finished at age 46.

MARY LOU RECOR

46er # 2214W

Winter hiking was inevitable for me. I was a passionate three-season hiker, finishing the Adirondack 46 in 1987 then moving on to hike in Vermont, New Hampshire, and Maine. In winter I cross-country skied until hiking seeped into ski season. My only obstacle was a husband who believed winter hiking was synonymous with misery, short dark days, waist-deep snowdrifts, and cold. He wasn't interested, and so we skied…a lot. Divorce in 1996 brought a reluctant freedom for me. At thirty-nine, with time on my hands, I could either sit home feeling sorry for myself or pursue my goal. I've gone on to climb all 116 peaks over 4,000 feet in the northeast in winter, though without the same sense of urgency or kinship I felt while climbing the 46.

I lead outings for the Green Mountain Club, including beginning backpacking and winter hiking workshops exclusively for women. I am past president of the Burlington Section and currently edit their newsletter. Twice yearly I write a column for the "Long Trail News" and am now writing a monthly column for "Vermont Sports Today." I assumed the presidency of the Adirondack 46ers in the spring of 2003 and through-hiked the Appalachian Trail that year. I have hiked the Northville-Placid Trail twice and the Long Trail once.

Climbing the Winter 46 has left me with a passel of memories: putting myself at the mercy of a local man with a shovel when my car slid into a snowbank on Corey's Road after a long day on the Sewards; watching sunset from the summit of Esther and then skiing down the Whiteface Veterans Memorial Highway by headlamp; wading across Indian Pass Brook and climbing Street and Nye with wet socks; soloing Sawteeth; basking in windless days on Haystack and Algonquin. Loneliness, friendship, tears, laughter, apprehension, confidence, humility, pride, challenge, accomplishment. Determination.

'…And miles to go before I sleep."

Allen, March 9, 1996:

A mutual acquaintance introduced me to Wil Desbiens, who gave me the names and phone numbers of two group leaders both of whom were climbing Allen Mountain the last weekend of that winter— nineteen miles round-trip. Sobering. Well, I thought, this will be a test and if I can climb Allen, I can climb the rest. I called the first leader who was polite but firm that I wasn't welcome to join them. I don't blame him. They knew nothing of me and even my dubious "stair climber" credentials couldn't convince them. My second call to Carl Rosenthal was more encouraging; he told me he and his fiancée, Jadwiga, couldn't be responsible for me but I could tag along. Maybe he believed I'd think better of the whole thing and stay home.

My alarm went off at 3:30 the morning of the hike and I pulled into the trailhead parking area three hours later, just as Carl and Jadwiga were starting off. They must have wondered what kind of dope they'd saddled themselves with, one who couldn't even get there on time. After a few hastily exchanged words they headed down the trail into the cold, gray dawn. I was so completely alone. I thought about my soft, cozy bed. If I continued to hike in winter there would be more mornings like this. How easy to get back into my still-warm car and go home, forget the whole thing. It wasn't as though Carl and Jadwiga were counting on me; I was merely a tag-a-long. I opened the trunk and strapped on my snowshoes.

I caught up with them at the site of the former Twin Brooks Lean-to. We walked together from there, talking about our goals, our lives, our mutual acquaintances. Skylight Brook was frozen solid and we crossed with no thought of the raging torrent it would soon become. We scrambled up the last steep pitch, digging in with our snowshoe claws, to find four men seated around the canister. They were friendly as we passed the logbook, each signing our names. One of them remarked on my frosted lashes and eyebrows. Mindful of the long slog back, I followed Carl and Jadwiga down the icy slope; I parted from them four miles later at the lean-to site where they stopped to eat and rest.

The approaching dusk dropped the temperature below freezing; five miles to go. I fantasized about soaking in a hot bath and then snuggling into a warm bed. I was exhausted, hungry, alone, and discouraged. I considered secreting my snowshoes among the trees and retrieving them the next summer. I hated their cold metal. I hated the weight of my pack. I hated the remoteness of Allen. I hated my ex-husband. I felt like crying. Why had I gotten myself into this? Relief flooded through me as I finally caught sight of my little gray car in the darkness, comforting in its familiarity. Well, I thought, you've climbed Allen so you can climb the rest. Besides, I had nine months to reconsider. I met John Jaeger while volunteering to answer telephones for Vermont Public Radio. We started talking about winter hiking; he had climbed a few mountains in Vermont and I...well, I had climbed Allen. We teamed up in the 1996-97 season to climb Giant, Rocky Peak Ridge, the Wolf Jaws, Armstrong, Couchsachraga, and Panther.

Panther and Couchsachraga, January 1, 1997:

I'd planned to climb Mt. Washington today, but -17° and seventy mph winds neatly squelched my obsession; the idea of climbing the Santanoni Range took its place. My rationalization went something like, "even if it's windy we'll be in the trees most of the time." The problem was we lingered too long over breakfast—at seventeen below that's easy to do—and were an hour late getting to the trailhead. Only Wil Desbiens showed up, who felt it was too cold to hike in such a remote area with so small a group; that left John Jaeger and me—not an inspiring picture. We set off on the creaking snow. It didn't take long to warm up, even for me, a person who wears mittens from September to May. We did have some difficulty putting on crampons, but after moderate cursing (a method I've found remarkably effective in some circumstances), we got them on.

The day turned out to be absolutely gorgeous! We spent time vainly looking for the herd path to Couchsachraga, became frustrated and climbed Panther. Flush from the success of achieving one trailless summit, we tackled Couchie again and made it. Back at Times Square we watched the sun wane over Santanoni. The mountain will be there another day.

Cliff, January 8, 1997:

We drove to the remote trailhead at Tahawus for the long hike to Cliff Mountain. We crossed on the ice at Flowed Land and hiked up the frozen Opalescent to the abandoned Sanford Lake-Marcy Trail, where we followed snowshoe prints. I left my pack below the steep section not far from the summit to make the final distance to the top easier. The mercury had not risen above zero; we signed the canister logbook quickly before hurrying back down. I learned a valuable lesson—I discovered that some hungry varmint had ransacked my pack, stealing my peanut butter and jam sandwich on baguette, dried cranberries, and chocolate-covered raisins. Ed Robertson once told me, "She who leaves her pack dies." Good advice.

As we crossed back over Flowed Lands the sun was setting and the cold was unrelenting. Many people were spending the night in the lean-tos, hardier souls than I! Even with chemical hand warmers and expedition-quality mittens, my fingers were frigid. I suffer with Raynaud's Syndrome, a condition in which my fingers and toes turn white in cold temperatures as the blood rushes to my body's core to keep it warm, leaving my extremities pale and useless. I lose dexterity and the simplest tasks become difficult, like pinch-releasing fastex buckles. Over time I have learned to compensate by taking only brief rest stops, eating regularly, wearing well-insulated mittens and packing hand warmers. Even then, sometimes the day is just too cold.

A three-quarter moon rose above the trees reflecting off snowy branches and casting evergreen shadows across the trail; it was magical. We walked without artificial light. Tahawus always seems a lonely place, especially so in winter. By now my hands were so cold and stiff, John had to help me put the key in the door lock and remove my snowshoes. Otherwise, I might have become the first person to drive a standard transmission while wearing Sherpa snowshoes.

Marcy, Skylight, and Gray, February 9, 1997:

Carl and Jadwiga Rosenthal drove from Connecticut; Ed Robertson from Massachusetts; Wil Desbiens and Claudia Warren from New York; and John Jaeger and I from Vermont to meet for what was to became my favorite hike in my quest for the Winter 46. At first light, we left the Adirondack Loj and reached the summit of Marcy around 10 A.M. to enjoy a crystal view and fierce wind—a mere thirty-second summit. From there we followed a ski track down toward Gray.

The bushwhack was a breeze until the third person in line, who happened to be me, dropped into a spruce trap—fortunately only up to my waist. We came up with the "third person rule" of spruce traps: the first two people in a group are able to cross without falling through and it's the third who must suffer. No reason, it's just a law of nature. We headed toward Skylight; from the summit we marveled at massive stark-white Marcy, bold against intense blue sky. I was inspired, almost giddy, as I began my quick glissade back down the trail. My body gained momentum as I ran, sliding, laughing. Suddenly my crampon caught on a branch just beneath the surface and I sprawled face first into the snow, my arms buried up to my elbows. I struggled to sit up, looking around for witnesses. None but the fragile vegetation. My pride was safe.

We regrouped at Four Corners and hiked down to Lake Colden, crossing it as the late afternoon sun glowed out of the west. Our elongated shadows reached over the white, frozen surface to the other end of the lake and the path home. Only the soft creaking of snowshoes against crust broke the late day silence. John, Wil, Paul Plante, and I made plans to climb the trailless Dixes later that month. The rumors among the winter hiking community were that the snow was so deep in the Elk Lake area that it was taking two, three, even four attempts to summit. Did that deter us? Absolutely not.

Macomb, South Dix, East Dix, and Hough, February 23, 1997:

The previous week the Adirondacks had undergone a thaw-refreeze cycle that consolidated the snow and hardened the surface. We walked in to the base of the Macomb slide on frozen crust, sinking only an inch or two even without snowshoes. It was easy going for a while until we were about three-fourths of the way up the slide. To that point I could kick small steps in the snow with my boots. John had gone ahead without needing crampons. I, on the other hand, was not so agile. I hated my crampons and avoided wearing them until I had no choice. They never went on easily, especially in cold temperatures, and once on I didn't trust them to stay secure.

So there I was, hanging by my toes on the Macomb slide, unable to go farther up or retreat down. Stuck. My knees started to shake as the precariousness of my position hit me. My calves tightened, attempting to hold me steady. My heart raced and my breath quickened. While I prayed for the strength to keep going, Wil and Paul sidled across the slope to help. They supported me as I tentatively bent down to strap on my snowshoes. Then Paul insisted I hang onto a rope while he held the other end as we made our way to the top. I was humbled.

From Macomb we bushwhacked to South and then East Dix, still among my favorites. The first time I climbed here was on a blind date arranged by a hiking friend. She assured me that the guy was in shape and willing to climb all four peaks. We made it to the top of Macomb when he decided he'd had enough and insisted I continue on while he waited there for me. So I did. Five hours later I rejoined him on Macomb. His first words to me were, "I was worried about you, little lady." Needless to say that was our last date, but it was also my first solo trailless peaks.

I love the walk along the ridge, with East Dix the reward at the end.

It has always seemed so remote to me, especially when approached from Elk Lake. There is a subtlety about East Dix. Most tourists don't decide while driving up the Interstate to climb it the way they might Dix or Giant. It takes planning. They don't tell friends at home, "I climbed East Dix" the way they would Marcy or Whiteface. East Dix requires effort; it's a place to be alone, a haven for the introvert.

Paul and Wil had already climbed Hough; John and I discussed whether to continue on. I sensed Wil had doubts about my judgment, but we took out the map and set a course despite his misgivings; we climbed Hough without incident. The descent via Lillian Brook was steeper than I had imagined. Where I could, I slid cautiously on my butt using my snowshoe crampons for braking. At times I slid my pack down ahead of me to make my descent easier. What would happen if I slipped and hurt myself? How much time would pass before John reached Elk Lake Road and returned with rescuers? How would I feel sitting here hurt in the cold for hours—probably overnight— alone? I was relieved when the terrain leveled and I could relax.

At home, afterward, I took apart my crampons, completely removing the leather straps. I discovered they had been improperly and illogically laced, which was why I always had so much trouble securing them to my boots. I spent an hour reconfiguring the straps. Now before every winter hiking season I sit in my living room and practice.

Haystack, February 1, 1998:

Haystack is one mountain I agonized over. Next to Algonquin I figured it would be my biggest challenge. Because these are open, rocky summits and I'd be spending a lot of time above tree line; I wanted calm days when there was more snow than ice. Today was the perfect day. Wil Desbiens, John Jaeger, and I left the Adirondack Loj at 6:45 A.M. The six-mile trail to the summit wasn't broken out and we had some fun backsliding on the snow-covered ice. But from Little Haystack to the summit of Haystack, the going was relatively easy, mostly snow and bare rock. After all the horror stories I'd heard, this trip turned out to be a real pleasure. With only a slight breeze blowing on the summit, we had time to enjoy great views of Marcy, Skylight, Basin, and the range. I couldn't have had a better day!

Finishing on Porter and Cascade is anticlimactic, they're so tame compared with some of the other peaks; I saved these for my final peaks because I could climb them any time. If I could have chosen the best hike to finish it would have been the climb of Marcy, Gray, and Skylight. I think everyone feels a bit let down when they reach a goal they've been working toward for a long time. I've made good friends; spending time hiking with people whose company I enjoy is as important as the challenge of reaching the summit. So some of the letdown comes from knowing I won't see some of those people again, or not in the same circumstances with the same sense of common purpose.

Mary Lou began the Winter 46 at age 39 and finished at age 41.

24

PEGGY MACKELLAR

46er #2857W

I was born March 18, 1958, the only girl between two boys. I rarely did anything athletic as a child since I was very involved in my church, academic activities, and practicing piano. I spent summers at my grandparents in a rural area of Vermont and developed an appreciation of natural beauty. Some summers our family would venture to Acadia National Park in Maine and camp.

I recall a glorious trip across the United States when I was twelve, when my family visited many National Parks. At the Grand Canyon I thought, "Someday I would like to walk that," as I looked down the Plateau Trail. Our family camped at Zion National Park and went on a day hike up a trail with many switchbacks and a long stretch to a viewpoint; my dad and I were the only ones in our family who made it all the way. Since then, I've hiked in New England, the Grand Canyon, the Smoky Mountains, and in British Columbia, Alberta, Quebec, and Nova Scotia. The Parc de la Gaspésie on the Gaspé Peninsula is especially good.

I work as dental hygienist for a general dental office and one day a week as a public health dental hygienist providing care to elementary students. I still have music for a hobby, occasionally singing at weddings, playing the piano, and playing weekly with a hand-bell choir. I'm a "renaissance woman" in the variety of my interests: canoeing, cross-country and downhill skiing, water-skiing, baking, gardening, basic construction, and home renovation. I look for opportunities to use my French and often meet hikers from Quebec. Friends remark that my socializing is seasonal. In summer it's too hot, buggy, and crowded in the woods so I hike every weekend I can during fall and winter; since I need to get up very early, I leave events early or don't go.

I'm currently a director of the Forty-Sixers Club, member of the Adirondack Mt. Club, the Adirondack Nature Conservancy, and Azure Mt. Friends, the group that restored that fire tower. When I started climbing trailless mountains and talking about the 46 High Peaks, I'm not sure what my family thought! We had a saying: "You can do hard things if you try." At times hiking conditions are "hard" and I don't necessarily enjoy it, but I know I can get by this "hardship" if I try.

My hiking experiences started with a first memorable backpack: An acquaintance complained that his girlfriend wouldn't go camping or hiking, declaring: "Women don't go backpacking." I replied, "Yes, they do; I'll go with you to prove it." And when a close friend suddenly died, I decided that this hike might be just what I needed to help me heal my pain. A steady drizzle began as we started on the trail, but Indian Pass was beautiful—the grayness made the red, gold, and orange of the leaves more stunning. My hiking companion went way ahead of me, I felt alone, my thoughts on my friend's funeral. Climbing up through the mud and difficult rocks was a severe mental struggle. My companion was waiting on the summit rock and then quickly left me behind again; the "death march" continued until we reached the Adirondack Loj. I was too tired to even eat; I crawled into my sleeping bag and didn't move again.

I declared that there must be another way back to the car! My friend said he knew one; I crammed my blistered, swollen feet into soggy boots. Hiking at my maximum speed, he still quickly left me behind. Breathless, I finally reached the Wright trail junction where he waited. Without my pack I decided that I could climb the half-mile to the summit; from Wright I saw what looked like ant-sized hikers crawling up a huge mountain nearby. My spirits plummeted when my friend explained that we were going up that mountain, Algonquin. I was abandoned until tree line. Thick clouds had moved in. He'd go ahead to a cairn or blaze; when I arrived he'd search for the next one. Other (male) hikers on the summit inquired whether "he was trying to kill me." On the steep trail down to Lake Colden my toes smashed into the front of my boots—but I was thankful not to be rubbing my heel blisters. The rest of the hike is a blank.

An amazing thing happened after this ordeal. Five toenails fell off, my heels didn't heal from the blisters for weeks, I couldn't walk normally up and down stairs—but I started asking where to buy backpacking equipment and how to join the Adirondack Mountain Club. How could this be? That weekend transformed me; I had found the power within to do things I wouldn't have thought myself capable of. I had learned that I was not a quitter and discovered the healing power of nature and hiking in particular. It is a powerful thing to realize that your limitations are not greater than you thought they were. It is reassuring to have a powerful tool to cope with the stresses of life that is as simple as putting one foot in front of the other.

Within two years I moved to Plattsburgh, NY, to be closer to the High Peaks and finished my remaining peaks. In winter I hiked Cascade and Porter, then Wright and Phelps, and conquered Colden on a terribly scary day. I became well-equipped for seriously attempting the Winter 46.

Climbing the Winter 46 was an adventure and a challenge and a pain in the derriere too, at times. I discovered my inner strength to be greater than I had previously thought. There's a close correlation between weather and my frustration level, also between low blood sugar and frustration levels. I'm no longer intimidated by darkness or cold, though I give winter conditions respect. There is little or no margin for error in winter, but I have confidence in my ability to make correct judgments. I found that the bonds of winter friendship go incredibly deep, with each of us helping the others to achieve. It was an exciting adventure from which I have derived enormous pleasure.

Colden, March 12, 1994:

My most frightening winter experience was when I climbed Colden. I had very limited winter experience and so made several crucial errors in judgment. Mark Goulet needed Colden and wanted to climb from the lake. It was overcast and light snow was falling as we crossed the ice on Avalanche Lake. The summit was shrouded in clouds. We struggled with trail breaking, deep snow, and steepness for three hours! Nearing tree line I became increasingly nervous— the winds had picked up and it was snowing hard—but Mark insisted that we go forward.

The conditions had deteriorated to an almost total whiteout. On an earlier trip to Colden, I felt like I would have fallen all the way down to the lake if I made one wrong step; today my snowshoe crampon slipped and I slid eight feet down the open rock; it took time to summon the courage to keep going. We changed to instep crampons for better traction, but removing our mittens was dangerous—our fingers were chilled by the wind and one of my mittens almost blew away. We were unsure of the way across the open ledges due to the whiteout. We fell into drifted-in depressions and got snow up under our shells and down our mittens. I couldn't stand up in the wind any more and crawled across the summit.

Just about when total hysteria was overtaking me, I looked through my tears and glimpsed a cross-country skier a short distance in front of us! The swirling snow obscured him but I was suddenly hopeful that my body wouldn't be found in the spring. We crawled as fast as we could toward the spot where he'd stood and barely made out tracks going back down to Lake Arnold and safety. We squinted against the driving snow to try to follow them; they sometimes were already blown in but we made it over the north summit and down into the trees. After eating we became almost giddy as we butt-slid down. This harrowing experience has affected my Winter 46er attempts; I will not go above tree line when the weather is extreme in any season. It is not a risk worth taking.

Allen, December 21, 1996:

I consider this trek my real start of the Winter 46. That was the day I fell in with "The Bad Crowd" and their influence took hold of my life for the next three winters! Mike Bush had contacted me about doing the Winter 46 and said the first hike would be Allen, "to get it out of the way before conditions got impossible." The other six hikers were considerably more experienced. Allen took twelve hours in summer and I could only imagine how grueling it would be now! I almost turned back at the Allen Brook waterfall because I already hurt so much; but Marta Bolton encouraged me gently, saying, "You can do it; we'll help you." Her encouragement when I was scared on the steep slide was also invaluable and her sense of humor when Bill's altimeter proved to be off by 500 feet kept me going. At the summit I was hardly capable of even smiling for a photo at the can.

A lone hiker came up and let out a "yeee-hoo!" It was Mike McLean, who summitted thirty-six of the 46 peaks with me in winter. The influence of The Bad Crowd spread over him, too. Thanks to his "babysitting" me with a slow pace and keeping me distracted with good conversation, I somehow made it back to the trailhead. I had Vic Pomerville's car keys and wanted to warm up the car, but my legs were so weak that I couldn't climb into the driver's seat to do it! I managed to crawl into the back and sat, comatose, until the others returned.

"How are you?" Marta asked, so nicely that I let a few tears roll down my cheeks. I replied, "I hurt from the roots of my hair to my toenails. I don't know if I've ever felt this bad in my whole entire life." "I'm going to see a doctor tomorrow," she replied with her characteristic humor, "to have my head examined!" She's on her fifth round of the Winter 46, and said she still found this fourteen and a half hour hike grueling. I slept for most of the next two days and an anti-inflammatory prescription is all that made it possible for me to even move my leaden legs. A week later the group invited me to go to Santanoni but I still could hardly walk!

I arranged my schedule to hike one day mid-week as well as weekends. My winter skills and tolerance, physical strength, and stamina increased to the point where I could trail-break with the best of them. It seems ridiculous and humorous and impossible that I would climb Allen again on the last day of winter! We went for a love of friends (two were 46ing), adventure, affection for the mountains, personal challenge, and our psychic need to be in the peaks winter or summer.

Lower Wolf Jaw, January 1, 1997:

I have finally recovered enough from the horror of my hike to Allen that I am able to walk and hike again. I was looking forward to an easy day with only one relatively short peak on the agenda. I decided to hike in spite of the -21° temperature, and was surprised and pleased to discover that, dressed properly, I wasn't cold in this extreme temperature. On the summit the temperature showed a balmy 18°, a temperature inversion where it is colder in the valleys.

I tried eating my trail mix directly out of the baggie by putting my face into the Cheerios, chocolate chips, etc. but got a Cheerio stuck on the end of my runny nose! After that I didn't have to share anymore! I got my first taste of butt sliding (and the bruises that come with it!) on the descent. The best way to start a New Year is not by staying up late and drinking, but by going to bed early and going on a wonderful hike on January 1.

Macomb, January 4, 1997:

Macomb is probably my favorite of the Winter 46 and high on my list in any season because of the slide and its fabulous views. It's easier to ascend the slide with instep crampons than it is on loose gravel. The cloud ceiling was too low to get views—then suddenly we climbed above the clouds and the High Peaks rose up through them like islands in a gray sea! As we climbed higher the clouds dissipated entirely. We celebrated Vic Pomerville's Winter 46 peak.

On our descent, I had a mini-adventure on the ice flow just above the rock face at the top of the slide. Having little experience with my instep crampons, I lost my footing, fell down hard, slid past Vic and stopped only by grabbing a death-hold on a small spruce. Had I continued to slide I would have had a nasty fall over the ten-foot rock face and who knows where I would have stopped. I was very cautious around ice after that. We slid quickly on our butts down the snow-covered slide. What fun! In early January, the snow may not be as deep as you wish it were and you may have interesting bruises to prove this! When the snow is deep, the first person down gets so much snow piling up between the legs that it actually stops you; the next sliders have increasingly exhilarating slides!

Tabletop, Jan. 24, 1997:

I winter camped at Marcy Dam when I first climbed Tabletop. We used a North Face VE-25 tent, Quallofil sleeping bags rated to -20°, Thermarests and a Whisperlite stove. We hadn't known about snow stakes and although we'd tied our tent to a tree, it blew over and was upside down when we returned. We couldn't get a fire started; we learned later that you need sterno or bits of fake fireplace logs because the wood is frozen. I also learned that my propane Bluet stove won't work when it's too cold out. Proper layering of clothes kept me comfortably warm even if I did look like the Michelin Man (temps were 0-10°). A deck of cards provided entertainment, with a single candle lantern hung from the ceiling for light. Outhouses don't smell in the winter! There are no bugs, less people, and wildlife is more easily seen. We've seen mink, pine martens, fishers, snowshoe hares, owls, and the friendly chickadees that try to share your oatmeal while you are trying to eat it yourself! Bears don't steal your food since they're hibernating.

The Tabletop herd path is free from the obstacles of summer such as rocks, roots, and mud holes. We saw many rabbit tracks, but no bunnies. We noticed where a mouse had been plucked from the snow as he crossed an open area—his trail ended where the bird's wingtips had brushed the snow. We arrived at the canister in waist-high snow with Marcy gleaming in the sun! This is one of the many pleasures of winter hiking, seeing views others cannot imagine; in summer this summit is viewless unless you climb a small spruce. While sitting on the snow you can see the phenomenal view of Marcy in winter splendor, the Great Range, Whiteface, Colden, the MacIntyre Range—peaks by now my friends—stretched out in glory.

Marcy, February 15, 1997:

I was very nervous about the weather, which was cloudy with light snow and wind that reminded me strongly of how the terror on Mt. Colden had started. I tried to get the group to change plans and stay below tree line, but they were confident that I could make it with them even if conditions weren't ideal. At Indian Falls I was dismayed to see darker clouds moving in while the snow fell harder; I should've gone back. Again, The Bad Crowd reassured me and encouraged me to continue. We had to break trail through deep and drifty snow starting a mile past Indian Falls. The balsams looked wonderful with icicles hanging on almost every branch. The sun made occasional appearances but then disappeared and the wind picked up, causing the falling snow to go sideways in a perfect whiteout. My worst fears were being realized.

We huddled together at the Phelps junction and Mike Bush used his compass to determine the direction; I knew he was extremely competent and I trusted him completely as he carefully explained how he had figured the heading at home and how we reverse it to return to exactly the same spot in spite of the whiteout. We started up the trail single file, with three people in front and three behind me. Conditions had deteriorated so badly that the first person couldn't see the seventh even though we were on each other's heels. I kept my head bowed to protect my face from the wind and blowing granular snow, but also to hide my tears of fear, which I couldn't control. It was sometimes impossible to tell the sky from the ground or to judge how far up or down I was stepping.

Somehow, everyone made it to the top and Mike McLean found the summit plaque on the snow-covered rock. We took pictures, and in one I look like I'm flying through clouds—you can't see the summit rock I'm standing on; an ice chunk is blowing by in front of Mike McLean! Thank goodness for the compass bearing, because our tracks were completely blown away. The descent was cautious; it would have been easy to slip and fall off a cliff due to the limited visibility. The compass heading was checked several times and surely enough we did return to the exact same spot, as Mike Bush had promised. Even with this success, I still change my hiking plans if it's snowing or the summits are shrouded in clouds.

Seward, Donaldson, and Emmons, March 19, 1997:

Everyone knows that it's rare to get the three Sewards in a daytrip and that if you do get them it takes fourteen to fifteen hours. They are all wrong—try doing it with us. John Bennett and Mike

McLean put snowmobiles on their pickups to get to the trailhead, but to our surprise we drove down a well-plowed road. It was the beginning of as smooth a day as anyone could wish for. We started at 6 o'clock on a hard-packed trail and reached Donaldson's summit via Calkins Brook at 9:30! And Emmons at 10:30! The day was extremely sunny, deep blue skies, icicles hanging off the balsams that made them look like decorated Christmas trees, and temperatures of 25-30° on the summits. The High Peaks, though far away, were spectacular.

Mike led most of the time because he's "impatient" by his own definition, but we tried to get him to rest after he fell into his tenth spruce trap. At Seward's summit at 1 o'clock, we were disconcerted to discover the can was buried. After futile digging, Marta remembered that if she went off the summit away from Donaldson and came back up, the can was practically in her face. John hit the can with his pole. We tied surveyor's tape on the tree. We were back to the cars by 4:35; Marta thinks this ten-hour, thirty-five-minute trip may be the fastest time to climb the three Sewards anyone has ever done. We were impressed with ourselves and proud of what strong winter hikers we have become this year.

Saddleback and Basin, December 27, 1997:

Our group had seven women and only three men on this high-adventure day. Sally Hoy and Bill Johnson carried climbing ropes; I had purchased full crampons just for the occasion. We put on full crampons for the descent down the cliffs, and I actually felt more secure than in summer. About halfway down, we hung a fifty-foot rope to aid us for the ascent later. The snow was incredibly deep as we slowly made our way up Basin; trail markers, when we could find them, were at snow level! We were off the trail and I think we missed the scariest part of the narrow trail along the cliff.

We struggled back up the cliffs of Saddleback. My straps had gotten clogged with snow, the buckles had frozen and I found it impossible to tighten them enough; the right crampon fell off several times and eventually I used it in my right hand instead of on my foot! When I got to the rope I had great difficulty navigating that section—without the rope it would have been impossible. About half way up there was an expanse of smooth open bedrock with a small crack under an overhang—on the left side. I wrapped the rope around my wrist. Panic gripped me as my crampon-less right foot kept slipping and I clung to the rope with one hand. I rested to prepare for a more energetic push and took several deep breaths; with all my strength and gumption I hauled myself up, hand over hand, using my left crampon whenever I could. Connie grabbed my wrist to help me up the last part. Even the two college kids and the men had a tough time. This section of trail is not to be taken lightly at any season and proper gear is a MUST in winter.

Dix, February 18, 1998—46th Peak:

Marta Bolton, Mike Bush, John Bennett, Gary Mavis, Mike McLean, and I started up to Round Pond at 6:15 A.M. We encountered sleet, wet snow, wind, and hail the size of peppercorns; the High Peaks were shrouded in thick clouds. Mike Bush suggested that the slide ascent was easier than the trail—but then we had a twenty-minute bushwhack back to the trail. My pack caught constantly because I'd attached a rolled-up foam pad for Mike McLean's swimsuit Winter 46 pose; he lay on a beach towel on the rocky summit in his swim trunks and sunglasses. The wind had such force that it stung the face, but it didn't squelch our exuberance. Mike Bush opened champagne and Marta pulled out Winter 46er Rocker patches.

Len Grubbs and the Winter Outdoor Leadership group reported that the trail was very icy, so we bushwhacked back through the thick stuff and butt-slid down the open slide, whooping loudly. It has been an extremely meaningful experience to hike with these true blue friends. Perhaps it's because of the extreme nature of the conditions that bonds go so deep and are so pure.

Peggy began the Winter 46 at age 32 and finished at age 39.

25

ANN SPENCER

46er # 3179W

Mountain hiking for me didn't begin until after we moved to Potsdam, NY, in 1971. As I was growing up, my mother moved us to our cottage in Northern Michigan for the summer, where we swam, rowed tubby wooden boats, fished, and did all the summer things. In the winter we'd go sledding and downhill skiing without the benefit of a tow. During my freshman year in college, I hiked in New Hampshire. The next summer I worked as a camp counselor and in the fall switched my major to Physical Education. After graduation, I taught until our twins were born. After that I stayed active teaching adult education fitness and Swedish gymnastics classes.

As a young family living in Lexington, Kentucky, we started hiking. A favorite getaway was the Red River Gorge area. Activities then were swimming, rowing, sailing, downhill skiing, canoeing, dance, aerobics, and cross-country skiing. When we moved to Northern New York and joined ADK, it was great to find a group of people with similar interests. We still camped and hiked with our four children and as they became active in scouting, sports, and church groups, we did too. I was busy with community and church volunteerism, and found time to earn a nursing degree and work as a Hospice Nurse. As the children left for college we became much more active with ADK. In the late 1980s, I began hiking and skiing with the Clarkson University Women's hiking group. I was so enthralled with some of the places we'd visit that I could hardly wait to take my husband there on the weekends. It was from these experiences that mountain hiking became an important part of my life. Armond and I became 46ers in 1992.

Winter climbing has been a grand adventure, and I've always said that as long as it was fun I'd keep climbing. By 1992, we had climbed five peaks in winter and earned our "V" badges. I was quite proud, but little did I know what was to come! We kept on doing winter hikes for the pure enjoyment of it, and actually it wasn't until 1998 after I had climbed almost all of them, that finishing the Winter 46 became important to me—and then only after we'd climbed Allen.

When Armond and hiking companions did the trip in 1997 without me (I had an ADK meeting in Lake George), I was sure I wouldn't finish. After all, who wanted to go back to Allen? Armond and I have hiked together on all the 46, done most of them twice and some several times, but we would never have become Winter 46ers without the help of our good friends, John and Susan Omohundro, who went back to so many peaks for the third and fourth time to climb them with us.

I served a six-year term on the Board of Governors of the Adirondack Mountain Club from 1993 through 1998, and also served on the Executive Committee for the last three years of that term. This means I spent a lot of Saturdays in Lake George. Fitting in hikes with consideration of the weather, work, and meetings took some doing. Our minister joked about our being "Foul Weather Christians," because if the weather was nice on Sunday we'd be out on a hike somewhere.

I've been asked, given my "I'll do it as long as it's fun," "Were they all fun?" Each in its own way was special. Climbing Sawteeth too soon after a bout with the flu made that peak most difficult, and doing a very steep bushwhack up South Dix while I was sick with a cold was hard. Donaldson and Emmons had fresh, wet snow with a great distance to cover off trail. A first hike of the season, Seymour on December 21, was more than I wanted to finish—the mountain was crowded with hikers ascending and descending, my knee hurt, and I decided to turn around. Redfield was also easier than I expected, with the trail broken out. Dix was more difficult than I remembered—the last steep mile was very hard in extremely deep snow. My favorite is Colden! Among other favorites are Haystack, Gothics, Armstrong, Allen, and Phelps.

Big Slide, March 17, 1989:

Big Slide on St. Patrick's Day 1989, was my first winter peak. I was extremely excited to be asked to be the fourth with three other women. The day was typical for March, overcast and spitting snow, but the weather didn't dampen the excitement. We drove up to the parking area called the Garden after coffee at the Noonmark and strapped on our snowshoes. I had rented mine from the Outing Club at Clarkson.

Almost immediately we were into ice. After a hard fall, one of my companions switched to crampons. After I had trouble on a rise, I switched to my rented crampons and spent the rest of the day in them. I remember sending pictures of "Mom in Crampons" to my grown-up sons, and our daughter who was home on a college break couldn't believe what her mother was doing. It was a real thrill to make the climb. We did have to scout around in a birch forest to find the trail and, on the return trip, we were all glad that we didn't act on the idea of making a loop down to Johns Brook. The views were limited, lunch was eaten in a hurry, but I was hooked. Three of the four of us have finished the Winter 46.

Colden, February 27, 1993:

My absolute favorite climb was Colden. We chose to climb the new slide on Colden's east face. It was crisp and clear and Marcy looked close enough to reach out and touch. It was a beautiful day as we started out on skis, carrying snowshoes and boots. Carrying the snowshoes wasn't a problem, but the Sorels are bulky and hung outside the pack. We were able to ski to Marcy Dam where we stashed the skis, changed boots, and started on snowshoes.

Our plan was to climb the east slide and descend the yellow trail to Lake Arnold; we checked at Lake Arnold and the trail was broken out; we continued down to the base of the slide, losing 500' of ascent on the way. The day got better and better, with brilliant Adirondack blue sky and wonderful sunshine. The climb was steep and we took turns breaking trail. At the top of the slide it became very steep, so we appreciated the rope John tied to a twig in the snow.

Reaching the summit was a real high. We marveled at the views, marveled at two young men who came up the Trap Dike, and generally reveled in the feeling of being up here. When it was time to start down, we found a yellow marker or two and then they seemed to disappear. They were under the snow! After we searched for the trail toward Lake Arnold with little success and after a spruce hole swallowed my 6'3" husband, we decided to retreat from that direction and head for another.

There was a trail broken out heading north. We figured that someone had bushwhacked down to Avalanche Lake, so we followed. After awhile the track started to turn and turn and head uphill, and after an hour we found ourselves back on the summit. We finally headed down the red trail to Lake Colden.

We hit the lake just at dark, but by the light of a sliver of a moon and a star-filled sky we walked back out to Marcy Dam and carried our skis back to the car at South Meadow without using flashlights. This was the last time we started so late but not the last time we finished well after dark. The only real problem with finishing late is that in some parts of the Adirondacks, finding a place to eat dinner seems as tough as finding the canister.

Sawteeth, March 5, 1995:

Climbing Sawteeth after a bout with the flu was probably the most challenging climb I did. I skied on the Wednesday before the Saturday climb to test my strength and thought I was in good enough shape to try it. As soon as we started up I had trouble, but the leader was caring enough to keep the group together. We've always maintained that hiking with a group means hiking with the group, which means, of course, that you travel as fast as the slowest hiker. Since it would be a trip up and back in this case I tried to convince him to keep going, that I'd see them at the top, but he wouldn't do that.

Being a drag on the group was very uncomfortable for me but we made it. I'm not sure if it was the summit high or something else, but I managed to lead the way and be the first one down which helped my pride. I think that the whole enterprise, the hiking and the camping, is as much a mental challenge as a physical one.

Livingston Lean-to, Cliff, Redfield, February 14 and 16, 1998:

Our first planned trip to Cliff and Redfield in 1997 was unsuccessful. We'd gone in with a large group and camped at the Livingston Lean-to at Flowed Lands. We decided that in order to climb some of the distant peaks we would have to camp. We had gathered information from ADK books, from friends, and from warm weather camping experience.

What a sight we were on our first winter trip—bulging backpacks, papoosing day packs, and plastic toboggans heaped with gear, well laced with bungee cords. We discovered that with one pulling and one pushing with a ski pole in the tuna can attached to the sled, we could move along quite well, except for the occasional toboggan rollover. Righting it was a struggle. Going downhill was an adventure too, till we added a braking line for the "pusher." Braking was often more difficult for me than pulling. We soon learned to pack more efficiently.

We also learned that, in cold weather, one needs to be quick getting the tent up, getting out of damp clothes and into dry ones. We become very focused on getting the tents up, getting water or melting snow, and getting the calories in before climbing into our tents and warm bags. Sometimes water gathering was a real challenge. Finding water was much better than melting snow, the simple acts of breaking thru the ice, scooping up a bucket of water and getting back up the bank were very exciting.

I had two bad camping experiences, both of which I believe came from not getting enough calories in very cold weather. On the first—the unsuccessful trip to Cliff and Redfield—we hadn't had a big lunch and didn't snack on the way in. Our dinner wasn't good and it was extremely cold; I felt cold overnight. In the morning there was pressure from the group to hurry, and to add insult to injury, I broke a tooth on a frozen breakfast bar!

Before we even got to Uphill Brook Lean-to I knew I couldn't keep up, so Armond and I turned back. Either by good luck and conditions or more careful planning, this is the only time we both turned back on a try for a peak. On our way out we met Carol and David White on their way in. Armond, especially, was glad to learn that failed trips are not all that uncommon (this was their second attempt to summit Cliff). Since then, as we have learned more and more about winter camping, we now go out in the winter just for the fun of camping.

In 1998, we climbed Cliff as a day trip from the south, crossing the south end of Flowed Lands up a route Bruce Wadsworth had told me about. On a beautiful day and with a great bunch of trail-breakers, we made the summit with ease and I had enough energy to lead the pack on the way out. Two days later Susan Omohundro, Tom Wheeler, Armond, and I went in to climb Redfield. The trail had been broken out and was in great shape, and the weather was Adirondack beautiful. I remember this hike as one of the easiest among the trailless peaks. Once again I was psyched enough to lead the way back to the car.

Seymour, December 21, 1997; March 13, 1998:

When we went in to climb Seymour, we were anticipating one of our quiet Winter Solstice parties, but found the Blueberry Lean-to and the Ward Brook Lean-to full with what seemed like a cast of thousands camped nearby. This was the first day that climbs "counted" as winter climbs. When we woke up in the morning, my little thermometer showed fifteen below zero. Getting started was tough. As we were preparing, another large group came in. Then people were passing us on the way up and after a while, we had to keep stepping off to avoid sliders coming down. It was the first hike of the season, I was tired, and my knee hurt.

It suddenly dawned on me that the serene Winter Solstice we had anticipated was not going to happen. I'd always said I'd do this as long as it was fun and this was far from fun. I still didn't have the strong need to finish the Winter 46, so asked my husband to go on up without me. As it happened I was fairly near the summit but didn't care, I wanted to go down.

What is funny about Seymour is the fact that a few years earlier, I had convinced Armond, Susan and John, Tim Davis, and Stacy Stone to climb Seymour as a day hike in the winter. Well, not actually winter, but on the twenty-ninth of March. It seemed like winter. We skied as far as we could, then switched to snowshoes, then crampons, and had a wonderful day. We celebrated our fete with a dinner in Saranac Lake.

On March 13, 1998, Armond and I went back to climb Seymour. He had finished his Winter 46 in February, and I had decided that I was so close, with only Seymour, Macomb, and East Dix to go, that I wanted to finish too. Armond had decided to retire in 1998 and we were going to move to Michigan, so this was my best shot at finishing. Other than the walk from Algonquin to Iroquois, this is the only time we broke the "rule of four" on a trailless peak. Weather, work, and meetings had made setting up a trip difficult.

There had been a good snowfall so the track wasn't clear, but it was a nice day. We were able to follow slight depressions in the snow, but got sidetracked by following a false path to a false summit. When we looked through the trees and saw higher land off to our left, my heart fell because it was getting close to "turnaround time" and it looked like we still had quite a ways to go. We persevered and just when I was ready to call a halt to turn back because it was so late, Armond, who was about thirty feet ahead of me said, "Oh, just a little farther, we've gotta be almost there!" Imagine my surprise that, as he was saying this, he was standing by the canister with a huge grin on his face. Even though we broke the rules, this is one of his most memorable hikes. A true trailless experience.

East Dix, March 20, 1998—46th peak:

There had been quite a bit of conversation on the 46er e-mail list about whether March 21 counted as winter. We decided to go on Friday, partly because we are purists but mostly because of weather forecasts. Our other fourteen hikes this winter had all been in beautiful weather. Reading Barb Harris's account of the moonlit ridge walk, a call from Marta Bolton, and reading Barbara McMartin's description in her "Discover the Adirondack High Peaks," made us confident that we should try the South Fork approach. With Armond and our faithful companions, John and Susan Omohundro, we began the easy bushwhack up Elizabethtown 4 Peak. From there it's a ridge walk over Spotted Mountain and on to East Dix. I understand that the views are spectacular but we were so high in the clouds that seeing our boot laces was a feat! After stopping in the "Lady Bushes," I had to yell for someone to wait for me—it was that hard to see. The woods were dripping, but not too unpleasant, and the bushwhack was rather civilized. The snow had a crust that held us up, so walking was not too difficult.

It's hard to describe the feeling that one has when finishing such a quest as the Winter 46 has been. I think my companions were almost as psyched as I was, at least I know my husband was. He had finished on Emmons three weeks earlier and seemed even more excited on East Dix. We were happy to arrive at the summit at 2:40 P.M., still within Solar Winter. Imagine our surprise, while we were snacking on a chocolate rabbit at the summit, to have three men come up from South Dix. They were even more surprised to see us.

The descent was fairly easy; so not long after dark we were back, sipping the celebratory champagne. I don't know how the tradition of celebrating the 46th with food or drink came to be, but my most memorable feast, after my chocolate bunnies and Armond's pink gooey marshmallow cakes on Emmons, was the shrimp and cocktail sauce with David and Carol White on Hough. On the way home, as the high and the glow of having finished was replaced by the realization of what we had done, I couldn't help thinking, "Maybe now my life will get back to normal?"

Ann began the Winter 46 at age 52 and finished at age 60.

26

LINDA COOLEY

46er # 3448W

Climbing the 46 was very much a family affair. For me it was as much about doing things together as it was about climbing the peaks. We started the all-season 46 when our sons were seven and ten, and finished the Winter 46 when they were sixteen and nineteen. In that time, they went from being children to being almost full-grown men. I started out carrying their food, water, and spare clothes (so that they moved along at a reasonable rate) and finished with them carrying my snowshoes, crampons and water (so that I moved along at a reasonable rate). The experiences climbing the 46 helped me to see my sons as individuals—not as just "my sons." On the trail we were four people working and climbing together—not just a traditional family unit. I learned to appreciate their strengths and abilities and judgment far better than I might have any other way.

Before we started doing the 46, I'd hiked only occasionally. The longest trip my husband and I had done was a ten-day trip on the West Coast Trail in British Columbia in 1974. We hiked for days along the coast without seeing another party. Most of our recreational time was spent in canoes, either in whitewater or flatwater. Before kids arrived, we did a lot of racing. But kids put a dent in the training schedule as well as the race schedule and we moved on to recreational canoeing. Winters were spent on cross-country skis. The four of us raced, the kids in Bill Koch League races and Bob and I on the adult circuit.

Summers we started short hikes like Whiteface Landing or Copperas Ponds or Racquette Falls. We did Giant in the summer of 1990 and the kids were hooked! It was a gorgeous, clear day, perfect for viewing all the peaks. The kids wanted to know the names of all of them. Then they declared they wanted to do them all. After completing the Summer 46 the next logical step was to undertake the Winter 46.

But winter hiking was different than summer and we learned as we went along. First lesson learned was on Street and Nye. Start early, preferably before sunrise. It's easier to walk in the dark when you're fresh and it is getting lighter, than after a long day of spruce traps, icy slopes, and deep powder! It is easier to do most climbs as day trips rather than hike in loads of equipment to spend the night and then have to hike out without getting a peak—like we did for Couchsachraga. Carrying all the gear to stay overnight and cooking and dressing in the winter is such a project, even if we did successfully summit. Recently we've added a GPS to our list of "must have" equipment, especially since there are no canisters now to tell you when you have summitted.

Today I prefer winter hiking because there are no bugs, minimal mud, better views, and no crowds. And there is nothing to compare to the "free" ride home, sliding down a steep slope on snowshoes on the trail you worked so hard to break on the way in. We've done fewer High Peaks and more trailless peaks since completing the Winter 46.

Bob and I have been hiking without kids, typical empty nesters. Kilburn and Slide in the Sentinels are interesting day trips as well as Jay Mountain Range. We also tried South Dix from Route 9. We've done Slide and Hunter Mountains, 4,000ers in the Catskills, and lesser peaks like Ampersand and Hurricane Mountains. One of our more memorable hikes was an August day when the four of us hiked up Cascade Mt. starting at 6 P.M. We spent two hours watching the setting sun and the lights of Lake Placid come on and returned to our car with headlamps.

Canoeing has become more important since we finished the 46 peaks and the kids left for college. We spent a week in sea kayaks on the coast of Nova Scotia. Kayaking didn't seem natural after so many years with a canoe paddle so we ended up with sea canoes, large touring single canoes which we can catamaran together when the winds and waves get to be overwhelming. They are extremely stable but not very sleek or fast. We've started exploring Lake Champlain and Lake George in these boats. We're doing a lot of marathon canoe racing; our big accomplishment recently was doing the 90-Miler, a three-day canoe race from Old Forge to Saranac Lake.

I have a PhD in physical chemistry and am assistant professor of chemistry at the College of St. Rose in Albany. While climbing the Winter 46, I was assistant professor at SUNY College of Agriculture and Technology at Cobleskill or at other times a chemistry teacher at Albany Academy, a private college-prep school my sons attended. I did teach them and both ended up majoring in chemistry at Middlebury College! Bob is an orthopedic surgeon in Schenectady.

Street and Nye, December 29, 1994:

Bob, Mike, Rick, and I started this peak late, 8:15 A.M., and paid for it at the other end. We never made this mistake again. We carried crampons and snowshoes as well as a two-person tent, stove, headlamps with spare batteries, and plenty of layers of clothes to stay warm. The crampons were never needed and the snowshoes were never used, although they might have been useful near the top of Street. Headlamps and spare batteries were necessary. We were just lucky that we didn't need the tent or stove or extra warm clothing.

We made it to Nye easier than in summer, because the herd paths going off in all directions were buried in snow. We'd run into another party near the start, but never saw them or their tracks again until we were descending Street. We followed their footprints down but they seemed to be swinging back uphill, so we left their trail and bushwhacked straight down. This choice probably put us one or two valleys away from where we intended to be.

As the afternoon wore on there was a lot of family discussion—

were we lost or not? Bob was certain we were in the right place. We were headed down hill, we were following a stream that must end up in Indian Pass Brook, and if we got to Indian Pass Brook we were essentially out. The rest of us were willing to grant him that much. Our questions were more concerned with how far from the car would we end up when we got to Indian Pass Brook, and was this really the best way to do this? Shouldn't we be over just one or two more ridges? As the sun got lower in the sky, the question of how many valleys over we were became more important to everyone but Bob.

Headlamps came out and discussions quieted down. Headlamps are great but when you have no idea where the trail is, the little spotlight does not foster much confidence; after an hour and a half spare batteries came out. Even our beagle was walking with her tail between her legs; she was as tired and discouraged as we were. The stop time was designated as 7:30 P.M. If we didn't come across our trail or the brook by then, we would get out the two-person tent and squeeze everyone in for the night. At 7:25 we crossed over the small stream we were following and discovered our tracks from the morning! Still another hour of hiking, but we felt so much better being where we had been earlier in the day.

Years later the mention of Street and Nye still brings heated family discussion as to whether or not we were lost or just a little off the mark. Bob is still convinced we were just where we wanted to be; all we needed was more daylight or a faster pace. But we learned a lesson on our first winter peak…start early. It's always better to start in the dark, when you still know where you are and are fresh, and finish with a few rays of sun on your back.

Skylight and Gray, February 19, 1996:

Bob, Mike, Rick, and I walked in from the Adirondack Loj and up past Lake Arnold. Temperatures were cold but the trail was well packed until we started climbing up from Four Corners. I put on my new Atlas snowshoes, lightweight and supposed to enable me to move faster. Instead I had to stop every twenty minutes or so and reattach them. We ended up wrapping straps around my boots and through the snowshoes and still I couldn't keep them on my feet. I cursed them the whole way up Skylight. On the way down we ran into another hiker with the same snowshoes—same complaint. His were tied on with rope as successfully as mine were strapped on.

The view from Skylight was great but we didn't stay long. Bob, as usual, lobbied to add Gray to our itinerary. After all, it was so close! Marcy was also close but we planned on saving that for our 46th peak. So off we went even though we hadn't studied descriptions of the herd path; soon after crossing the dam, we lost it. The powder was very deep; even with snowshoes we were post-holing two feet or more. We scrambled up a rock face we should have gone around by using veggie holds (holding onto trees). The only way I made it up was following the rest of my family and stopping every twenty feet to readjust my wonderful new snowshoes.

No one remembers the view once we got to the top. We found the canister and were surprised to see someone had been there two days earlier, for there was no indication that anyone had been there in months. I wore my snowshoes until I reached the well-packed trail; I almost left them there. This was their first and last trip! The climb back to Lake Arnold was exhausting; it's hard going uphill to go home. Even the slight uphill finish to the Loj, twelve hours after starting, can be too much on a trip like this.

Haystack and Basin, March 17, 1996:

We prefer to winter camp in March or maybe February; days are longer and usually warmer than December or January. The extra minutes of daylight mean a lot when you're tired from a long day of hiking. Bob, Mike, Rick, and I had reservations for Meyer Lean-to, an ADK-owned lean-to near Johns Brook Lodge. The advantage of using this club-owned lean-to was a guaranteed place to spend the night and no need to carry a tent. Without that guarantee we would have carried a heavy four-person tent. Sleeping bags, polypads to sleep on, lots of layers of warm clothing, extra socks, stove, cook kit, and food for three days was more than enough for the four of us to handle.

In the morning, we were lucky enough to find parking in the Garden and packed in our gear to the lean-to where we repacked for a day trip, and started up Haystack. We had to use crampons going up Little Haystack as well as Haystack itself. The problem was the peaks were not evenly covered. It was too icy in spots to brave it without crampons but too bare in other places to walk on rock without ruining them. The crampons went on and off and then on and off again; I lost track how many times we did this. This did nothing to increase our speed! The views were far better than when we climbed Haystack in the summer, but I did not appreciate it much after the scramble up the icy, rocky face. I was just grateful, briefly, for level ground and dreading the steep descent.

We returned to the lean-to in daylight but had to cook and eat by headlamp. We had carried in water for one day of hiking, but then had to heat water from Johns Brook for dinner and for the next morning. We usually start with coffee, hot chocolate, or hot cider. Dinner is some kind of freeze-dried "wonder." Add hot water and wait ten minutes. In winter that means reheat for several minutes or you'll be eating a cold meal. Dinner is served in a cup and dishwater is started. It's difficult determining if the water is boiling in the winter; the water steams so much that in the light of the headlamp it's hard to tell when it begins to boil.

A great treat for us is to take a bottle of hot water with us in the sleeping bag. It warms the bag at night and then is ready to cook with in the morning. Boot liners and gloves are also brought into the sleeping bags for the night. Leaving them outside guarantees they will be completely frozen by dawn; frozen boots and gloves make your feet and hands cold and then wet, as the dampness from the previous day thaws.

The next day we arose before sunrise, but it was 8:30 before we started for Basin. Getting dressed and fed takes a long time when you start in the dark, but waiting for sunrise means an even later start. Putting cold liners into frozen boots and lacing them up is a project when temperatures are in the teens. Ice-cold water has to be boiled, water bottles filled with hot water, oatmeal eaten, coffee or hot chocolate made, cups washed, and daypacks packed. Nothing is done fast.

The hike to Basin was also slow. We wore crampons most of the way up the peak. On top the snow was deep and very soft; temperatures were in the forties. We spent an hour on the summit eating and sunning ourselves. There were great views in all directions. It was easy to forget the season—too warm, sunny, and windless on top to be winter! Many of my sons' friends had gone south for winter break. It was hard to believe they would've enjoyed sunning themselves on the beach as much we enjoyed sunning ourselves on Basin. I ended up with my first sunburn of the year! This was perfect snow for making snowmen and also perfect conditions for icing and balling up on our crampons. Descending, the snow built up in the crampons until it seemed like we were walking on high heels. The problem continued until the sun fell and temperatures dropped. That day we cooked in daylight, a pleasant treat, and hiked out the next day.

Marshall, February 16, 1997:

Bob and Mike had failed to climb Marshall last winter from Indian Pass trail so we decided to try going up via Herbert Brook. We started at Adirondack Loj, hiked over Avalanche Lake and on to Lake Colden. Walking across the lakes is much faster than walking around them. It's windy but if the sun is out it can be very pleasant. Being out in the middle of the lakes gives you a completely different perspective of the slides on Colden and of the size of Lake Colden. The lakes were covered with snow, unlike Cascade Lakes or Middle Saranac which are wind-swept and great for ice skating! Sometimes the snow thaws a bit and the traverse can get wet, but the ice itself is always solid. On later trips we found it easier to ski the lakes, but on this trip we were on snowshoes.

We followed old tracks up Herbert Brook, but then the snow became very deep and we lost the old trail. Spruce traps were everywhere! Mike won the award for falling in the deepest and most often; he was most often in the lead. On his prize-winning fall, Mike was in up to his chest. Our beagle was most upset to see him at eye level! It took hours to complete this climb. The return, however, was an example of the best part of winter hiking. We followed our tracks down, slipping and sliding with abandon. The boys jumped off large boulders to land explosively in three feet or more of powder. I hated to see the descent end.

Saddleback, Gothics, Armstrong, and Upper Wolf Jaw, January 31, 1998:

The four of us started out expecting to do only Saddleback, but we easily reached the peak and the views were great. We could see Basin and Haystack in one direction and Dial, Nippletop, Colvin, and Blake in the other. We snacked and just enjoyed ourselves on this peak. We returned to the col between Saddleback and Gothics by 12:30 P.M. and then the lobbying by Bob began. It was such a beautiful day and it was still early. Why not do Gothics, Armstrong, and Upper Wolf Jaw? Why pass up such perfect conditions? We took a family vote and ended up pushing on.

It was a bit icy going up Gothics, but we still did not need crampons. We didn't need the cable either. In fact no one recalls even seeing the cable. These peaks were tough when we did them in the summer (90° +, not enough water, and a million black-flies around each one of us). On this trip Gothics was as memorable as Saddleback—great views and warm weather, everything winter hiking is supposed to be.

But after that, the trip is a blur. The views on Armstrong were still outstanding, but I was losing interest and energy and there was minimal time to stop if we were going to finish the trek. My body was also telling me it was quitting time. That was not good considering the descents we were facing after Armstrong. The descents were fast, often faster than we wanted. We slid down trying to control our speed with the bear claws on our snowshoes or with tree holds or veggie holds. Mike and Rick took turns leading. I think they were actually enjoying the sliding. I was third and just plain scared. Bob followed, to pick up the pieces.

The steep, icy drop between Armstrong and Upper Wolf Jaw was particularly scary. I don't remember seeing any ladders or cables. They were either buried in snow or ice or I was going too fast to notice. I don't remember being on top of Upper Wolf Jaw. But since I made it home I must have been there. I don't remember when we finished. All I know is that I eventually ended up on level ground that was not icy or slippery and I could simply walk without concentrating on where I was placing every footstep.

Dix, January 17, 1999:

Bob, Rick, and I got an early start on this peak (6:45 A.M.), anticipating a long day. The sun just started to rise as we were crossing

Round Pond. The sunlight through the woods was just beautiful—the colors changed every minute. There was a lot of snow, but our son Mike and his friends from Middlebury had packed the trail well the day before. I had only two complaints. One, they must have been running; their strides were so long that I often had to take two steps to their one. And two, they could have picked a better way off the new slide and into the woods—we ascended the slide and then cut over to pick up the old trail. I've done this cut in the summer with no trouble finding the trail, but in the winter it was another story. Mike and friends missed the trail and then bushwhacked through some very thick bush. We had a choice of following them, knowing they eventually made it, or striking out on our own and breaking trail ourselves. We elected to stay with them. Eventually we made it back to the actual trail and pushed on to the top.

The day remained bright and clear. The snow got deeper and deeper as we neared the top. We had to use veggie holds as well as ski poles to push and pull our way up the slope. Near where the trail from Elk Lake joined our trail the slope flattened out and we had a chance to admire the snow-covered trees. These trees are stunted and usually not very pretty in the summer, but this day they were beautiful. On the summit we could see forever in all directions. We could see Giant in the distance as well as Dial and Nippletop, the Great Range, and snow-covered Elk Lake. And it was pleasantly warm. What a combination! We spent almost forty-five minutes on top, eating and comparing the present views with what we had seen when we finished our Summer 46 on this peak, on a cloudy, foggy morning in August 1994.

The trip down was fast. Rick perfected his "telemark" maneuvers on snowshoes as we descended the very steep sections off the top. We were out by 5 o'clock. A long and tiring day but nowhere near as long or tiring if Mike and his friends had not packed the trail the day before. We saw no one all day.

Couchsachraga, January 23, 1999:

The dreaded mountain! We had attempted this peak once before and not made it. We had carried heavy packs five-plus miles into Bradley Pond Lean-to, climbed to Panther, and then returned to the lean-to to spend the night before going after Santanoni and Couch-sachraga. We had woken during the night to high winds and then in the morning to pounding rain. All the way through breakfast we'd debated whether to hike in the rain or come back another day. We had chosen "another day," and this was it!

Bob, Rick, and I left home in Schenectady at 4 A.M. and arrived at the trailhead at 5:30 in light rain and fog. We might have given up again if we had found an empty parking lot and deep unpacked trail. There was a van and another car in the parking lot and a well-packed trail. We decided to go for it in spite of the rain and the fog. Three guys who had spent the night in the lean-to passed us on their way to Couchi. But not too far ahead their trail veered off towards Panther. We had to decide whether to follow them or head off in the direction we thought was right; we decided to head out on our own. We found Times Square, took a compass reading, and headed towards Couchi. We never saw them or their trail again.

Because of the fog, all we could do was trust the compass. We never found the usual herd path and ended up blazing our own, often fighting to go between or around or over trees that seemed to grow everywhere. Even when we turned sideways to get through them, the trees would often have the last say, grabbing at some strap or side pocket on our packs or ski poles and pulling us back. And if we weren't pushing to get around them we often ended up falling through them. This was the first trip I remember personally having problems with spruce traps. Usually I bring up the rear and avoid the problem areas. But on this trip the snow was different. Bob and Rick could walk safely through an area and then I would fall through. I never fell through more than thigh deep, but it was always unnerving as well as exhausting.

After we had dropped down what seemed like forever, we came upon a steep uphill; the compass said to go up. The big advantage to going straight up was not having to fight with spruce trees anymore. At the top we arrived at a ridge and found an obvious old trail that we followed to the canister. It was still cold, wet, and foggy, with no views anywhere. Great trip! Plus we still had to retrace our steps nearly 800' back up to Times Square, and 2,400' down to our car, and then drive home. And it was already 2 P.M. No one was in good spirits.

The return trip was almost as slow as the way in. At the junction where our trail veered off towards the steep climb we had to decide: Follow someone else's trail and assume they came from Times Square or follow our own. We followed our own. Even that was difficult to do. Our trail had been wind blown or the snow had melted and our tracks were no longer visible. We fell through where we hadn't before or we fell deeper than we had before! Rick was feeding me candy bars to keep me going.

We finally made it back to Times Square at 4:30 P.M. Darkness was upon us, but we were through the worst of the bushwhack and our spirits lifted. Our path from Bradley Pond to the car had become a small creek during the day and we had to walk around it or through it. We finished at 8 P.M., with two out of three headlamps totally run down. This was our longest day of hiking ever! In the car was cold pizza that never tasted so good.

Bob repeated this hike a couple weeks later with Mike during Mike's winter break. They had no trail but they had clear conditions, could see where they were going, and easily found the peak. With their extra time they visited Panther for great views. I am still not convinced that it would ever be worth repeating this peak, great views or not!

Linda started the Winter 46 at age 46 and finished at age 50.

CONNIE SOUTHMAYD MORRISON

46er #3875W

I was born in July 1947 in Jay, New York, the granddaughter five generations removed from one of the original settlers—which makes me a rarity, a native Forty-Sixer. I grew up on the AuSable River, swimming in it in summers and skating on it in winters. My parents are avid outdoorsmen with a great appreciation for the beauty around us. I graduated from AuSable Forks High School, State University College at Brockport, and earned a Master's Degree from State University College at Potsdam.

The availability of a teaching position brought us joyfully back to this area. My husband, Don, a recently retired elementary school principal, has completed the 46, as has our youngest daughter. Don and

I have climbed Mt. Katahdin in Maine and Camel's Hump in Vermont. He hiked the Appalachian Trail. We have three daughters, Heather, Stephanie, and Meredith. It was Meredith that suggested that we climb "all" the mountains. "Not all in one summer!" I said. And so it began...I 46ed in the summer of 1996.

I am a Physical Education teacher at AuSable Valley Central School and enjoy many recreational activities, including alpine skiing, cross-country skiing, telemark skiing, water skiing, camping, swimming, white water canoeing, rock climbing, skating, and boating. I've always had a love for the mountains, but until I began hiking I never experienced such a personal relationship with them. I find spiritual renewal in the glorious beauty of our lakes, brooks, woods, and mountains.

I have a strong religious faith and am active in my church. I feel strongly about the preservation of the environment—I support ADK, the Nature Conservancy, and have done trail work for both ADK and the Forty Sixers, earning the 346-hour conservation badge for trail work—one of only eight women at the time to do so. It is very satisfying to improve the way for others and keep them on the right path! It is also frightening to observe environmental damage to our balsams, spruce, and other trees—as well as damage to the lakes from acid rain and over-use of salt on our roads. I want my grandchildren to discover these wonders and I hope the natural world can be preserved for them. It's thrilling to see the return of moose and turkeys to our area.

We began the quest for the Winter 46 in January 1996; fellow teachers who were Winter 46ers urged me on. I continue to climb with others who aspire to be 46ers. Most of my climbing has been in the Adirondacks—close to the mountains I love. I enjoy the lesser peaks and like the quiet time away from the masses. I admire the women who climbed with me and showed me the way—Marta Bolton, Barb Harris, and Peggy MacKellar. I would never have made it without the strong support and friendship of the "Geezer Gang"—Bill Johnson, Vic Pomerville, and Mike Bush. We have endured many adversities together. I have found great friendships with other hikers and spent some of the best and hardest days of my life in the woods.

I feel truly blessed to be able to make it "to the top." Winter climbing tested me like nothing ever has before; I understand the term, "mental toughness." The Allen Mt. trip became a yardstick: if I could survive that, I could do pretty much anything by putting one foot ahead of the other. We as women, mothers, and teachers know that we're strong—but winter hiking gives one a new confidence and a new strength to overcome seemingly impossible obstacles. Life is good.

Seymour, February 10, 1996:

At 6:15 A.M. the sun rose promising a gorgeous winter day; the sky was a spectacular blue. Ampersand Mt. and the Sawtooth Range sparkled like gems with their frosty crowns. A rest stop at Blueberry Lean-to provided refreshment. At Ward Brook Lean-to, evidence of an old trail tempted us; as it got steeper Vic and Bill questioned the direction of our unknown predecessor. Soon snowshoes were required. Wow! Was it steep. In one spot we crawled up a nearly vertical slope. Vic went first, then Bill, and then I got about twelve feet up, lost my footing and slid all the way back down. Vic threw Barb a rope.

The views were spectacular, looking down on Ampersand, all white and sparkly; Colden, Whiteface, and Giant rose in the distance. We were seemingly no nearer the top. We were lost. Up, up, up, we went, taking turns breaking trail. The snow was very deep and we pulled ourselves up by hanging onto trees; snow fell from branches and melted on us.

Finally, Vic lucked onto the herd path and it was a very short distance to the top, arriving at 12:45. We laughed from the sheer exhaustion of making a success out of a tough climb. I spent most of the descent sliding on the seat of my pants—laughing all the way. I felt about eight years old. It seemed impossible that we had climbed so steeply and so far. A rush of cold air gave warning that my Gore-Tex pants and long johns had parted company on a root. Sadly, my jacket did not escape unscathed either. It was an expensive slide down!

Donaldson, February 19, 1996:

We left home at 4:10 A.M. to meet Sally Hoy, a friend of Barb Harris, to climb the Seward Range. The slippery road into the parking lot began with unexpected excitement as the car went into a skid, slid sideways, and bumped into the snow bank—finally coming to a rest facing the wrong direction. That was an adrenaline rush! We left the parking lot at 5:45 A.M. at -2°, planning to climb Donaldson, Emmons, and with luck Seward. After Calkins Brook we lost our way.

After climbing steeply to over 4,000' and being no nearer the summit of Donaldson, we knew we were in trouble. We were unable to go forward and a precipitous drop between Donaldson and us eliminated any progress in that direction. Down we went and again tried to bushwhack toward Donaldson, only to be thwarted again by sharp drop-offs, deep snow, and thick trees. Impossible! We descended to 3,500' where we were able to bushwhack to the herd path. It's mighty discouraging to be forced to retreat and lose that hard-fought altitude; this is the time for learning mental toughness.

We had a visual of our goal, Emmons. The rate we were traveling and the advancing time made reaching it and returning a dangerous move. The winds were frigid; our faces froze as we smiled for photos, but we enjoyed the blue sky, bright sun, and snow-covered trees on the way down—a twelve hour day.

Allen, December 21, 1996:

We left the Tahawus parking lot at 5:30 A.M. and staggered back fourteen and a half hours later. It was a mistake to attempt such a long hike for the first winter climb of the year. After the former Twin Brook Lean-to site, we lost our way. This became the routine; much time was lost, retracing steps repeatedly and it became increasingly discouraging—on a hike of this distance and magnitude, one cannot afford to waste either time or energy. Bill, Vic, and Mike took turns leading. The steep climb from Allen Falls was a pattern of five steps forward and rest, five steps and rest. The deep snow forced a slow pace, but by covering the ice on the slide it helped give our snowshoes purchase. The sky was blue and the sun bright but the temperature didn't get above 10°. It was 2 o'clock by the time we reached the summit.

We were almost back to Twin Brook, but in the dark we got turned around and were going the wrong way—until Mike Bush noticed that the moon was in the wrong place! It was tough retracing; we had five more long, cold miles to go. Beautiful moon. Both my head-lamp and flashlight ran out of batteries but I didn't need them. I have never been more tired in my life! Allen has become the rule by which the difficulty of all other hikes is measured. It was the hard-est and most exhausting hike that I have ever done. There were times near the end where I was not sure I could finish it—the temptation to lie down in the snow and sleep was so great!

Redfield, January 11, 1997:

We left the Adirondack Loj at 6:00 A.M. The temperature was 5° and there was a wicked wind chill. The trip up to Avalanche Lean-to and Lake Arnold was a battle in the deep snow. The nice downhill to Feldspar Lean-to brought worrisome thoughts about the return climb up when we'd be weary. The climb up Redfield was tough—every-one got caught in spruce traps! Where one or two people would pass by smoothly the next hiker would sink, so one never knew where the best route would be. We found the canister at one o'clock. Swallowing frozen food was difficult. Returning, the 7.2-mile sign to Adiron-dack Loj was demoralizing—but after climbing Allen it wasn't that bad! We put one foot slowly in front of the other, digging deep inside for the tenacity required to reach the car and warmth and rest. We got back with headlamps at 6:30 P.M. My new Tubbs snowshoes with rugged crampons work great.

Giant and Rocky Peak Ridge, February 8, 1997:

We left the car at 7 A.M. at -5°. We were convinced there'd be many hikers breaking the trail ahead of us—hah! No such luck. Snow-shoes were required and the snow was very slick. Every step up was a struggle and at times we went back three for every one forward. We noticed some guys behind us; I yelled, "Hurry!" hoping for trail-breaking help but they were smart and stayed back. The flu last week may have caused my breathlessness—I was struggling.

We saw tracks where a lynx was closing in on a rabbit. The sky became blue and the sun was bright. The views on the open ridge were awesome. When we reached Giant's summit I considered turning back, but Bill shared his hot chocolate and I got a second wind. We started for Rocky Peak on unbroken trail—Bill thought left, Mike thought right, and Marta and I were just floundering in the very deep snow; we decided to let some Canadian hikers pass and break trail.

Rocky's 360-degree views offered a panorama of High Peaks. Back at the col we decided to bushwhack down rather than reclimbing 800' back up Giant. But the deep snow made us think hard about this; I looked at the long climb back up Giant, the unbroken bushwhack downhill, and was ambivalent. Starting down, Bill took a fall and nearly disappeared out of sight. Just as we were beginning to question our sanity we found old tracks. Our snowshoes no longer sank four feet at every step; we followed a stream nearly out to the road—it was a good exit.

Marcy and Gray, February 20, 1997:

We left the Adirondack Loj parking lot at 6:50 A.M. The new snow sparkled like diamonds at Marcy Dam. The trip was quiet and lovely; everything was cobalt blue, sunshine yellow, and blinding white. Marcy was magnificent. We had to really dig in the snowshoe crampons to climb Marcy. The rocky face was crusty, frozen snow and ice—steep, slippery, and unrelenting. It was a challenge to our lower legs to press in the crampons for a bite. The thought of those chairlifts on Whiteface, so clear in the distance, was tormenting! The wind had made waves of the snow and in some places, feathers. You feel like you're on top of the world.

We slid down on our bottoms toward Gray; it was fun! At tree line, we switched from crampons back into snowshoes and picked our way through the snow-covered spruces with great caution, but could not avoid sudden drops into unbelievable spruce-traps. Once I dropped completely out of sight. Not fun! You never knew how far down you would sink; often it required help from others to extract yourself. It was exhausting to get out of them!

We found the stick that Ed Bunk had left to mark the canister tree on Gray; Marta dug down a long way before discovering it. Descending toward Skylight, suddenly a terrifying collapse into seemingly bottomless snow got me in over my head, and I'm tall! Had I been alone I don't know if I could have escaped the last spruce-trap; I could not reach my snowshoes. My "geezer gang" would have enforced the seventy-pound rule—they'd come back for you when you were down to seventy pounds and could be carried out!

Gothics, Armstrong, and Upper Wolf Jaw, March 1, 1997:

The trail was very icy. Reaching open rock on Gothics, we put on crampons and used fingernails to clutch our way up the icy face. The bottom of the cable was broken and the rest of it was so frozen-in as to be useless. Marta could walk straight up with her full crampons, where the rest of us could not with only insteps. The mountains around us were spectacular with their white crowns—Whiteface, Haystack, Basin, Marcy, Saddleback, the MacIntyre Range, Phelps, Tabletop, and Big Slide. Mike found an ice ax frozen in the path and rescued it.

The climb was incredible. We were saved by Bill's rope as we reached an ice flow that could not be circumvented; Marta walked across it and tied a rope to a tree; Bill held the other end as we edged across. At the end he tied it around himself and we three held on for dear life. A slip would have been disastrous. The mountain totally fell away—anyone sliding out of control there would drop 1,000'. It was terrifying! After this experience I went directly to the Mountaineer and purchased full crampons.

The winds at the top of the south summit were wild and so was the view. We could see storm clouds blowing up rapidly; the sky above us was still blue and the sun was shining brightly, but it was about to change dramatically. The clouds began blowing by us at incredible speeds, ending all views and sunshine for the day. The strong winds were frightening. We moved on towards Armstrong, encountering very icy spots; the oncoming rain was imminent. I took a nasty fall ten feet down an icy face, but was unhurt, falling on my back and pack. When we reached the cliff off Armstrong, I slid down on my bottom but lost my ski pole on the way; Bill recovered it in a great display of athletic talent as he slid by. Hard rain began to fall.

Saddleback and Basin, December 27, 1997:

A team of ten left the Keene Valley Garden parking area at 6:40 A.M. My terrible cold left me little stamina for trail breaking. By the time we arrived at the col it was snowing hard. The trip up Saddleback was tough—the snow kept breaking away, forcing us two steps back for one step up. We finally reached the summit at noon; the wind was blowing hard as we changed to full crampons. Everyone was worried about the descent down the cliff. Our destination, Basin, would appear and then be lost in clouds and snow. As we feared, the rock was ice-covered and treacherous! Peggy, the brave, sought the route; four of our strongest members used their muscle to get the rest safely down. We used a rope and left it in place for the return. We all wondered how on earth we would get back up!

We didn't know then that Sally Hoy broke her finger and Ellen Ohnmacht pulled a muscle during the descent. At the base of the cliff the snow was very deep; we quickly changed to snowshoes and slid down the rest of the way. We climbed the first steep section of Basin and then moved on to the second. The trail breaking was exhausting! By 2:00 P.M. we had struggled to the summit. We took photos and started down around the scary cliff that drops away very far below; it was icy and required great care to avoid sliding over the edge. It was windy; we all dug in our crampons and one after the other cautiously edged our way down. Everyone was anxious to get past this treacherous point. Bill is cautious in the descent because he injured his tailbone sliding down Seymour and is still painfully conscious of the injury. Andy rescued me when I slid down a steep, icy pitch into a tree.

Soon we were back to the ascent of Saddleback. It was a struggle just to climb to the dreaded cliffs. On the last very steep pitch we stopped to put on crampons and then clawed our way up. Stephanie and Andy found handholds and they scrambled easily over the first hurdle. The rest of us are neither as strong, agile, or young! They managed to ascend the next section of cliff and tied a rope. Even with boosts from Mike and Bill and having the rope, I made several futile attempts before a hand from Andy got me up; I slashed my gaiter with my crampon. Peggy and I managed to get up over the next hard part with the help of the rope.

Bill and Mike were pushing everyone up. We were a strong team, determined to meet the challenge. Barb's crampons broke. I stayed by the rope and shouted encouragement and helped pull. Steph and Andy went ahead to assist on the next part. Bill and Mike came last after seeing that everyone was up. They were very cold after staying for an hour on the exposed cliffs. It was nearly dark when we all reached the top; it had taken an hour to climb this little way. The cliffs on

Saddleback were my most feared climb. I am happy that I have done it.

Macomb, March 7, 1998:

We put on our dancing slippers as we left the trail; it had been snowing from the time we left home and continued most of the day. We arrived at the slide and could see only part of the way up as the rest was obscured by snow and fog—God's way of protecting us from what lay ahead. One had to kick in steps to move upward; one misstep would result in a 1,000-foot slide down! As we climbed higher, it became a test of courage and nerve. We reached the top of the slide and found it difficult to stay on the herd path; several times we found it, only to lose it again. Finally we headed toward the tallest trees visible in the fog and found the can at 11:30. Descending, I took a fall that will leave bruises; I felt great anxiety about getting safely down the steep and icy drop ahead. It was a kick; we lay down on our backs and laughed all the way.

Dix, February 20, 1999—46th Peak:

We left the parking lot at 6 A.M. in high spirits. We reached Round Pond and crossed on the ice. Soon the sun came up and the new snow sparkled like diamonds. Someone had skied down the slide. We had to drive our crampons into the crusty snow on the steep trail to make any progress. The sun was shining but there was no view as the air was full of flurries. We finally reached the summit and Bill and I climbed the remaining few steps together. It was 10:55.

We reveled in the moment: we are genuine Winter 46ers. We had begun the quest together and were surrounded by wonderful friends. We had endured many adversities and it was fitting that we could all share this moment; we received gifts of Winter 46er sweatshirts with our numbers on them, cards, winter patches, and fuzzy critters. The joyous party celebrated with shrimp, cheese, crackers, and champagne to toast this wonderful day. What a great day and such special friends. God bless them.

Connie began the Winter 46 at age 48 and finished at age 51.

SUSAN KIRK

46er # 4270W

In high school, I was as unlikely a candidate for winter hiking as you could get. I hated sports and was always the last one chosen for a team. I was awkward and uncoordinated. I think I got a C in gym. Years later after finishing a hard rock climb, I remembered how I just couldn't get off the ground on those dreaded gym ropes. After high school and Nursing School, I joined a gym and did some small local hiking, but never really got the hiking fever.

In 1986, a girlfriend from work and I decided to hike the highest peak in New England, Mt. Washington. That September, we drove to New Hampshire and went into the Appalachian Mountain Club's Pinkham Notch camp. The caretaker looked at us and immediately referred us to a hike up small Pine Mt, 2,405 feet and three miles round-trip—instead of our prized Mt. Washington, 6,288' and 8.2 miles round-trip. We were not to be denied! Looking back on that hike I realize how foolish we were. Inexperienced novices trying to hike one of the more challenging peaks—with disregard to the weather, which wasn't that great and as I know now, changes frequently and suddenly. After we summitted and arrived safely back, I decided this kind of hiking was for me! I loved the steep challenge and the beautiful views.

I joined the Appalachian Mountain Club in 1987. After a trip with the Connecticut AMC chapter in 1988 to celebrate the 100-year anniversary of the High Huts in the White Mountains, I started to climb 4,000-footers in all seasons. Not peak-bagging so much as peak-exploring; a new peak was for me like opening a new present each time I climbed a different one. The adventure of hiking somewhere I'd never been before was so exciting. I loved the roar of the wind in the mountains. It was on that trip that I really got hooked. I met other hikers who had climbed the forty-eight 4,000-footers in New Hampshire and I was determined to do them all, finishing on West Bond. Since completing a number of lists (the New Hampshire 4,000-footers, New England 4,000-footers and Hundred Highest), I rehiked many of my favorite peaks again and again—and soon found I didn't want to stop hiking when winter came!

So I started to climb in winter and figured I might as well start the lists all over again. I started with club trips and then expanded to almost every free winter weekend. At the time I was working every other weekend and so my winter weekends were very precious to me. I finished the winter New Hampshire 4,000-footers on Mt. Zealand on February 23, 1992, and started working on the New England 4,000-footers in winter. But my winter hiking slowed to almost a stop when I returned to school. I had been a licensed practical nurse and decided to return to nursing school to pursue a Registered Nurse degree. How sad I was—while in school all I could think of was the wilderness and hiking. But I needed to work full-time and go to school full-time, not easy, and it left no free time for hiking.

Back in 1990, I had taken the AMC rock-climbing course and also learned to ice climb. It was exciting, challenging, and dangerous. In 1991, I climbed Mt. Rainier with Nola Royce, another Winter 46er, and other friends. Nola had climbed Denali and Mt. Rainier previously and a few high peaks in Russia including Peak Communism. She was a role model and had a lot of high-altitude experience, including the Winter 111ers in Northeastern USA, the fourth woman to do so. After talking with Nola, I decided that I, too, would attempt all those peaks—and so began my winter hiking in the Adirondacks.

Besides the AMC, I belong to the Adirondack Mt. Club Albany chapter; Catskill 3500, aspirant; Adirondack Forty-Sixers; New Haven Hiking Club, in Connecticut; Randolph Mt. Club, in New Hampshire; Green Mt. Club in Vermont; and the Rochester Winter Mountaineering Society (RWMS). The RWMS is an interesting group; you have to hike a winter beginner overnight with them before they will allow you to join. I try to lead or co-lead a trip into Baxter State Park in Maine every winter.

I also belong to the Appalachian Trail Conference. I support the ATC and maintain my section of the Appalachian Trail in Connecticut (after spending hours, often alone, on a section of trail you start to think of it as your section). I maintain the section of AT from CT Route 341 to Schaghticole Mt, including the Mt. Algo shelter. The section is short—about 2.5 miles—but steep and contains a million water bars (O.K., maybe twenty-five), but they all have to be cleaned out two or more times a year with a Hazel hoe. Sometimes I think some folks believe the trails appear for them to hike on without thought to the hours and hours of service volunteers spend working on them! The shelter also requires attention and education to the users. As the trail maintainer, I frequently find the remnants of a "No fires" sign burned up in a forbidden campfire ring.

I must admit that when I started the Adirondack High Peaks in winter I felt a little smug; after all, I had been winter hiking for years—just how hard could they be? I felt I was a seasoned winter hiker, having completed the sixty-five winter 4,000-footers in the Northeast. Well, I was in for a surprise. Unlike the forty-eight New Hampshire 4,000ers that are frequently broken out—not so for the Adirondack 46. I did my share of trail breaking in New Hampshire, but nothing like the breaking we did in the Adirondacks! My first winter peak was Redfield, climbed with the Albany chapter on the first day of winter, 1996. I found a bushwhack and a non-broken trail full of spruce traps. Another challenge—trailless peaks—and I loved it. I fell and ended upside down with only my snowshoes sticking out. How embarrassing! The group pulled me out and I certainly felt a little more humble.

I was really learning to love the Adirondacks. They were far wilder than anything I had previously hiked, except for Baxter State Park in Maine. With the large number of bushwhacks, I enjoyed finding and signing the canisters; it was fun to see who had signed in before you. The winter hiking community is a committed group and you soon get to know quite a few winter hikers. Each winter peak was like opening a Christmas present; each one different and wonderful at the same time. I became the fifth woman to complete the 111 4,000ers in winter—and found the ADK 46ers the most challenging.

One of the most amazing and beautiful sights in the Adirondacks when I was climbing there was the Hale-Bopp comet. The comet was clearly visible against the dark, remote Adirondack night sky. After a long day of winter hiking the Santanoni's, on the way out I noticed the comet. I asked the group to turn off their headlamps. We stood in silence and awe at how something millions of miles away was visible to us in that dark wilderness sky.

Besides hiking the treasured wilderness, I also enjoy collecting antiquarian mountaineering books, old guidebooks from New England and New York, the West, and Europe. I enjoy old journals such as Appalachia's, "American Alpine." I love reading old trail descriptions and try to imagine what the old abandoned trails were like. I have one 1950 guidebook, "The Adirondack Trails, Northeastern Section," and one to the Northville-Placid Trail. In that little green guidebook is a note regarding winter mountaineering awards: "An individual award, the winter mountaineering emblem, may be earned by anyone who climbs five Adirondack peaks over 4,000' in elevation between December 21 and March 21. For questionnaire, write club secretary and fill out same and return with fifty cents."

I presently live in Middletown, CT, and work in Hartford, CT, as a Registered Nurse on a medical/surgical care unit on the tenth floor of a busy, inner-city hospital. I am also on the hospital's bio-terrorism task force; I will be on a team to help protect our patients and community in the event of a smallpox outbreak.

As for training to winter hike, I try to train all the time—I mean I climb up ten floors to my hospital unit rather than take the elevator. If I am biking, I try to bike hilly, steep terrain to keep up my fitness level. If I can't get away to hike, I do three-mile loops around the reservoir near where I live. I also bike in the summer, thirty-five- to sixty-five-mile rides three times weekly, mixed with occasional century (one hundred) mile rides. Connecticut has over six hundred miles of blue-blazed hiking trails. I live very close to the Mattabesset blue-blazed trail and can head out to it from my doorstep. A few years ago, I trained for half marathons by running on local trails that had the added benefit of increasing endurance for winter hiking. But in 1998, I developed arthritis in my back and feet and found running just too painful.

For hiking in any season I always carry Gore-Tex jacket and pants, wool hat and mittens, fleece jacket, two quarts of water, compass, and space blanket all year round. In winter, if traveling alone, I bring a bivy sack or sleeping bag, down suit, metal cup, and candle to melt snow if necessary. Above tree line I also carry a facemask and goggles. I carry snowshoes all winter long even if the trail is broken. In the event you are up high and suddenly have to drop down because of bad weather; snowshoes would be a necessity— plus carrying them is good training. For skiing or snowshoeing into a winter camp, a plastic sled is great. I have a Mountain Smith sled that I have used since 1990; it can handle a lot of gear. Making a sled is easy; serious winter climbers often use a child's plastic sled and other pieces and a harness for the waist.

A winter hobby of mine is looking for moose racks! While skiing into Redington Ponds Range in Maine a few years ago, I met a snowmobiler who had a large moose rack on the back of his machine. After chatting a little he explained: he goes out in winter looking for racks in the snow; moose lose them in the fall. The fellow shared the trick to finding them in the snow. He said, "Look for something that looks like an upside down pumpkin stem." The racks are heavy and fall point side down. Thus the part that would attach to the moose skull will be sticking out of the snow—very much like a pumpkin stem.

A few weeks later I was snowshoeing into Elephant Mt. in Maine with friends; I saw what looked like a pumpkin stem upside down sticking out of the snow. Wow! I was impressed. My friends were amazed the rack had only one horn that must have weighed twenty pounds. I never keep them. I just enjoy looking for them. Lastly, I feel when hiking, "Do no harm"—like the philosophy of medicine. Leave only footprints.

Street and Nye, March 15, 1998:

The coldest backpack I did in the Adirondacks was into Street and Nye with the Rochester Winter Mountaineering Society. The RWMS is committed to winter backpacking and although they almost always climb the peak, they also enjoy the beauty of just being out in the winter. This trip into Street and Nye was a longer approach via the Northville-Placid Trail, starting the bushwhack above Wanika Falls. We bushwhacked Wanika Falls Brook into the col between the two peaks. We set up camp in the col using our snowshoes and shovels to make tent platforms out of the snow. It is often necessary to even out the snow by building such platforms in order to camp on a level spot.

That night the temperature was 30 degrees below zero. I was excited—another first for me. I was prepared; the forecast was for the extreme cold to continue. I had my -30° below zero North Face sleeping bag and my down suit on, plus two hats and down booties. The down suit was from my old ice climbing days. It could get mighty cold standing around belaying someone else on an ice climb. Even with all that clothing I was just barely comfortable. My tent-mates thought the down suit was overkill but I was glad I had it.

That night I had to get up to use the bushes and marveled at the beautiful night sky. So many stars! I think the cold makes the sky so much clearer. Nothing is so wonderful as the night sky from a remote backpack in the Adirondacks. Oh—we didn't find the canisters on that trip, but did the following year. Was the snow so deep, possibly were they buried? I was thrilled, however—I had never camped out before in such cold conditions and had climbed a rarely used winter route into Street and Nye.

Skylight and Gray, January 25, 1997:

Another Adirondack adventure began with a backpack into

Feldspar Lean-to. The plan was to hike in, set up camp, and climb Skylight and Gray. It was warm and rainy on the hike in and turned to snow as we reached higher altitude. As the group unpacked, someone left two large candy bars on the ground near his pack for just a moment. Well, the next thing we knew a pine marten raced out of the woods and grabbed the candy and fled. We were amazed. I think the pine marten had a racket, shaking down winter hikers. We could hear him all night screeching and running around the shelter sites. For a tiny animal they are ferocious.

This was the winter backpack where I learned if anything is damp, put it in your sleeping bag. During the night the temperature dropped to -10°. I usually would put my boots in a bag under my head and they would be O.K. In the morning my boots had frozen solid, since the felt liners had been damp. Many people only hike in plastic boots, thus avoiding that problem; I even have plastic boots for mountaineering or ice climbs, but for winter hikes I prefer Sorels. So in the morning I tried everything to thaw them out and finally just walked out with those frozen boots rubbing my heels raw. Another lesson for me. Now I always hike with extra liners and just stick the boots in a plastic bag and cram them into the toe of the sleeping bag.

Sue began the Winter 46 at age 44 and finished at age 46.

JADWIGA ROSENTHAL

46er # 4476W

I was born in the foothills of the beautiful, rugged Polish Tatra Mountains. Because my family had very meager financial resources I had to find things to do by myself, and I became attracted to the beauty of the outdoors. It was always an escape for me to see the beauty of the mountains, rivers, flower-filled meadows, and birds. At sixteen, I moved to Szczecin near the Baltic Sea to live with and help an older sister who was expecting her third child. A year later I enrolled in night technical high school and went to work, both full time, six days a week as a clerk in a factory sweat-shop. Because I realized that the job would never get any better, after a year I quit even though I was in desperate financial straits. At eighteen I moved from my sister's to live as a boarder in someone's home. I had an 8' x 8' room with no kitchen and a shared bathroom without hot water. I earned enough to pay rent and buy subsistence food. I would go for extended periods without a hot meal. After graduating high school, I enrolled in a five-year college and continued to work full time as a typist and payroll clerk in a furniture factory.

In my last year of college, I met my first husband who was a U.S.

citizen in the Danish Merchant Marine; a year after graduating, I moved to the United States and married him. One year later my son, Matthew, was born. Three years after his birth I got divorced. I had trouble finding work because my English was poor, so I went to school to learn English. I was able to survive and raise my son with some child support and by doing odd jobs, like cleaning homes, taking care of older persons, and sewing.

Fortunately, a woman for whom I was altering clothes mentioned that she knew of a job in her husband's company doing accounts payable, receivable, and payroll. I got that job on a temporary basis and stayed there for three years. During that time I was able to buy a small house. Because of my experience there, I was able to get a better job working for the State of Connecticut. Finally I had a decent job with good pay and full benefits.

In 1989, a friend at work introduced me to the Appalachian Mountain Club activities. This came at a good time because my son was now old enough that he didn't require as much attention. I joined the club and did some weekend hiking in the White Mountains of New Hampshire and I fell in love with it. I was able to transport myself away from day-to-day problems.

In November 1994, on a hike in Connecticut, I met the man who was to be my second husband. After the hike Carl and I went out to supper. Because it was November, he asked me what I had for winter hiking equipment. I was surprised that you could hike in the winter! I got some equipment and, in December, we climbed Mount Adams in the Whites.

Carl had started working on his Winter 46s. On New Year's weekend we went on my first trip to the Adirondacks. We climbed Wright and Algonquin the first day. The wind on Wright was so strong I crawled on all fours. The next day we hiked Phelps and it was warm and rainy. After that weekend I was ready for more. I even enjoyed my first trailless peak, Marshall. It reminded me of playing in the woods while I was growing up in Poland.

We kept going to the Adirondacks for winter weekends for three years, during which I climbed thirty-nine of the 46 winter peaks. The following September shortly before getting married, I lifted some books while moving to my husband's house and injured my back severely. I was in terrible pain. I required surgery for a ruptured disc. I was bedridden for three months and afraid that I would never be able to hike again. That January I was feeling well enough to try a little hiking, but I was bitterly disappointed when I re-injured myself.

Now I was suffering again and went back to seeing doctors. One doctor told me that that was how it was going to be for the rest of my life. However, I took physical therapy and acupuncture and started doing stretching exercises. By September, I was ready to give hiking another try. This time I was delighted that I felt no worse after the hike. I continued to hike in the fall. I was anxious for winter to start so I could finish the Winter 46. My first hike was to Colvin and Blake. When that went well I was able to do Cliff. We did Haystack as a backpack from Grace Camp. I finished the Sewards on a backpack with the Rochester Winter Mountaineering Society.

I have since gone on to complete the 100 highest peaks in New England and the Catskill 3500 peaks in winter. This means I have qualified for the Northeast 111 (now 115) in winter. I celebrated Valentine's Day of 2003 by finishing on New Hampshire's Mt. Carrigain on a gorgeous, very cold and windy day.

Two of my most notable hiking achievements would be hiking Gannett and Granite Peaks, the high points of Wyoming and Montana, respectively, and are considered the most difficult state highpoints to reach in the contiguous 48 states. My husband and I retired to Center Conway, New Hampshire. We are close to New Hampshire's White Mountains and western Maine mountains. I belong to a fitness center where I do yoga, water aerobics, the treadmill, and lift weights. Of course when the weather is nice we go hiking.

Marcy, December 31, 1995:

To celebrate the New Year 1996, Carl, some friends and I headed to the Adirondacks for the weekend. On December 30, we started out to do Iroquois by going over Algonquin. Unfortunately there were whiteout conditions almost as soon as we emerged above tree line. We stumbled around for a while and made the decision to go back. While our friends went cross-country skiing, Carl and I wanted one more chance to climb a peak and we thought we could climb Marcy, a very popular peak, safely by ourselves. We started from the

Adirondack Loj around 7 A.M. and, once again as we emerged from the trees, we encountered whiteout conditions almost as dense as the day before. Again we stumbled around and were just about to give up when a skier came up from behind and passed us. We looked and saw he had left a trail that we could just barely follow.

We followed his tracks and met up with him on his way back. He said he had made the summit and that he was able to do it only because he skied Marcy quite often. We continued on to the summit and then turned around in the increasing whiteout. We soon found that most of our tracks, both the skier's and our own, were now covered up by blowing snow. For a while things were pretty scary, but luckily we were periodically able to spot the holes made by our ski poles. That was just enough for us to make it safely below tree line!

Redfield, December 21, 1996:

Carl and I saw a write-up in "Cloudsplitter," the magazine for the Albany Chapter of the ADK, for a hike described here. The article suggested taking advantage of the lack of early season snow to do an ambitious Leader's Choice hike in the High Peaks. We called the leader and he felt that doing Redfield and Cliff would be possible.

So on a cold, sunny December 21, ten of us left the Upper Works Trailhead at Tahawus by 5:30 A.M. As we walked along we became aware of more and more snow. Still we were making good time until we came to Uphill Brook Lean-to; after a break we almost immediately had problems finding the herd path to Redfield. Soon somebody had fallen into Uphill Brook! That had to be taken care of immediately, then two other people fell into the brook and had to change clothing. We did find a good herd path and eventually all made it to the summit around 3 P.M., where nice views were seen on this sunny day. The leader looked over to Cliff and said, "Some parties could make that summit today but I don't think we will."

Back at the lean-to we unanimously agreed that doing Cliff was not possible today. Soon it became apparent that one of our party was ill; he was nauseous and faltering. The leader and others in his carpool kept the safety gear and stayed with him. Everybody else was told to go ahead; soon this smaller group started to bog down. One of us had to rest periodically; we all got out about the same time, 10 P.M.—it had taken us sixteen-and-a-half hours to climb Redfield! While it was true that there was less snow than later in the winter, many of our group had not been in mid-winter shape. We "enjoyed" supper that night at a gas station in Schroon Lake.

Allen, March 9, 1996:

Again we called about a Leader's Choice hike in the "Cloud-splitter." The leader, Wil Desbien, said that he had hurt his knee and would not be hiking, but that he knew of four strong hikers who were going to climb Allen. They didn't want anyone else to hike with them but had no objection if others followed them in. We showed up at the trailhead half an hour after the four had started. Only one other person was there, a woman named Mary Lou Recor, who had called us.

We had an easy time of it until we started up the slide. Even though the trail had just been broken, there was still tons of loose snow; every step had to be fought for. Many steps were given up by sliding back and then having to climb up again. Finally we reached the summit. The four hikers were still there. We thanked them for breaking the trail and we followed them down. As hard as it was going up the slide, it was as much a pleasure going down. There was enough snow so we could sit and slide down the whole way. We continued out and noticed that it had taken thirteen hours and twenty minutes to climb Allen.

Macomb, South Dix, East Dix, and Hough, March 16, 1996:

We called Wil this week and thanked him for suggesting Allen; did he have any suggestions for this Saturday? He said the trailless Dixes would be a good bet. Again we showed up at the trailhead and again there was only one other person there, a woman named Jane. We found the trail up Macomb to be broken, and put on crampons up the slide. We met a couple at the summit who camped at Slide Brook Lean-to and the five of us uneventfully climbed South Dix and East Dix, followed a broken trail to Hough. The three of us headed down from Hough—a spectacularly beautiful day and we bagged four summits! We noticed that the hike had taken us thirteen hours and twenty minutes. Wil had suggested two hikes on beautiful successive Saturdays where we met one woman at the trailhead each time and each hike had taken thirteen hours and twenty minutes!

Colvin and Blake, January 17, 1999:

This was my first hike in the Adirondacks since I injured my back. Early in the morning on a very cold crispy day, seven of us headed down Lake Road. When we got to the trailhead we were excited to see that the trail was broken; shortly before the Colvin summit we met people camping who hadn't gone to Blake, so we began breaking trail from Colvin towards Blake. We were still doing well on time as we started up Blake.

Even though we put our best trailbreakers in front, a lot of fresh-fallen unconsolidated snow slowed things down drastically. In the very steep places at the beginning we often found ourselves sliding backwards. At times someone above pulled me and someone else pushed from below. It took two hours to go the half mile to the summit of Blake. I was exhilarated to be there but at the same time exhausted and worried about making it back up and down Colvin's very steep pitches.

The others were happy for me to have climbed my first Adirondack High Peak in almost two years! One friend encouraged me to take one step at a time on the way back up Colvin. The sun had set by the time we re-summitted Colvin. On the long walk out in the dark I was tired but no longer worried, and I allowed myself to savor the satisfaction of being able to hike again in the Adirondack High Peaks in winter.

Donaldson, Emmons, and Seward, March 12-14, 1999:

The last three peaks on my list were Seward, Donaldson, and Emmons. Carl and I signed up for a three-day backpack with the Rochester Winter Mountaineering Society led by Neil Andrews. I enjoy backpacking but winter has extra challenges such as carrying additional weight, keeping one's hands warm enough to function, and making water from snow. We met our group of seven for breakfast in Saranac Lake. I was the only woman.

We drove in four cars to the winter parking lot just before the iron bridge on Corey's Road. We got into a Jeep and the leader's brand new four-wheel-drive truck to drive to the summer trailhead, 3.3 miles away. It was not an easy drive! It had snowed recently and several times we had to get out and push or shovel, but we got there. It's a good thing, because backpacking even from the nearer parking area tested the limits of my strength.

I was still recovering from my back injury and my asthma was acting up. Just moving forward with the heavy winter pack on the level trail was difficult. Under cloudy skies, we started in on the Blueberry Foot Trail for 1.3 miles and turned right on the Calkins Brook Horse Trail. Where that trail makes a sharp right we went left and headed up Donaldson on what is referred to as the Calkins Brook herd path. As the herd path got steeper and went over trees and rocks, I had difficulty in many places pulling myself up. Often I had to ask Carl for help lifting my leg so I could get over an obstacle.

Finally we got high enough on Donaldson that we could pitch our tents in a relatively open area. By now the weather had become clear, cold, and beautiful. We climbed a little way to the summit and then headed for Emmons, reaching it at 3 P.M. Back at our campsite we quickly changed into dry undergarments to stay warm. We finished dinner in the dark and put hot water bottles in our sleeping bags to keep them warm overnight. They sure felt good on my feet!

The next morning was still cold and clear. Packing up the tent warmed us. We had to put the heavy packs back on and head to Seward. Looking towards Seward we could see a steep rock wall ahead of us. Relying on his compass and familiarity with the area, the leader did a wonderful job of getting us around the wall and turning us straight for the summit.

I had done it! Finished the Adirondack 46 in winter. I broke into tears and thanked the others for their help in getting to the top. All that remained was to get down safely to Blueberry Lean-to. There was a lot of snow and it was very steep. I kept falling and needed help getting back up. Finally we made it to the lean-to. The next morning brought a warm, sunny day. The Jeep ride back out to the winter trailhead was not as bad as the ride in!

Jadwiga began the Winter 46 at age 48 and finished at age 52.

30

SALLY HOY

46er # 2924W

Zorro was always a hero of mine! I was undefeated for four years of fencing matches in high school, named one of the top ten fencers in the 1960s in New Jersey. When our kids were younger I was active with the Bill Koch Ski League—played soccer on skis—and was a den leader and brownie leader, coached soccer for the YMCA, as well as modified field hockey. I'm a past president of the Glens Falls-Saratoga Chapter of the Adirondack Mt. Club. I was a nursery school teacher for six years and taught in Junior-Senior High School for fifteen years. I've served as president of the Glens Falls Symphony and on the board of the Glens Falls Home for Women.

My daughter, Kate, and I completed the Summer 46 together when she was thirteen years old. Running, cross-country skiing, and downhill skiing are activities that keep me in shape. I finished the Northeast 111 in July 1999 and completed the Northville-Placid Trail with Barb Harris. We did this 134-mile trail through remote parts of the Adirondack Park in sections, spotting cars.

Forty-Sixing was originally a three-season assault, and I couldn't imagine what I was about to get into when I donned a pair of snowshoes in February 1995 to lead a hike for our chapter up Cascade and Porter. What a difference a season makes! Bugs, roots, and mud were replaced by darkness, spruce traps, frozen this-and-that, and generally no summit lounging. I found Winter 46ing more of a mind game, getting up at 3:30 A.M. for the drive north when my body said, "No!" Most of the climbs of our hiking group were day trips—but some were at night, the Allen Mt. marathon took seventeen hours. One unexpected difficulty was near the summit of Allen when a fellow in our party broke the metal part of his snowshoe and had to rig it together with a stout stick and twistums. We could barely keep awake driving home; one in the party pulled over to sleep.

But winter hiking has been a joy (most of the time). My body functions better in cold. You can do just about anything when you set your mind to it—it is a powerful thing. Winter hiking has given me another sense of that pioneering spirit, in addition to providing a beauteous backdrop given to us by God's creative hand.

Phelps, January 15, 1996:

I trekked alone up Phelps in -15°, with a backdrop of incredibly blue skies. Real cold seems to give clarity to my surroundings. Sounds of my snowshoe steps are crisp. Ice-laden branches sparkle like jewels as do the snowflakes and they all belong to me. The silence lends peacefulness to my soul. Higher up, latticed fingers of snow-encased branches against the deep blue framework of sky are a sight to behold.

They say not to hike alone in winter, but Phelps is a friendly destination and other hardy souls would surely follow. I recall a hike I led with my school kids on a June 1 when biting rain and a snow-patched trail confronted us. The summit was unbearable and snow still crowned Mt. Marcy. You can never be sure what the mountains will bring, for me preparation is the main thing. Many times I have wanted to lighten my winter pack for faster traveling, but wisely, I have resisted.

A couple of rangers in the warming hut were amassing a search effort for a father and son over in the vicinity of Algonquin. They were later found in fairly good condition with minor frostbite and bruised egos. The trail up to Phelp's summit was like a sidewalk and the wind was non-existent. I had this place to myself. In this freeze I didn't stop long for sips of my tomato soup or food. Movements had to be quick. Exposure of my hands to that cold was minimal but occasionally necessary; windmills and arm swings were employed to warm up chilled fingers and the stork stance was used for toes. Since then I have put foot warmers in my boots before the hike if the temperature is that cold.

Chickadees are so friendly at Marcy Dam. They land on your hat and gloves looking for a handout. It just so happened that I had some sunflower seeds for my friends.

Santanoni and Panther, March 9, 1997:

No sooner had we headed down the trail than we had the feeling of being followed. The twinkling stars illuminated the darkness at that time of morning and we knew the day would be a beautiful Harris-Hoy-Ohnmacht (H2O) blue-sky day. But we still couldn't shake the feeling that something was out there. We trudged onward.

At Times Square, a base camp above 4,000' for three trailless mountains, a bright orange tent was set up and I was tempted to tell the girls that I was staying for a nap while they went on; but the day was incredibly gorgeous and the mountains beckoned. We signed in at the canisters on Santanoni and Panther and then descended. As darkness fell we were convinced that we were being followed. We stopped, waited, looked up, and were finally introduced to our mysterious companion. Bopp was the name. Bopp would be on our hikes for the next few outings and each time was a thrill and a heavenly inspiration. But just as mysteriously as Bopp had appeared, Bopp was gone. In my lifetime I will probably not see Bopp again. Hail to Bopp. Hale Bopp.

Saddleback and Basin, December 27, 1997:

Anyone who has ever been to Saddleback knows that a steep,

rocky descent lay between here and Basin Mt. In wintertime, ice forms on that pitch. Many people retreat the way they came and climb Basin from a different way on a different day. Our group of ten did not retreat after summitting at 11:30 A.M. Bill Johnson expertly tied my green rope to a boulder with a stout knot and, one by one, we descended icy cliffs in crampons to a jumping-off area. I jumped the remaining ten feet, but because of my backpack, I pitched forward onto my head and hands, breaking my ring finger on my right hand. Initially it hurt but the cold kept the swelling to a minimum. I duct taped it to the neighboring finger and continued on to Basin. I had broken fingers before so this was nothing to worry about. Zippers were a bit of a problem, though. Off with crampons and on with snowshoes between the summits—Help, Barb!

Remember the rope? It was left purposely back on Saddleback. On the return, a possible abort via Chicken Coop Brook was discussed but the snow was too deep, and so up those cliffs went ten very determined people. Barb's crampons kept coming off! The descent off Saddleback was a delight of butt slides to the Gothics col.

Haystack, January 15, 1998:

Seymour Ellis, Barb Harris, and I left at 6:30 A.M. for the summit of Haystack, later to be joined by Mike Bush, Vic Pomerville, and Marta Bolton past Indian Falls. With snow and wind kicking up, this tenacious group plodded toward their destination without the aid of snowshoes. Going up the chute to the base of Little Haystack was challenging, particularly with the very large crevasse formed near the base; some wondered how they were going to avoid the pit on the return.

Before going out onto the exposed area of Little Haystack, everyone put on more clothes—we looked like the Pillsbury Doughboys. Icy rocks came into view and crampons were affixed to everyone's feet; the wind and blowing snow were incredible.

A bottle of champagne was almost opened in honor of Barb Harris's 46th peak in winter. The plastic cork did not cooperate and Barb did not offer to carry the bottle out. She also tried to sell her snowshoes for $5.00 right then and there, but no takers. Good thing, because they were needed on the way out because of the constant snow. Mike would have offered to sell back her snowshoes for $10.00!

Marshall, February 22, 1998:

Hoy, Harris, and Ohnmacht were at it again on Marshall under their famous blue skies. A 6:40 A.M. start meant no headlamps! At Upper Works register a comment was left: "Diff." Did this mean "difficult" or "different?" At Flowed Lands, this trio met two gals from Maine and Virginia who had been camping and were very surprised and happy to know that other women were out in the woods. Not another soul would they encounter. Full crampons were donned for better grip up the icy brook. A faded path led away from the far reaches of the brook, up—then up more steeply—and then down steeply, ending up at the beaver area they'd been looking for. "Diff" obviously meant, "go a different way." Here was a snow message, "too cold."

A forty-five minute lounge on Marshall with grand views was enjoyed. Back at the beaver area, three snow angels were left behind to keep watch. On the descent, Ellen, in the lead, noticed and warned the other two by inscribing in the snow, snow fleas! They were everywhere—a zillion! Barb asked, as she contemplated dropping drawers for a much-needed pit stop, "How high can these fleas jump?"

Another Upper Works adventure:

As we slipped out into the 5 o'clock darkness the chill grabbed me in a stranglehold forcing me to cough. My nose hairs quickly stuck together and the beginnings of a headache started just above my left eyebrow. We had just driven into the Upper Works parking lot, Barb in her Tracker and me in my SUV. The plan was to do Cliff, but when you share the mountains as much as Barb and I have, you intuitively know what each other is thinking. In harmony we grumbled, "It's too frickin' cold. Let's reschedule."

We said goodbye. She parted while I used the privy. My fingers barely functioned, tending to my zippers. I proceeded down the narrow road toward the main highway seven miles away. Rounding a curve I lost control of the car, swerved to the left, then the right, and over the snow bank. The job was complete with back wheels in the air and a flat, too.

While surveying the situation only two solutions came to mind—stay with the car or walk to the main highway. I kicked the tire some, swore some, and then it dawned on me. I was quite alone on a Sunday morning in January with most mountaineers in bed not willing to face the cold that was chilling and rattling my bones. Decisions under Draconian situations can be daunting, but fear had not entered my psyche yet, only frustration and a feeling of foolishness. My pack contained a thermos of hot soup, two sandwiches, gorp, and candy bars. I figured it would take me under three hours to walk to the main highway. I put the pack on. Then I took the pack off, for I knew I had a full tank of gas that I could run on and off until someone drove by—maybe today, tomorrow for sure, because my husband would make the call to the National Guard by then.

Pack on, pack off, pack…brrrr…do some jumping jacks…what is that I see…an angel appeared in the distance! I am saved! Barb had almost returned to the main highway when she realized she hadn't seen my headlights. She turned around and found me jumping up and down in the road. I hopped into her car and we drove out to the highway to make a cell phone call to AAA; we waited an hour for the tow truck and in that time only one car came by. Finally the tow truck arrived from Pottersville and this driver rolls his window down, shakes his head and asks, "Ladies, do you know how cold it is?" That's why we canceled. "It's 32° below zero!" As with most experiences a lesson is learned: Always leave remote areas together.

Sally began the Winter 46 at age 46 and finished at age 50.

NANCY ELLEN COPELAND

46er #4468W

This has been the most rewarding winter of my life. I have accomplished one of my biggest endeavors, climbing all 46 High Peaks in the winter in one season. With eighteen journeys out to the woods on rainy, sleety, snowy, and twenty-below days, I have enjoyed every minute of it! I have learned lifelong skills not only in climbing but in friendship—things I believe cannot be taught in classrooms.

I learned how to find my way up trailless peaks in trackless snow, and how to persist in bushwhacking to a summit when you are off the usual course. Somehow, after checking your compass thirty times, and after five hours of bushwhacking, you go around the corner and are able to just see the canister almost completely covered in snow. You have worked for this moment all day and here it is right in front of you! You can't fully express the degree of joyfulness and delight you feel inside. You sit down, eat your lunch, sign in, and see who preceded you and how they climbed the mountain. This experience drives me back every weekend for more. This is truly climbing in the Adirondacks, for me.

I've had many climbs I'll never forget, such as climbing the Lower Great Range and Sawteeth in January when it rained the whole trip. By the end of the day, my whole body was so cold—especially my feet which were soaking wet. This taught me a lesson: always bring more than just one pair of extra socks and gloves, as well as other spare clothing. When I first started hiking in the winter, I was under-equipped; for example, I did not have crampons for the Upper Great Range. As time went on, I felt it was good to carry more than you think you may need. One of the most important items to me were my gloves; if my hands were cold I could barely even climb.

As I look back, I think to myself, what an achievement! When I started to climb that first day in late December, I never thought that I would finish my winter round that season. I was thinking more along the lines that I would finish when I was twenty or something. I still can't believe it happened. However, I know that I could not have finished if I did not have the grace of God in my climbing. There were times when I was wondering if I was going to find my way out or even to a summit, and I would pray to God for help. A few times I did do the mountains by myself and I really did not mind it. It gave me time to think.

I started hiking when I was in sixth grade on a class trip to Giant Mountain. I had never hiked before, and it was the year I began my all-season round of the 46, which I finished when I was in the eighth grade. Other sports that I pursue are running marathons, soccer, swimming, and snowboarding. Winter is my favorite climbing season because there are not so many people and you get the summits to yourself; the views are so wonderful in the winter! One of my favorites is the view of Indian Pass and the slides of Colden from Iroquois. The most difficult peak for me was Allen. We could not find Allen Brook, so we had to bushwhack up the side of the mountain. This took us a very long time—we didn't get out until 10 P.M. and we had started at 5:30 in the morning.

In general, I would assess my experience of climbing the Winter 46 as a very good learning experience and a very enjoyable time. I think climbing, that winter, changed me for life. It made me think about things I would never have thought of otherwise. I believe my mental outlook on life changed in some ways. Two examples are that setting goals for yourself is a very good thing, and that you can learn a lot from the environment you live in. I think everyone my age should have to set goals in life, because it really helps you to understand what your mind and body can do when you put your mind to it.

Saddleback, Basin, Marcy, Tabletop, and Phelps, March 13, 1999:

Two of my all-time favorite hikes were my last two climbs, one with my brother Billy. It was a perfect day until the wind picked up, but nevertheless we climbed Saddleback, Basin, Marcy, Tabletop, and Phelps in one day—a once-in-a-lifetime experience. We also tried for Haystack but couldn't make it because of high winds on Little Haystack. On Marcy the wind wasn't as strong, but I could hardly stand up! People were saying it was fifty mph with sixty mph gusts. This experience helped me face my fears of wind that I have had for several years. However, it also reminded me how powerful the wind is, and how it is nothing to play around in.

Earlier that day on Saddleback and Basin, we enjoyed ourselves because the wind was not as strong and we were able to stay on top for some time. Later, clouds came in but we enjoyed views on Phelps. We actually did not rush but had a good time and enjoyed the mountains.

Haystack, Marcy, and Tabletop, March 20, 1999:

My final peak was the Haystack trip with Johnathan Esper. We did Haystack, Marcy, and Tabletop all on the last day of winter, starting at 7 A.M. at the Garden in Keene Valley. We were on Haystack at 11:11, my final High Peak, on a beautiful day with no wind. I was so happy —we took many pictures; this is definitely my favorite mountain. Coming down Marcy we had a blast, sliding down makes the descent so much fun if you can't bring skis up the mountain. This is a Johnathan and Nancy ritual—getting all snowy. My favorite mountains for sliding were Algonquin (below tree line), Giant, Whiteface, Dix, and Skylight. One of my fondest memories of sliding was coming down Giant when I went off a small cliff and went headfirst into the snow; to me, it was the best experience of sliding.

Nancy Ellen started and finished the Winter 46 at age 15.

32

MARIAN ZIMMERMAN

46er #2910W

From my earliest days, the out-doors has been an integral part of my life. My love for the environment was fostered by my parents who gardened and recycled long before recycling was seen as important. It was also nurtured by my mother's commitment to outdoor education and community activism. She led Girl Scout troops on weekend camping trips and my sisters and I were included; these were wonderful times for me as was the week that I spent at summer camp every year. For twenty years my mother taught swimming lessons to buy a tract of land and keep it as park land instead of allowing it to be developed.

I hiked Mt. Katahdin as a graduate student at the University of Maine where I was pursuing ecology and natural resource conservation studies; but it wasn't until after I completed graduate school and went to the Blackfeet Indian Reservation adjacent to Glacier National Park in Montana that I began to hike in earnest. For two summers I completed my workday early and took to the trail for the afternoon and evening. Long summer days made for a lot of miles into the high mountain cirques and alpine lakes where I discovered beautiful vistas and the delight of delicate flowers.

From then on hiking became part of the way I enjoyed exploring new areas. The winter between my summers on the Blackfeet Reservation, I traveled throughout the Southwest and hiked extensively. Jobs with the U.S. Fish and Wildlife Service took me to Portland, Oregon; to eastern Oregon; to Flagstaff, Arizona; and to Anchorage, Alaska. Work typically revolved around the water—rivers, lakes, and marine environments—but I found hiking filled an important portion of my spare time as a way to connect deeply with the natural world.

I moved to Albany, NY, in the summer of 2001, when I decided to enter the Sisters of Mercy. I missed the wide-open vistas of the West—the Rockies, Grand Canyon, Cascades, Chugach Mountains, but rediscovered the hardwood forests of my youth. I met people who introduced me to the Adirondacks and Catskills; they provided a different kind of hiking than I had grown accustomed to in the West. No, the mountains weren't as high and trails were shorter, but they were steeper and often rougher. That caught me by surprise. And the idea of climbing to a summit was also novel; I was used to hiking to a col to cross over into an adjacent drainage, but not head for the peaks; open alpine zones made it not necessary to summit in order to see.

Hiking in the Adirondacks began with a Columbus Day weekend trip to hike Phelps, Wright, and Algonquin with Sister Kathleen Pritty and several other women. The following spring, Sister Fran Husselbeck suggested a hike to Wittenberg and Cornell Mountains in the Catskills. My day off was midweek so I often hiked alone. The Catskills were particularly good as the trails are shorter and the area is close to Albany; the Catskills were also perfect training ground for learning to use map and compass to hike trailless peaks. I felt that it would be difficult to get seriously lost. Successfully completing them built confidence in my ability; I learned how to keep my head and use my resources when the unexpected arose or an unplanned difficulty occurred.

The Catskills made another important contribution to my hiking endeavors. To complete them, the 3500 Club requires four winter hikes to introduce people to the beauty of winter hiking. It all started innocently enough. We had a winter where the snows were late in coming and there was no cross-country skiing nearby, so I decided to complete my winter peaks. They did their magic and thus began my winter hiking. I completed the winter Catskills on Wittenberg and Cornell on a gorgeous day, twelve hours before the "storm of the century." I assumed then that I would hike the Catskills and that would be it, for I didn't believe I could hike the Adirondacks in winter; I found the idea of winter hiking there overwhelming, even terrifying. They seemed exponentially more dangerous and difficult.

My first winter peaks in the Adirondacks were the Santanoni's in March 1991. Spring break at Rensselaer Polytechnical Institute freed up a little extra time. I was finishing my regular season 46, so off I headed with my backpack to Bradley Pond for an early start. It was a windy, frigid night and I wore every article of clothing I'd brought! I met Craig Leroy and Nick Ringelberg who were trying to complete all the Winter 46 in one season; we summitted the three peaks and I returned to Bradley Pond to head out. When I came back with my friend, Julie Martini, to hike Street and Nye, Craig and Nick were there; Craig suggested that we hike together, as we both lived in Troy. He was always talking about the Winter 46; I maintained I had no interest in hiking them, that doing the Catskills was enough for me. Also, I had left the Capital District for Latin America the summer after I completed the winter Catskills.

When I returned I worked a series of temporary jobs while job hunting. I needed something to keep my spirits up, so one day I made the leap and called Craig to go hiking; we decided to hike Mt. Colden. Why I didn't call it quits then I'm not sure; I'd only hiked six of the peaks in winter, but I became committed to completing the Winter 46. Gone was my reticence, replaced by a healthy respect for the mountains and the need to visit them on their terms. To experience their sublime beauty draped in winter garb fills me with awe and delight.

The next winter I started the season with a reunion hike with my friend Janine Mauche. We hiked Big Slide on a frigid day, -15° when we arrived at the Garden trailhead. Brrr! Craig's knee began to act up again and I began hikes with Leo Briand, Dave Graves, Bob Zayhowski, and other ADKers.

Colden, February 9, 1997:

On a beautiful day, Craig LeRoy and I hiked from Tahawus to Flowed Lands on a well-traveled trail and crossed the edge of Lake Colden to the junction. A foot of new, untracked snow made the going slow as we hiked up the steep trail from the lake. We couldn't tell where the trail went; after much searching I was ready to turn back but Craig persisted. Above tree line, the windswept rocks were icy and we encountered a short, steep, icy stretch about a quarter-mile from the summit where crampons would have been helpful, but the lateness and brisk cold winds urged us to keep moving.

Quickly enjoying the summit beauty and satisfaction of having made it, we headed back—it was late. Descending that icy stretch was more difficult going down and I slipped and tore the muscles, tendons, and ligaments in my left ankle. It was 4 o'clock and we were a good seven miles from the car, so I said to myself, "O.K., you have a choice. You can find a way to walk out of here or you can go home tomorrow in a box!" I slid down the mountain on my butt, changed into dry clothes and limped out to Tahawus, a long, slow trip. It was late, but we made it out warm and dry. My ankle took the rest of the winter season and then some to heal.

Marcy, March 7, 1998:

I decided to climb Marcy alone, feeling pretty confident that I would encounter other hikers along the Van Hoevenberg Trail. Just before Little Marcy I finally met other hikers who were on their way to Marcy and hoped to hike Skylight and Gray as well. Above tree line the wind howled and snow came at us horizontally. I waited for the others in the lee of the rocky outcrop on the summit and then we started down the back side toward Four Corners, but after a couple of cairns we were in a total whiteout! It was such an eerie feeling. We were reluctant to travel just by compass bearing; we did not want to end up deep in Panther Gorge! We turned back.

Haystack, Basin, and Saddleback—Almost, February 20, 1999:

Dave Graves was sick so Bob Zayhowski and I decided to hike something that Dave had already done. We were unable to get to the

Garden parking lot due to ice, so we parked in town and walked an extra two miles to the trailhead. At Johns Brook Lodge, we met other hikers who described icy conditions on the peaks. We bare-booted it past Bushnell Falls and Slant Rock until the pitch became so steep we needed crampons. We summitted Haystack with only minor difficulty in icy spots, and then dropped below tree line beyond Little Haystack to eat lunch. We continued on to Basin where conditions were good as was our progress.

As we climbed near the summit of Basin the wind increased, additional layers of clothing were needed. Coming down Basin, very steep spots required care but we negotiated them without undue difficulty and continued making good progress. We arrived at the steep rocky outcrop of Saddleback at 3:20 P.M. as two hikers were descending. This was a particularly difficult spot, and we spent over an hour trying to find our way around the thin skin of ice and snow cover. We decided to try and work our way east along the edge of the rocks. Eventually we came to a place twenty feet below the summit that was impassable; we doubled back and picked up the regular trail on the rocks.

We were so close! Once up to the summit it was an easy hike back to Johns Brook Lodge and the Garden. Bob and I had been having an on-going dialogue whether it was doable under these conditions. Finally, Bob impressed upon me to give up the quest and as I was turning around, I lost my footing. I will never know what happened, but in turning to go back I somehow slipped and fell some sixty feet.

Much of what happened after that remains in a fog. What I knew, after Bob helped me up, was that I was not going to be walking out. He took me to the two hikers, Maciek Domanski and Arek Pasikowski, that we had met on arriving at the base of the rocks and left me in their care for the night as he retraced to go for help. Luckily the men were camping in the col between Basin and Saddleback about a quarter-mile from where I fell. When I returned later to the site I was amazed that I was able to cover that distance. What I remember is the pain of them putting me into Maciek's sleeping bag. We were fortunate that it was relatively warm outside, 10-20°. I could not have asked for two kinder, more thoughtful helpers than

Maciek and Arek. They stayed up the entire night heating tea to keep me hydrated and warm. One funny tidbit was that as they sat up through the night with me they talked constantly to keep awake. In my fog I thought that my French had really gotten away from me, for I didn't understand anything they were saying! I realized later they were speaking in Polish!

The next morning I was air lifted out to an emergency room. The paramedic explained my options and suggested that a sling would probably be less painful, given my injuries. I agreed—only to learn once off the ground that the sling only offered leg but no upper body support. That is when I discovered that I had no use of my right arm to hold onto the cable! As I dangled from the cable while they drew me up 200 feet into the helicopter I realized that, of necessity, I had to dig deep to find the strength to hold on with only one arm. Once in the helicopter I tried to relax and enjoy the magnificent day and the beauty of the mountains. My ability to focus lasted perhaps a total of thirty seconds. I remember nothing else until hours later.

My accident once again terminated the hiking season prematurely, but it launched me into a whole other venture—that of healing my broken body. My injuries were extensive and required multiple hospitalizations and surgeries, as well as months of disability leave from work. But to focus on them would be to miss the real story of the responsiveness of the Adirondack hiking community and my own inner processes as a result of the experience. This has proven to be a time of rich learning as well as a time of seeing the hiking community and my other friends at their very best. Hikers that I barely knew helped me in so many ways. Some helped retrieve my gear that was left behind on the mountain; some invited me to dinner to break the boredom of convalescence; some drove me places because I was not driving. Someone was always there to lend a hand when I needed one.

Haystack, Basin, and Saddleback: Second Time Around, December 28, 1999

This was my first hike after my accident. I repeated this hike with Janine Mauche DuMond (minus the part to Haystack). This was a time to make my peace with the mountain and survey the scene. Craig LeRoy and I summitted Saddleback from the Orebed Trail. It was windy so we did not linger; I looked down on the rocky outcrop where I had fallen. The rocks had a layer of ice and little snow. I was grateful that, for this time at least, I did not have to negotiate those rocks. Someday I will return for that. For the moment it was enough to know that I was ready to go forward with the rest of my winter hikes.

Sawteeth, Gothics, and Armstrong, January 15, 2000:

Dave Graves, Bob Zayhowski, and I hiked in from the Ausable Club on a -15° day, leaving simultaneously with a group of hikers of the Rochester Winter Mountaineering Society. We were treated to a splendid view to the southwest on Sawteeth; at 0° with a steady breeze coming up over the ridge, we didn't linger. Richard Preis of the RWMS joined us to Pyramid and Gothics. None of us had brought snowshoes because there had been so little snow; there were spots where it would have been easier. We arrived on Gothics to a toasty 10° and no wind. The view was magnificent...we could see forever. Two hikers were clearly visible seated on the summit of Saddleback!

We pressed on to Armstrong to enjoy lunch and the spectacular scenery. Bob and Dave went ahead to make sure the Beaver Meadow Trail was tracked; it was getting late. Richard and I were treated to sighting a mink near the summit of Armstrong. At a Flowed Lands lean-to we had the delight of watching a pine marten circling around us.

South Dix and Hough, February 26, 2000:

This hike holds a special place in my heart, a "reunion hike" with Maciek Domanski and Arkadiusz Paskowski who helped me when I fell on Saddleback last year. I had updated them on my recovery throughout the year. We decided a reunion hike would be a nice way to reconnect and celebrate. Our day was relatively warm and started off clear. After crossing West Mill Brook and climbing onto the shoulder of South Dix, the snow on the trees melted on us. Traversing around to the slide leading to the summit, the visibility decreased. On the slide Arek had trouble with his legs cramping; at the summit he decided he needed to turn back. This concerned me, but there were quite a few people from the Glens Falls group in the area, so I knew he would find help if needed (which he did not).

Maciek and I continued on over Puff to Hough and conditions actually improved—warm weather had consolidated the snow and today's cooler temperatures made for firm footing. Retracing, we got below the slide on South Dix before being caught by the dark. Wet, soft snow made for slower going; we were relieved to find the ice shelf across the brook still intact. Arek was back in good spirits. This was a special day commemorating a chance encounter that brought us together and made an important difference in my life.

Donaldson, Emmons, and Seward, March 7, 2000:

Extensive route-finding three days ago netted Pete Hickey and me only Donaldson, so I made an Internet inquiry about someone interested in hiking the Sewards. Inge Aiken responded and even though she only needed Seward she was game to try for all three. Inge agreed to continue to Emmons so I could be sure of summitting at least one of the other peaks; I did not want to put all my eggs in the Seward basket, run into difficulties, and come home with only Donaldson again. What a good sport! By now it was warming and the snow was sticking to our snowshoes and slowing us down; it took an extra hour to go over to Emmons and back.

Off Donaldson, we scouted for the herd path to Seward to no avail. At 1:20 we proceeded along the height of land; this was working fairly well until we ended up at the base of the cliffs to the west of the summit; we did not want to scale them, but to the east was a sheer drop off. We decided to traverse around the cliffs, hiking for what seemed a long time until we could start to climb, and then ascended a steep, heavily vegetated slope. Progress was exceedingly slow. At 3:30 we were still struggling with a dense tangle of spruces, but decided to continue in hopes of finding another way out rather than having to retrace our steps. Finally we broke out near the ridge and it was an easy hike to the summit. We could not find the canister. We walked right by it and over to the next false summit. Only when we ran out of high ground did we look back and see it tucked under trees—within feet of where we had walked.

Now—how to depart? Neither the herd path to Ward Brook nor to the Donaldson col were evident. As it was now 4 o'clock and we were not going to be out before dark, we opted to retrace; by 5:20

we were back to the Calkins Brook herd path and got down to the brook crossing by dark. Our tracks were "melting" in the wet snow; the remaining walk out, snow conditions, and our weariness made for a slow trip—but we were jubilant at having hiked all three peaks!

Dix and Hough, March 18, 2000—46th peak:

At last the day to complete my winter hikes dawned, clear and initially very cold. Leo Briand, Dave Marcy, Nina White, Richard Preis, Bob Zaykowski, Pete Hickey, and I started early because although I only needed Dix, there were others who wanted to continue on to Hough. I wanted to do both because we had had no views when I was on Hough last month—and because signing a canister register on my last hike seemed fitting. Off we went on a most perfect morning—the day warmed to a comfortable temperature. I was worried about crossing the North Bouquet because of previous warm weather and we had found smaller stream crossings with open water. Whole stretches of the river were open, but when we arrived at the lean-to, we found just enough ice on rocks to permit a dry passage. This was a huge hurdle successfully negotiated.

At the base of the slide some donned snowshoes or crampons and up we went; leaving the slide for the trying quarter-mile stretch to the trail required traversing a steep slope in unconsolidated snow—hard work. I put on snowshoes and then crampons; the rest of the group had gotten ahead of me while I wrestled with my footgear, but what a great bunch! They waited for me ten minutes from the summit so I could lead the way.

We were treated to spectacular 360-degree views as we summitted at 12:50. It was calm, clear, and warm enough to linger on top and savor our accomplishment; we could see forever and enjoyed picking out the many spots we've visited. We celebrated by waving Tibetan peace flags and taking multiple photos, then we ate lunch. We headed over the Beckhorn and arrived at Hough at 3 o'clock—leaving our packs in the col to bushwhack out the South Branch of the Boquet.

Before dark descended we lost a lot of elevation, but had miles to hike back. The delight of it was that the full moon illuminated our way so brightly that we did not need headlamps. It was magical as we watched the mountains profiled against the night sky. It was a perfect day and evening—the kind you hope for and dream of for your last hike.

Marian began the Winter 46 at age 40 and finished at age 49.

DONNA JERDO

46er # 3703W

I was born in Ticonderoga, New York, on March 18, 1952. I have an older sister, Patty, and two younger brothers, Joe and Michael. My parents' families came from northern Italy. I took accordion and piano lessons for what seemed forever. One of my father's favorite songs was "Climb Every Mountain."

Living close to Lake Champlain, our family did a lot of fishing, especially in the winter and even at night. Ice fishing is a great sport here in the Adirondacks. We fished in a shanty with a lantern; my father had a gas stove that not only served as a heater, but we also cooked on it. My mother operated a diner in Port Henry and served "ice fish" on the menu caught by us.

They didn't have school sports when I attended school in the late

1960s. After secretarial school in Plattsburgh, I married and had three children between 1973 and 1992. I've happily worked at the Essex County ARC for the past twenty-four years and just graduated from Empire State College with a Bachelor's degree in Business Administration. I'm the grandmother of two wonderful children and spend as much time as I can with my family.

My main activity over the years was walking—before work, on break, after work! I was a heavy smoker until 1992, but have not touched a cigarette since; I have so much more energy and that's when it all started! When my youngest, Jarrah, was two, my oldest daughter Julie hiked with friends and one day she suggested maybe that we'd like to hike on this mountain that my brother Michael hunts on in New Russia. I will never forget that day; my legs had turned to rubber! At the top of Blueberry Cobbles, I had had it! But when we saw the views from the top of "Baldy," I couldn't believe my eyes. My brother said he knew a guy that hiked all the 46 High Peaks and that maybe we should do it. I thought he was crazy.

Our very first High Peak in 1994 was Mt. Marcy! My husband Stewart and I hiked this with Jarrah on his back and with a friend. Hiking the highest peak in New York State—what were we thinking? A ranger on the summit told our friend to stay off the alpine growth; we didn't know what he was talking about. Another ranger warned him to wear boots, not sneakers. We didn't even bring a lot of food or water. Wow, have we learned from our mistakes.

One story about our experiences in the High Peaks will stay with me forever. Stewart and I, and Julie and her fiancé, Tom, decided to hike Gothics. After a great time on the summit we headed down and I decided to run ahead with my usual burst of energy after enjoying the views. I slipped on a small rock, heard a "pop" and down I went. My right leg from the knee down was facing to the right! Crying, I told everyone I couldn't walk; Stewart told me to get on his back and he would carry me down to the huge slanting boulder on the Beaver Meadow Trail. No sooner was I on Stewart's back than he twisted his ankle, spraining it badly. What a mess! At the boulder Julie made a splint for me out of the metal from Tom's backpack, but it was unsuccessful—I couldn't walk and it was very painful.

Tom went for help. A young man and his wife appeared and

offered to help. Although a small-framed guy, he tells me he is going to carry me on his back. Stewart would take over when he tired; at times on this steep, rugged descent, I dragged my body down the trail. What a nightmare. The ladder at Beaver Meadow Falls was the hardest; we made it just beyond the falls, five hours later, and in came the militia! People had come from Malone to assist. They strapped me to a sled and carried me to a waiting DEC truck on Lake Road and then the hospital.

Here we were, both of us 46ers, in wheelchairs! I bought a knee support and continued to climb small peaks like Mt. Jo, Pocomoonshine, and even Camel's Hump in Vermont. I went through months of physical therapy before the surgery of reconstructing my ACL knee ligament was done; I even participated in a research study for the next five years on reconstruction versus non-reconstruction of ACL's. We continue to hike and Stewart and I ran our first half marathon. For my fiftieth birthday, the one gift I asked my son Johnathan for was to hike Giant with me when he was on college break. His boots weren't suitable for wearing crampons so he had a difficult time; it snowed the whole day and was very icy. When he got to the summit he was the happiest I'd seen him in a while!

I think about all the hours spent wearing snowshoes or crampons, and when I finally take them off I feel as though I could run like a deer! I think about those nights before a hike, tossing and turning, and when finally getting to sleep the alarm goes off! I think about all the nights sitting at the kitchen table; Stewart would plan a route that didn't consist of just one peak but, "Hey, while we're there, we might as well hike a couple more!" My first hike without my husband was Giant with my sister-in-law; I have to admit I was a little nervous about going without a man. I have come a long way since then. Friends in the office and I usually take a day off to hike without men. It's a great time to share stories with each other and a lot of fun.

In addition to hiking I usually run every morning before work, walk during breaks, and have become more health conscious! I have been a vegetarian for fifteen years, but am very conscientious about getting enough protein and calcium. Good sleep and a healthy, positive attitude towards life also keep one in good shape! Hiking has heightened my appreciation of what God has created in the beauty around us, and brought me closer to the people I love. Hiking is a time to learn things about each other, to really get to know one another, to create memories that never fade. When my family hikes with me I can't explain how good it makes me feel. We always have a good laugh! When our friend Ed started hiking with us, he said not to ever ask him to hike in the winter. He became a Winter 46er in January 2003.

Stewart and I have developed a reputation—we never tell "newcomers" just how far each hike is or how tough it is; if you tell people the grueling details of some of the hikes you'd never get anyone to hike with you. We usually take newcomers up Cascade and Porter, then Phelps or Giant; if they like it, they come back for more! Now I tell them, "Read about it in 'Women With Altitude'." I think back to all the early mornings, late nights, the cuts and bruises, the sore muscles, fatigue, anxiety, hunger, and thirst—I wouldn't trade any of that for the world!

I have also learned that when you're hiking with children make it fun! Point out things to them such as the mushrooms, the funny-shaped trees, the flowers. Give them food and drink before they get hungry and thirsty. Compliment them on a job well done. I've learned that you can't force them! If they get tired let them rest. If they want to turn around, that's okay too. Just make it fun. I speak from experience. My advice to people who want to hike the High Peaks: Go for it! Be prepared. Don't hike alone. Tell people where you are going. Bring plenty of water and extra clothes. Watch the weather. Bring a map and compass and cell phone in case of emergency. Take your time. Enjoy the beauty of nature that surrounds you. Don't rush through this time in your life. Enjoy! The mountains aren't going anywhere. Climbing the peaks in the winter has given me a new definition of determination.

In the beginning, Stewart and I had no idea that we would climb all 46 High Peaks in the winter. We went from having no proper gear to carrying a cell phone for safety. We used to hike in the summer with only a fanny pack with enough water and food for the hike. Now we are prepared for everything. Proper clothing I'd recommend for winter trips are: sock liners, wool socks, gaiters, waterproof boots, snowshoes, and ten-point crampons (we graduated from inset crampons). I wear lined wind pants with polypro or thermax long underwear, duofold or polypro top, wicking sports bra, fleece, a wind parka that has zippers under the arms so your body can breathe and not hold heat in, waterproof mittens, neck gaiter, fleece headband, and extra clothes, "just in case." I have recently included lint from my clothes dryer—it's very light and can start a fire with no problem.

We call home to our kids or my mother every time we hit the summit and let them know when to expect us home. I need to thank my children for being so understanding and for tolerating us through all the times we weren't home or came home late. My husband Stewart, who led us through all these hikes, deserves a great "Thanks" from all of us. His knowledge of the woods and his memory made these successful hikes. Also, Amy and Ed have been wonderful hiking companions; both were dedicated and we have built wonderful friendships. This is a very big accomplishment for me and I am extremely proud of what I have done. I love the mountains and will continue to climb them till I can't walk anymore.

Dix, February 8, 1998:

We're starting to get serious about this winter hiking: we bought snowshoes, good boots, hiking sticks, hand warmers, you name it, we prepared for it! We started this fourteen-mile round-trip before sunrise, my first experience doing this. It was beautiful! The sunrise was spectacular. We crossed over frozen Round Pond (a little scary) but it saved time. The trail wasn't broken which made it difficult— the trail beyond the slide is so steep! The temperature was over 50° and we stayed on the summit for an hour; what a beautiful view. Coming down was fun—just sat and enjoyed the slide!

Big Slide, March 12, 1998:

We took the day off from work to hike in subzero temperatures! The forecast is calling for snow and an extremely cold day, and where are we? On top of a mountain! We took the trail over the Brothers, returning the same way. A short distance in, a friend turned around because he didn't feel well. This was probably the coldest day we had ever hiked—we estimated that with the wind chill it had to be forty below zero. It was so cold that our sandwiches were frozen. Stewart's beard and mustache were covered with ice. From the summit we watched the snow come in like a big white blanket; this was the extent of our view and it didn't take us long to leave that summit!

Lower Wolf Jaw, January 23, 1999:

This was an exciting hike. The first time Stewart and I had attempted this in the winter wasn't successful. It was right after the ice storm we had here and we completely lost the trail because there were trees down everywhere. We could still hear branches falling. This time Stewart's snowshoe had broken, and there was so much snow that Amy and I had a difficult time breaking trail. It was a long, tiring, tough hike up the Wedge Brook Trail. I remember the only way to continue to break trail was to focus on a certain point and not stop till I reached it. Amy would take over when I got tired. The snow was so heavy that our legs tired quickly. When we finally reached the summit it was beautiful! We even made snowmen when we got there!

Marshall, January 31, 1999:

Stewart, Amy Hayes, Ed Boyle and I left Upper Works to Flowed Lands, saving time by crossing over the ice. I love Flowed Lands, so much that I had a picture professionally painted of the mountains surrounding this place. To this day Ed will tell you that if this were his first winter hike, he would never hike another! It was a nice hike till about a quarter mile from the top; we should have stayed in the brook, but ventured off to the left of it too soon. We literally crawled through brush so thick a rabbit couldn't have squeezed through! We couldn't put on our snowshoes because they would have caught on this impenetrable "stuff." We fell into many spruce traps and had to pull each other out.

Haystack, January 29, 2000:

This was a twelve-hour day! The weather was beautiful. We went in from Johns Brook Lodge—I'd never been to the warming hut before. Took advantage of the hospitality on the way in and out. The packed trail ended from there, which starts to tire you. We missed the turn to Haystack, even after reading the sign that said: "Marcy, 1.5 miles." We must have gone a quarter to a half mile up beyond the turnoff to the left. Luckily, Amy happened to turn around and say, "I wonder what those two big mountains are back there?" I looked at Stewart's face and knew that those two big mountains were Little Haystack and Haystack! We immediately headed back down the trail and, later, had a pretty good laugh about it—back at the junction we noticed the other sign: "Haystack." Oh, I was a little upset!

Going up Little Haystack was a trip and a half! It was steep and icy. It's almost like we inched our way up and I remember saying, "Hey, I like this pace!" The strenuous hike up to the summit of Haystack was definitely worth it. It was the most awesome view ever! It was clear and we could see for miles. The sky was so blue! (Whenever I see such blue skies it makes me think of my father. I feel that he is always looking down on me.) The views were so spectacular that we didn't want to leave!

We knew we still had eight miles to go to the trailhead, so we headed down. I will never forget coming off Little Haystack. We just sat down and let go! I came down one section so fast that I lost my hiking pole, tried to grab a tree, and thought I pulled my arm out of the socket! Ed "inched" his way back up for my pole. What a lot of fun! Of course, coming out it got dark. We were cold and tired and hungry. A gentleman at the warming hut fixed us tea and coffee, we rested and got warm, then continued down. This is the best hike that I have taken in the winter!

Macomb, South Dix, East Dix, and Hough, March 4, 2000:

What a long day, but very eventful! We parked on I-87 at the first rest area south between exits 30 and 29. We followed West Mill Brook and when that split, we stayed to the left. When the route ended at a pond, we went around it and bushwhacked up this steep mountain that seemed forever. I asked Ed and Stewart, already on top, where the canister was and they said this mountain isn't Macomb. Amy and I thought they were kidding. We had gathered on the summit of Sunrise Mountain! Macomb was in sight but a long way off! Ugh! Off the backside of Sunrise to Macomb we went, breaking trail the whole way—and it was a long way!

Stewart navigated us right to the canister—he's very good at that. We met two hikers who had come in from Route 73 and decided to follow their trail out; we carried our cell phone and arranged for our son to pick us up on Route 73 to drive us to our starting point. We gave him an approximate time to meet us but our timing was way off! We headed to South Dix, enjoying awesome views on all these peaks. The weather was beautiful. We left our packs on South Dix and went on to Hough—that was a steep climb! Came back and went over to East Dix. By now our water supply was low. Our friend, Red, filtered the water that had collected in crevices on the summit rock—it didn't taste the greatest but it was wet!

We soon lost the hikers' trail we had planned to follow and bush-whacked the west side of Spotted Mountain and then Elizabethtown 4 peak, staying high but next to the Boquet River all the way out, and it brought us right to Route 73. Luckily my husband and Red have a good sense of direction. We bushwhacked for fourteen hours!

Couchsachraga and Santanoni, March 9, 2000:

We took the day off from work to do these two. This was the third time up to these peaks. On the way in to the trailhead we experienced a flat tire on our truck, and I knew that this wasn't going to be a good day! The forecast called for rain late in the day. Stewart and Ed changed the tire and the hike in was good. Got around Bradley Pond, started up to Times Square, and that route was good. Off we went to Couchsachraga, following a pretty decent trail until we got to the last climb up to the summit, then lost the path and made our own. What a long hike over there. That's okay—we need Couchsachraga! Okay, let's go to Santanoni.

We watched the black clouds roll in, heard thunder, and then saw the lightning! It had misted all day and it wasn't supposed to rain until later. Sure! I looked at Amy and said, "I'm scared." She replied, "So am I." I asked Stewart if he thought we should return another day. "Yeah, right, are you kidding, we're here, and we're going to bag this one." I put a lot of trust in my husband's judgment, so off we went.

I prayed so much on this hike. It was raining, thundering, light-ning, and snowing all the way up to the summit. On the summit the black clouds and lightning rolled all around us. We found the canister and headed out after a quick picture. The black clouds had passed but the rain started again back at Times Square. I want out of there. We'd left most of our water down at Bradley Pond. It rained all the way back to the truck. We were soaked through our ponchos. I won't ever forget the weather that we hiked through that day.

Saddleback and Basin, March 19, 2000—46th Peak:

A crew of nine of us left the Garden trailhead on a beautiful day. What an exciting feeling! I am ready for these, fully rested, and can't wait for that wonderful feeling of climbing them all in the winter. We stopped at a junction and I fed a bird out of my hand. We climbed over snow-covered ladders, (which I didn't realize at the time) up the steep trail to the junction to Gothics, and met a crew from Rochester at the summit of Saddleback. Having just ascended Saddleback returning from Basin, they told us we needed ropes to go down the cliff.

I thought at first that they were kidding when they told us. I was a little leery about attempting this rappelling. After I watched a couple of the guys do this I said, "I can do this!" So off I went! It was exciting, holding onto the rope and walking down backwards off the ledges. Then it hit me. We have to go back up! The first time we ascended Saddleback years ago I thought back then that we had lost our minds!

I looked over at Basin and was very anxious. One to go. I felt like I could run to the top I was so excited! As we topped the first "bump," many emotions started taking over. I was anxious, happy, nervous, sad—I had carried my father's picture with me, close to my heart. Going around the side and heading up to Basin, Stewart wanted me to go first. Suddenly our cell phone rang, a call about work, and Stewart reported that we were on top of a mountain!

When we got close to the summit I couldn't hold back my tears! I remember kissing my husband and thanking God and my father. Everyone hugged and we took many pictures. We didn't stay long on top because we were anxious to retrace the long route back and go celebrate our accomplishment with our hiking buddies and our family. One by one, we held the rope and slowly walked back up the rock cliffs of Saddleback. We were too excited to be nervous! It was fun.

Donna began the Winter 46 at age 45 and finished at age 48.

Other recorded Winter 46er women during the canister era through March 2001, from whom information was not received, are: Kathleen Gill, Marguerite Munch-Weber, and Janet Stein.

AFTERWORD

Many of us have characterized climbing the Winter 46 as the most adventurous thing we ever did, one of the happiest times of our lives, not only physically rewarding but emotionally fulfilling. We are spiritually nourished in the wild world. As one person said, "It is the most spiritual thing I do outside of church." Many speak of feeling a closeness to God out there. Winter climbing becomes almost addictive. For many of us, there is no better high.

Some of the greatest experiences are meeting other hikers and developing long-lasting friendships. Nearly everyone speaks of the camaraderie that develops. The bonds of winter friendship, male and female, young and old, go incredibly deep, with each of us helping the others achieve. We find to our delight that our long-time relationships are enhanced, feeling a deep sharing experience with our husbands, partners, and children.

Another powerful motivator is the discovery that you can do just about anything when you set your mind to it. There is nothing like winter mountain climbing to teach "mental toughness." We learn a lot about ourselves on the trail, about our vulnerabilities, but mostly about our strengths. Winter climbing tests us, teaches us that we are not quitters, and gives us a new confidence in our ability to make correct judgments and to overcome seemingly impossible obstacles. It is reassuring to have a powerful tool to cope with the stresses of life that is as simple as putting one foot in front of the other. In winter, this process takes the mind off everything else, requires full concentration and commitment. Many of us discovered that if we want something badly enough, we will do anything possible to reach that goal. We are survivors and use our knowledge to help us do that.

Not only is the sense of self-reliance increased, but also that of interdependence. As in many of life's pursuits, teamwork and cooperation are essential for success. What may be impossible for one individual to achieve—in this case, breaking trail many miles to a mountain summit through knee-deep snow—becomes possible. Many of us are very aware that climbing the 46 High Peaks in the winter was both an individual and a shared accomplishment.

The rewards of this sport are increased physical strength and fitness, self-confidence, and an ongoing process of maturing and self-knowledge. We learn good planning, patience, perseverance, stretching perceived limits, and inner strength. Our moments of living in an enchanted world are what bring us back again and again. The beauty of nature nourishes us and the elemental forces of nature thrill and humble us; every day out there is an exciting experience. Reaching a mountain summit, however many times it is repeated, is an experience of pure happiness. Would we do this again? Let me get my pack!

APPENDIX I

THE 46 ADIRONDACK HIGH PEAKS

High Peak	Rank in Height	Elevation
Algonquin Peak	2	5114'
Allen Mountain	26	4340'
Armstrong Mountain	22	4400'
Basin Mountain	9	4827'
Big Slide Moutnain	27	4240'
Blake	43	3960'
Cascade Mountain	36	4098'
Cliff Mountain	44	3960'
Mount Colden	11	4714'
Mount Colvin	39	4057'
Couchsachraga Peak	46	3820'
Dial Mountain	41	4020'
Dix Mountain	6	4857'
Mount Donaldson	33	4140'
East Dix	42	4012'
Mount Emmons	40	4040'
Esther Mountain	28	4240'
Giant Mountain	12	4627'
Gothics	10	4736'
Gray Peak	7	4840'

Mount Haystack	3	4960'
Hough Peak	23	4400'
Iroquois Peak	8	4840'
Lower Wolfjaw Mountain	30	4175'
Macomb Mountain	21	4405'
Mount Marcy	1	5344'
Mount Marshall	25	4360'
Nippletop	13	4620'
Nye Mountain	45	3895'
Panther Peak	18	4442'
Phelps Mountain	32	4161'
Porter Mountain	38	4059'
Mount Redfield	15	4606'
Rocky Peak Ridge	20	4420'
Saddleback Mountain	17	4515'
Santanoni Peak	14	4607'
Sawteeth	35	4100'
Seward Mountain	24	4361'
Seymour Mountain	34	4120'
Mount Skylight	4	4924'
South Dix	37	4060'
Street Mountain	31	4166'
Tabletop Mountain	19	4427'
Upper Wolfjaw Mountain	29	4185'
Whiteface Mountain	5	4867'
Wright Peak	16	4580'

APPENDIX II

CLIMBING THE PEAKS

Below are ascents from trailhead to summit and typical miles to a peak; all figures are round-trip. The shortest trip is 4.8 miles and a 1,940' ascent to 4,098' Cascade; the longest, up to twenty miles to 4,340' Allen—nearly half off-trail—and a 2,800' ascent. The shortest trek to 5,344' Marcy is 14.8 miles with a 3,166' ascent; many go on to 4,924' Skylight south of Marcy, or bushwhack to 4,840' Gray, west of Marcy—or both! Skylight is 17.2 miles via Lake Arnold from the Adirondack Loj; twenty miles from Upper Works.

Eight challenging peaks make up The Great Range: Lower and Upper Wolf Jaw (4,175' and 4,185'), Armstrong (4,400'), Gothics (4,736'), Saddleback (4,515'), Basin (4,827'), Haystack (4,960'), and Marcy (5,344'). These are near enough each other to tempt one to overreach. All present formidable challenges: cliffs, narrow trails with sharp drops, very steep trails, and exposed summits. Treks vary from 9.8 to 17.8 miles and ascents from 2,600' to 3,600'. Establishing base camp at the Johns Brook Lodge area, 677 feet higher than the Garden and 3.5 miles closer to the Range, makes the days easier.

The magnificent MacIntyre Range includes Algonquin (5,114'), Wright (4,580'), Iroquois (4,840'), and Marshall (4,360'). These peaks are famous for high wind and whiteout conditions in winter; the first three have large open summits. Algonquin is a 2,936' ascent and an eight-mile trek from the Loj; many climb Wright and/or Iroquois with Algonquin. Marshall is 13.8 miles and a 2,560' ascent from Upper Works; sixteen miles round-trip and a similar ascent from the Loj (335' ascent is lost over Avalanche Pass).

The five peaks of the Dix Range are climbed in many combinations from all directions. Dix (4,857'), the only peak here with a DEC-marked trail, is 13.6-miles and a 3,200' ascent via Round Pond; many bushwhack one mile from Dix to Hough (4,400') and 800' back up Dix. From Elk Lake, one must add four miles (round-trip) on unplowed road to South Dix (4,060'), East Dix (4,012'), Macomb (4,405') and Hough.

The Seward and Santanoni Ranges may be obstacles in many minds to achieving the Winter 46. Many camp to reduce the daunting number of miles per day. Seward (4,361'), Donaldson (4,140'), Emmons (4,040'), and Seymour (4,120') are approached via 10.8 miles on the Ward Brook Truck Trail, followed by eight miles off-trail over Seward, Donaldson, and Emmons and back, a total ascent of 3,380' (including retracing); or 6.6 miles on Ward Brook/Calkins Brook Truck Trails, followed by about ten miles off-trail; Seymour is usually climbed separately.

The Santanoni Range is approached via 4.3 miles on the Bradley Pond Trail and then off-trail about 1.5 miles and 2,400 feet up to "Times Square" on the Santanoni-Panther ridge from which 4,442' Panther, 4,607' Santanoni, and 3,820' Couchsachraga, are reached. The latter involves an 800' re-climb to Times Square.

Many peaks are climbed in pairs; ascents below include both: Nippletop (4,620') and Dial (4,020'), a 14.7-mile loop with 4,000' ascent; Giant (4,627') and Rocky Peak Ridge (4,420'), 8.2 miles and a 4,300' ascent; Street (4,166') and Nye (3,895'), eight miles off-trail and a 2,180' ascent with a tricky river crossing; Whiteface (4,867') with Esther (4,240', off-trail), ten miles and a 3,300' ascent; Redfield (4,606') and Cliff (3,960'), partially off-trail and 19-20 miles via the Loj or Upper Works; Cascade with Porter (4,059'), a 2,300' ascent in 6.2-miles; Colvin (4,057') and Blake (3,960'), 2,800' ascent in 14.6 miles.

Single peaks often climbed alone are Big Slide (4,240'), eight miles and a 2,800' ascent over the three Brothers or a 9.6-mile loop via Johns Brook Valley; Sawteeth (4,100'), 12.4-miles and a 2,900' ascent from Lake Road; Phelps (4,161'), 8.8 miles and a 1,982' ascent from the Loj; Tabletop (4,427') is off-trail from Indian Falls, which is 8.8 miles from the Loj, with an ascent of 2,250'; Colden (4,714'), via Lake Arnold 12.6 miles and a 2,535' ascent; via Lake Colden, losing ascent over Avalanche Pass, 14.8 miles and a 2,870' ascent.

Later surveys found Blake, Couchsachraga, Nye, and Cliff below 4,000', but the original 46 peaks are the requirement for 46er membership. MacNaughton is now measured at 4,000 feet but is not required.

APPENDIX III

GLOSSARY OF TERMS

BEARPAWS: A type of showshoe suitable for mountain climbing.

BELAY: To secure a climber by means of a rope attached to a projection.

BIVOUAC: Camping in the open with no shelter or improvised shelter.

BUSHWHACKING: Off-trail hiking with map and compass.

CAIRNS: Rock piles periodically placed, usually above tree line or on bare rock where markers are absent, to mark a route or indicate a summit.

COL: A pass or low point between two adjacent peaks.

CRAMPONS: Laced onto boots for stability on icy snowy surfaces, most crampons today have twelve points with two "front points" that enable the climber to balance on toes for very steep sections.

DIKE: A band of different-colored rock, usually with straight, well-defined sides, formed when igneous rock is intruded into existing rock.

FRONT-POINTING: Facing the mountain and using the front two points of twelve-point crampons to climb.

HERD PATH: Rough paths with no markers or maintenance created by climbers.

HITCH-UPS: Boardwalks and trail work fastened to cliffs and rocks.

LEAN-TO: A three-sided shelter with an over-hanging roof and one open side.

POST-HOLE: To sink deeply with each step into snow. These conditions require the use of snowshoes.

RIME ICE: An accumulation of granular ice tufts on the windward side of exposed objects such as rocks and trees, resembling hoarfrost.

SLAB: To traverse around a mountainside, in a riverbank or other sloped area, often making footing more difficult.

SPRUCE-HOLE: An often invisible hole in the snow created by many feet of snow blanketing small spruce trees, whose branches create spaces below the snow surface.

THE SWEEP: In a group of hikers, a person assigned to stay behind the slowest member to assure the safety of all.

SWITCHBACKS: A zigzag trail designed for surmounting a steep slope up a mountainside.

TREE HOLDS: Grasping trees to pull oneself up a steep slope.

VEGGIE HOLDS: Grasping bushes and smaller vegetation to pull oneself up a steep slope.

APPENDIX IV

WOMEN WINTER 46ers

From the End of the Canister Era Through 2005

Name	Date Completed	46er #
Christine Dresser*	01/17/2001	3166W
Elizabeth Moloff	12/29/2001	4789W
Patricia Schwankert	12/29/2001	4445W
Inge Aiken	01/28/2002	4688W
Linda Harwood	03/02/2002	2793W
Anne Gwynne	03/09/2002	4964W
Maria Hosmer-Briggs	02/23/2003	3872W
Ellen Cronan	03/16/2003	4889W
Barbara Bave	01/24/2004	3263W
Jacqueline Bave	01/24/2004	4469W
Christine Bourjade	02/14/2004	4967W
Lisa Bowdey	03/21/2004	4628W
Jeannette Donlon	01/09/2005	4805W
Nan Giblin	02/06/2005	5188W
Laurie Schweighardt	03/05/2005	5008W

Christine Dresser completed the Winter 46 before the canisters were removed in spring 2001, but was not a recorded Winter 46er for some years afterwards.